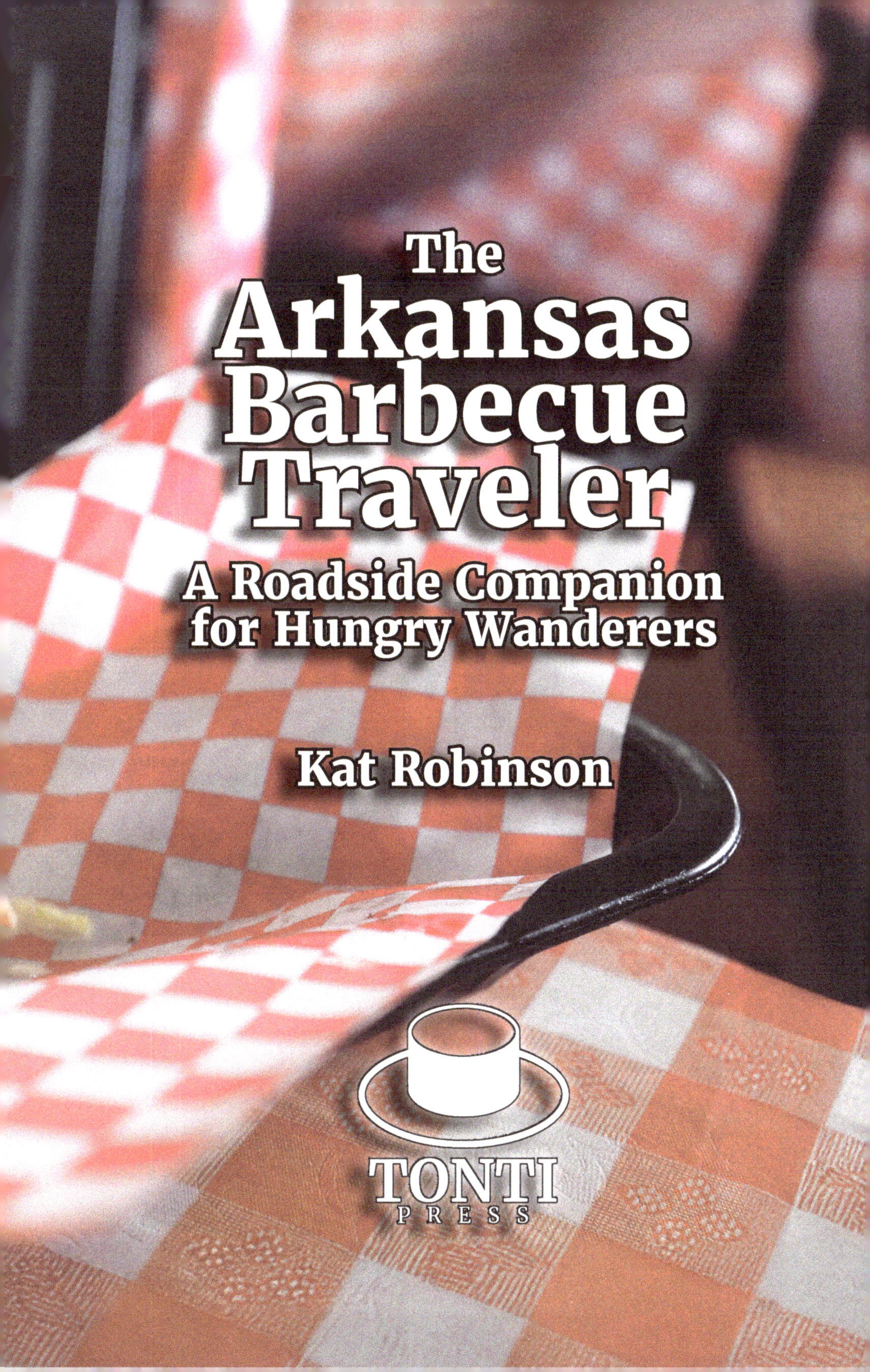

The Arkansas Barbecue Traveler

A Roadside Companion for Hungry Wanderers

Kat Robinson

Published by Tonti Press
Little Rock, Arkansas

Copyright © 2024 by Kat Robinson. All rights reserved.

Most photography by Kat Robinson
with additional photos provided by Grav Weldon,
archives across Arkansas,
and the restaurants themselves.

First published December 2024

Manufactured in the United States of America

ISBN: 978-1-952547-15-7

Library of Congress Control Number: 2024949778

Electronic release January 2025
ISBN: 978-1-952547-16-4

Notice: The information in this book is true and complete to the best of our knowledge. It is offered without guarantee on the part of the author. The author disclaims all liability in connection with the use of this book. All rights reserved. No part of this book may be reproduced or transmitted in any form whatsoever without prior written permission from the author or publisher, except in the case of brief quotations embodied in critical articles and reviews.

The author accepted no compensation for inclusion of any restaurant in this book. All photographs of food consist of edible, real food not enhanced with photographic tricks, manipulation or fakery. Some color editing and edging has been performed for printing purposes.

Map bases courtesy Arkansas Department of Transportation.

To Leif Hassell.
He knows why.

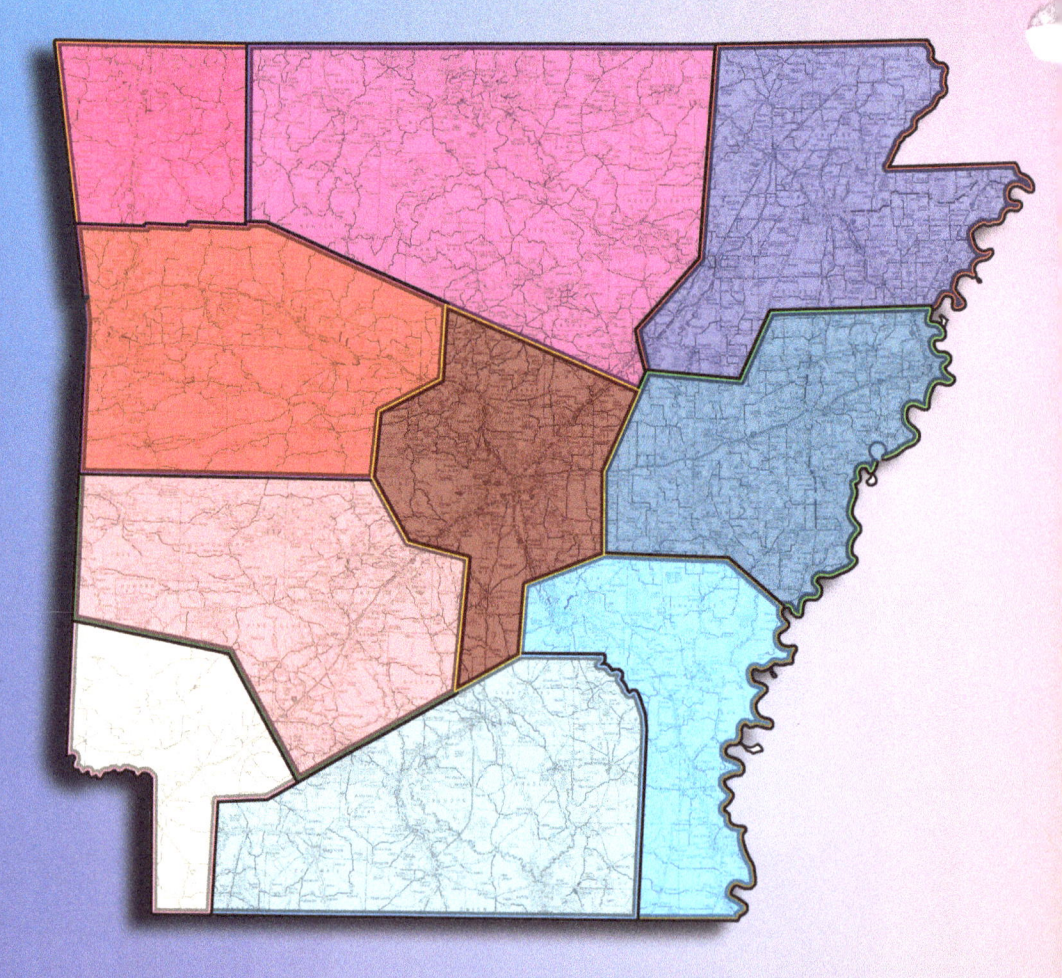

INTRODUCTION
8

THE UPPER DELTA
11

THE MIDDLE DELTA
51

THE LOWER DELTA & PINE BLUFF
81

LOWER ARKANSAS
90

SOUTHWEST ARKANSAS
113

THE OUACHITAS
123

THE ARKANSAS RIVER VALLEY
146

NORTHWEST ARKANSAS
180

NORTH CENTRAL ARKANSAS
221

CENTRAL ARKANSAS
259

INDEX
308

ACKNOWLEDGEMENTS
312

ABOUT THE AUTHOR
313

In hindsight, I may have bitten off more than I can chew.

In the spring of 2023, right on the heels of releasing my 12th book, *The Great Arkansas Pie Book*, I debated what would be my next project. I'd been fiddling with a documentary on catfish but was still seeking funding for the travel and equipment it would require. To be honest, the idea of building the restaurant compendium to pair with it seemed daunting at best. There's just so many times one can sit down to the Arkansas feast of catfish, hush puppies, coleslaw, brown beans, onion, lemon, and green tomato relish in a row before one finds themself exhausted.

There's a list I keep of possible book ideas that I will thumb back when I am seeking inspiration. On that list, I'd scrawled many things, but one had been crossed out - BARBECUE. A few years back, a colleague mentioned they were excited for a book from my esteemed friend Rex Nelson on the subject. I'd subsequently brought it up in conversation with him and found that no, that wasn't the case. While collecting information for *The Great Arkansas Pie Book*, my friend Rob Nelson (no relation to Rex) mentioned he was working on research into barbecue. Somehow that translated in my mind that he must be writing a book about it, and I once again crossed out the subject.

But it bothered me. You see, I felt that barbecue is something ingrained in Arkansas, something that's part of us, not just a food we eat but a culture that we own. I felt a need to delve into the topic, to reach back and find the roots of our love for the dishes that come from the smoker, and where we stand in the world when it comes to this. It felt like so much of what I needed to express in my research of Arkansas food. I didn't want to compete against my friend, though, so I reached out to see if he needed a collaborator on his book.

There was no book. Rob was researching barbecue to create a very specific barbecue restaurant. That restaurant, Brothers Meethouse, officially opened in November 2024.

I happily dove into putting together a book - one that I expected to take about six months to complete. I dove into archives at museums and talked to people across the food community, delved into what few books address the subject (mostly written by non-Arkansawyers), thumbed through old phone books and dug into obituaries, newspaper clippings and advertisements from ages past. My original thought was that I'd create an overall book defining Arkansas barbecue, with recipes and oral histories and a listing of the approximately 130 barbecue eateries I had already catalogued.

This is not that book.

You see, as I researched, the body of work expanded. I ditched the sections on how to barbecue, because there are hundreds of books talking about how to barbecue and I am not a pitmaster myself. I spent weeks researching, trying to narrow down one particular style of barbecue native to our state and found not one but four. I discovered, when interviewing experts from other states, I'd have my own state's barbecue talked down to me, as if I didn't understand what I'd been looking into for the past 17 years I've been studying Arkansas food. I began collecting oral histories from pit masters and pit mistresses and found there was so much more to this story.

I discovered something else - something much more astonishing. Arkansas is in a barbecue boom. Whether it's the explosion of food truck culture, a rush of a whole generation into retirement jobs, or a fervor to fulfill the hunger of a burgeoning barbecue loving populace, this state has seen a sudden and overwhelming rush of entrepreneurs diving into barbecue sales. Many have heard of the newer, large franchises that are developing here, particularly Wright's Barbecue and Blue Ember Smokehouse, but few have noted the escalation in the numbers of mom-and-pop shops selling barbecue - whether brick-and-mortar, food truck, or catering - all across the state.

I knew six months in, this would take a year. I knew a year in, I had at least six more months to go. I was sitting in my car in May of 2024, a full year into the research, having visited six different restaurants that day and interviewed individuals at four of them, feeling the aches of too much caffeine through my system, unable to get the taste of hickory smoke out of my mouth, leaned back and contemplating whether I'd overnight where I was at or try to make the drive back to Little Rock for the night to head out in another direction the next day. I was tired, I was trying to figure out how I was going to do justice to each of these restaurants where I'd spent anywhere from 30 minutes to four hours experiencing the space and interviewing the people in it, and still manage to comprehensively cover all of what we have to offer here, and the answer came to me. This isn't one book. It's just the first.

I have so many more interviews I'd like to complete. Time and scheduling and life in general has gotten in the way of being able to do the subject of Arkansas barbecue justice. There are simply not enough hours in the day, or week, or month. At the time of this writing, I am now more than 4000 hours into this project. I have driven more than 15,000 miles, visiting every county in the state on the search for purveyors and people who can tell the story of Arkansas smoke. I've spent, well, probably more money than I could ever recoup on this project, scouting restaurants and taking photographs, a whole half terrabyte of photos, maybe 20,000 or so. There have been days I've visited a dozen restaurants, and days I've worked from 3 a.m. to 9 p.m. editing photos, transcribing interviews, writing, and laying out the books. It has been all consuming.

In the end, I have in this book catalogued 399 barbecue operators in the state of Arkansas. That number doesn't cover multiple locations in the same city by the same owner and concept, nor does it cover all the locations of the mammoth Whole Hog Cafe, which originated in Pulaski County (I counted it once). I didn't count the myriad of barbecue chains or franchises that have barbecue on the menu - there's no Dickey's, no Corky's, no Crave, no RibCrib, and no, no Arby's. This book is a guide to each and every one of those Arkansas places where barbecue, smoked fresh daily, is offered. There are maps of the regions and check boxes for those who feel the need to do as I have, collect barbecue restaurants visited like Pokemon - gotta catch 'em all.

This book is a little late. Extraordinary unexpected expenses in my personal life slowed me down this time. But it is as complete a guide as I have been able to create at this time. Its goal is simple - here are our barbecue restaurants. Your taste buds are different from mine - I won't make declarations on which is better than another. The material is presented so you can let your own taste buds decide. And once you've enjoyed this appetizer, know there will be another soon. This spring, *The Arkansas Barbecue Classics* will arrive - histories and accounts from Arkansas's oldest barbecue restaurants, complete with full color photographs and stories you may not have heard about the people who bring smoked meats to the table in The Natural State. Two more will follow. Maybe three. We'll see.

Kat Robinson
November 2, 2024

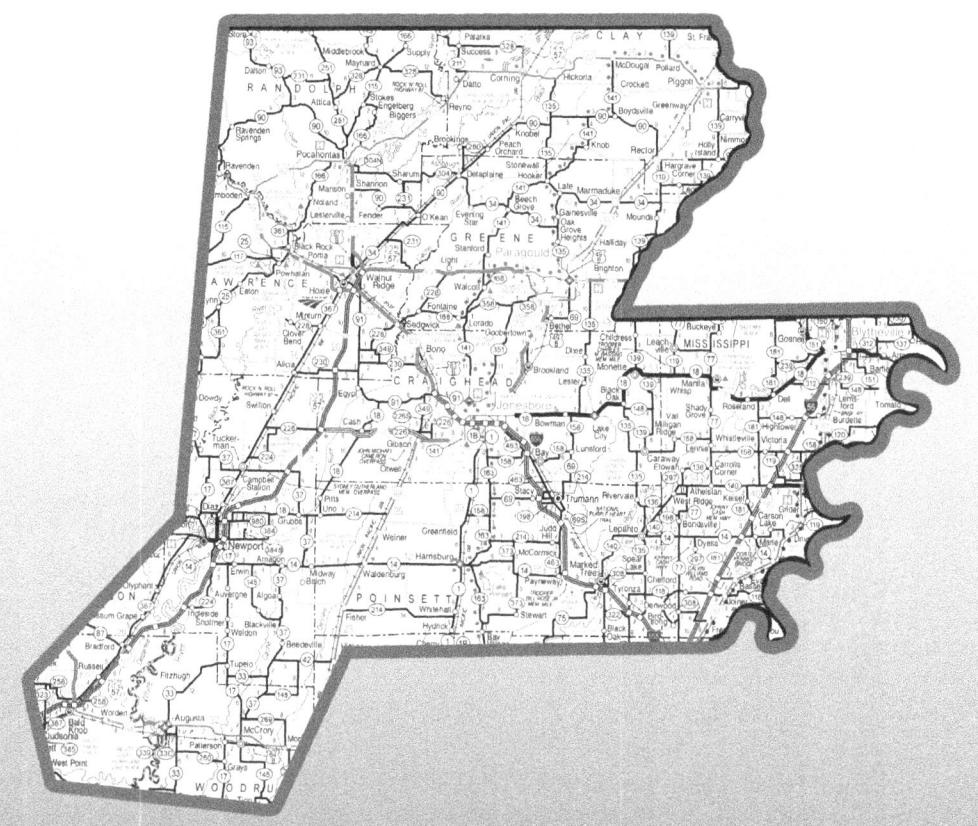

The Upper Delta

Kat Robinson

BULLDOG RESTAURANT

3614 Arkansas Highway 267 in Bald Knob
(501) 724-5195

Originally opened in 1978 by Bob and Lece Miller, The Bulldog Restaurant has served as the dairy bar at the heart of the Bald Knob community. Sisters Jennifer Muckleberg and Julie Roberts continue the tradition today, involving their whole family in an operation that feeds the town and hungry travelers seven days a week.

The barbecue here is smoked chicken and smoked pork, each pulled for serving on sandwiches or as part of a plate wiith two sides. The barbecue sauce is a secret, and the coleslaw is thick and creamy.

Because it's best known as a dairy bar, there are many who haven't gotten past the burgers and plate lunches on the menu. That diverse menu means the restaurant has something for everyone - from those barbecue sandwiches to fried catfish, breakfast to dinner, soft serve to pies to seasonally available strawberry or peach shortcakes. A good starting point for any culinary adventure.

The Arkansas Barbecue Traveler

GLENN'S SMOKEHOUSE
Regional food truck in Bradford
(501) 593-9616
GlennsSmokehouseSearcy.com

Charles and Gena Glenn started this food truck in 2023 to complement its brick-and-mortar in Searcy. This mobile catering truck is often spotted in Bradford, and at community functions throughout the region. Glenn's is best known for its Pig Pie - a layered creation with Frito corn chips covered by layers of baked beans, coleslaw, pulled pork, cheese, peppers, and barbecue sauce.

SMOKIN' JOE'S BBQ
966 North Jackson Street in McCrory
(870) 731-5637

Joe and Colleen Kyle saw a need to feed folks in this section of the Delta that's more than twenty miles to the nearest barbecue restaurant in any direction. With the help of their giant smoker Bertha, they turn out pork butts, chicken, Polish, spicy sausages, smoked bologna and occasionally brisket for customers every day. Pulled pork nachos are popular here..

13

Kat Robinson

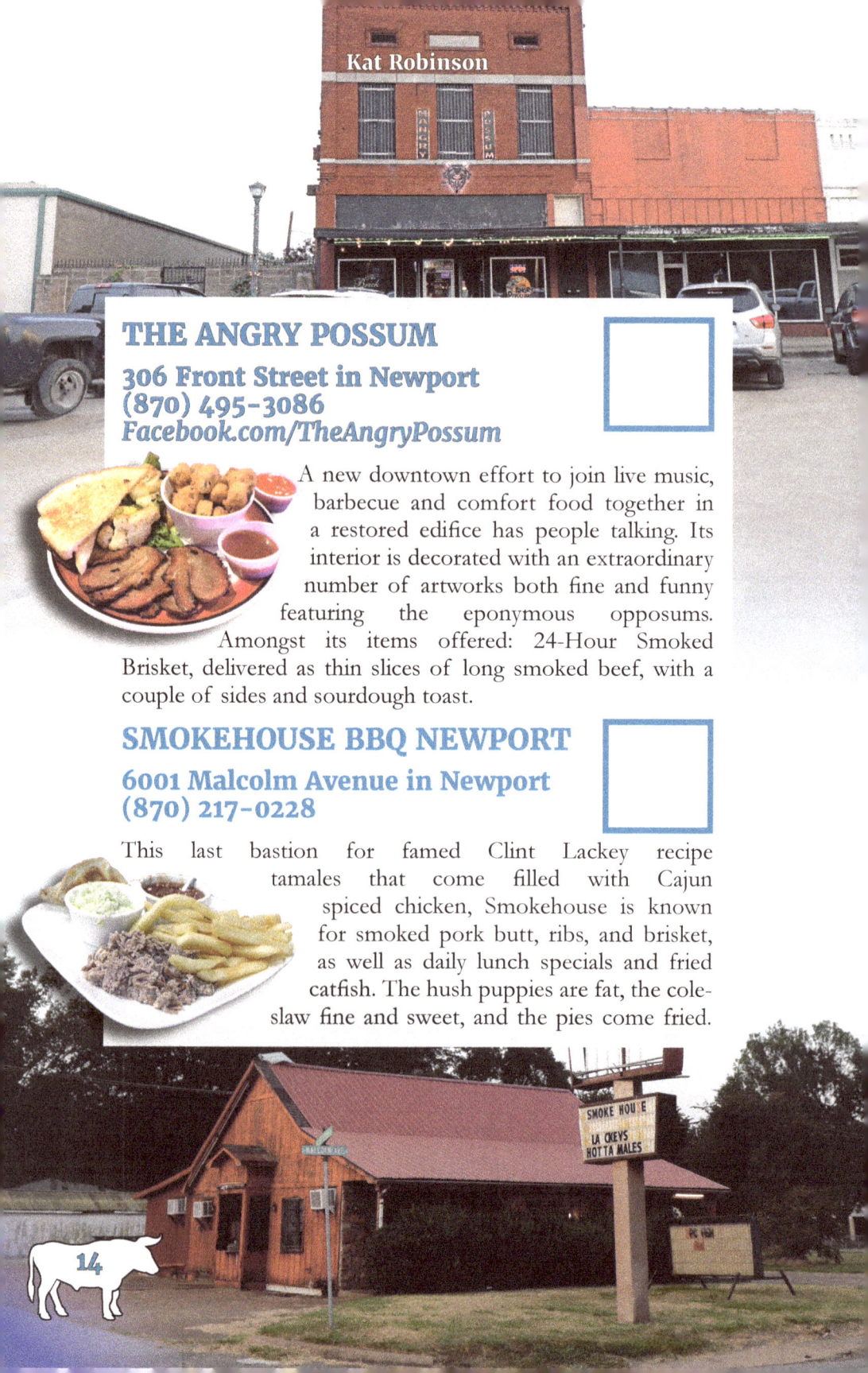

THE ANGRY POSSUM

306 Front Street in Newport
(870) 495-3086
Facebook.com/TheAngryPossum

A new downtown effort to join live music, barbecue and comfort food together in a restored edifice has people talking. Its interior is decorated with an extraordinary number of artworks both fine and funny featuring the eponymous opposums. Amongst its items offered: 24-Hour Smoked Brisket, delivered as thin slices of long smoked beef, with a couple of sides and sourdough toast.

SMOKEHOUSE BBQ NEWPORT

6001 Malcolm Avenue in Newport
(870) 217-0228

This last bastion for famed Clint Lackey recipe tamales that come filled with Cajun spiced chicken, Smokehouse is known for smoked pork butt, ribs, and brisket, as well as daily lunch specials and fried catfish. The hush puppies are fat, the coleslaw fine and sweet, and the pies come fried.

14

OLE HICKORY BAR-B-Q

320 Southwest Texas Street in Hoxie
(870) 886-2004

Ole Hickory (or Hickory House, back in the day) has been around Hoxie since at least 1983. Fire claimed the original building, and fire damaged the current building, too, back in 2020. But Ole Hickory continues to survive as the restaurant center of a hungry community.

It offers a lunch buffet that includes barbecue pork and catfish, baked beans, fried okra, mashed potatoes and gravy, a full salad bar, cobblers and so many different slices of cake. The barbecue comes smoked only with hickory, as the restaurant's name implies, and it's offered as plates, on that buffet, or in ample sandwiches with slaw and sauce.

Kat Robinson

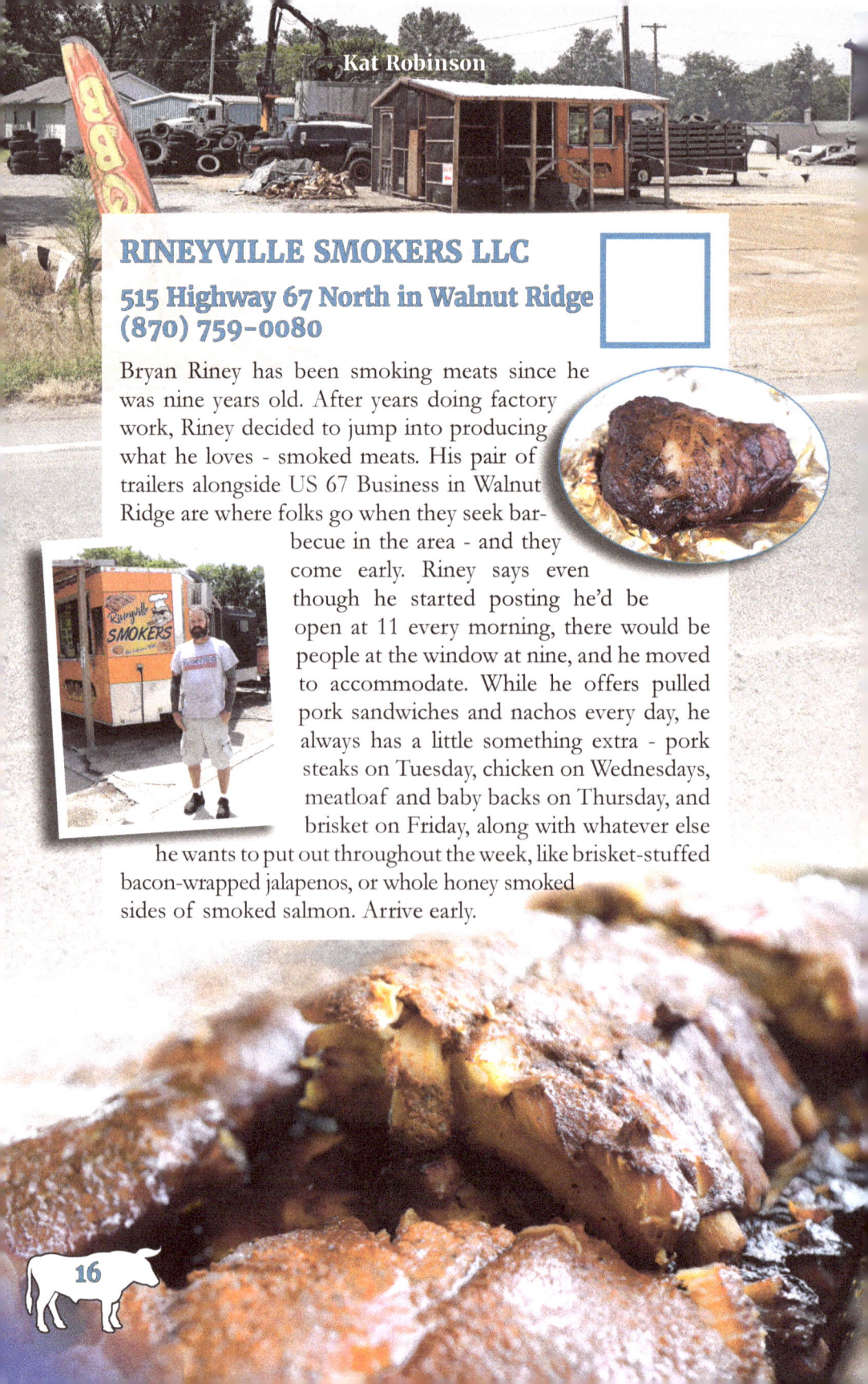

RINEYVILLE SMOKERS LLC

515 Highway 67 North in Walnut Ridge
(870) 759-0080

Bryan Riney has been smoking meats since he was nine years old. After years doing factory work, Riney decided to jump into producing what he loves - smoked meats. His pair of trailers alongside US 67 Business in Walnut Ridge are where folks go when they seek barbecue in the area - and they come early. Riney says even though he started posting he'd be open at 11 every morning, there would be people at the window at nine, and he moved to accommodate. While he offers pulled pork sandwiches and nachos every day, he always has a little something extra - pork steaks on Tuesday, chicken on Wednesdays, meatloaf and baby backs on Thursday, and brisket on Friday, along with whatever else he wants to put out throughout the week, like brisket-stuffed bacon-wrapped jalapenos, or whole honey smoked sides of smoked salmon. Arrive early.

The Arkansas Barbecue Traveler

BROWN'S DELTA BAR-B-Q

4007 US Highway 67 in Pocahontas
(870) 892-0142
Facebook.com/BrownsDeltaBarBQue

Dine in at lunch, or drive thru any other time of the day for hickory smoked meats and home cooking. Brown's is just as well known for its fish dinners and hamburger steak slathered in grilled onions as it is for pork spareribs, pulled chicken and pulled pork sandwiches and meals. Check the whiteboard for daily specials and a list of magnificent homemade pies.

GREENE'S BEANS BUNS & BBQ

2004 Airways Lane in Pocahontas
(870) 810-1100

Tony Greene spent more than a quarter century as a trucker before deciding to stick closer to his Pocahontas home. He started up his food truck, which recently went to brick-and-mortar, so he could feed his friends. And that he does, offering pulled pork, pork steaks, ribs, and brisket from his shack by the regional airport.

17

HILLBILLY JUNCTION

12859 Arkansas Highway in Maynard
(870) 202-5052

Maynard may not be much more than a spot in the road, but in that spot you'll find this old-style country restaurant that specializes in breakfast and lunches. If you get there after 2 p.m. you're just out of luck. The breakfasts are ample, the ham is smoked and fried, and the pulled pork plate is humongous.

HAROLD'S BAR-B-QUE

1108 West Main Street in Corning
(870) 857-2223
Facebook.com/HaroldsBBQCorning

Like barbecue? Want all of it at once? Harold's Bar-B-Que has you covered with The Shenanigator, an epic beast of a sandwich. It starts with smoked and fried bologna, then pulled pork, and sliced brisket, lettuce, tomato, onion, pickle, and barbecue sauce between two seedless, toasted buns. You'll need to unhinge your jaw for this one.

THE RANCH HOUSE at JAMES RANCH

51 James Ranch Road in Pocahontas
(870) 378-3529
Facebook.com/TheJamesRanchRanchHouse

Located on the James Ranch, this on-site eatery has frontage on the Eleven Point River. Live music is often offered, as is a smoked sausage and cheese platter and pork steak. Brisket, pork belly burnt ends and other smoked meats are often available.

SMOKIN' RAVEN

320 US Highway 63 in Ravenden
(870) 955-0970
Facebook.com/SmokinRaven

This tiny house along US Highway 63 in Ravenden has a smokehouse built into its end! Opened in 2022, Smokin' Raven offers chicken, sausage, pulled pork, brisket, and smoked potatoes on the regular, with frequent specials like smoked pinto beans and fried fish.

OINKY'S BBQ

318 West Northend Avenue in Paragould
(870) 236-4659
Facebook.com/OinkysBBQ

Pork is the only smoked meat Oinky's offers, but that's been enough to keep them going since the late 1990s. Judy Penny's rustic shop with its Wild West interiors has become one of those great local classics without any advertising. While the ribs have their own following, it's the Piggy Fries that get the most attention - a gigantic pile of crinkle cut fries topped with pulled pork butt, thick house barbecue sauce, and a heavy load of shredded cheese that melts on contact. It's a big plateful, enough to share and more than you could imagine for one meal (though some do try).

BAR-B-Q BARN

6115 West Kingshighway in Paragould
(870) 236-8999
Facebook.com/TheBarBQBarn

This longstanding Paragould restaurant on Crowley's Ridge's western edge has been open since 1975. Amy, Danny, and Isaac Hollis bought the place at the beginning of 2024 and are continuing the tradition of offering pulled pork and thick sliced smoked bologna alongside catfish, a slate of sides, including sweet corn, brown beans and fried okra, and slices of fresh baked pecan pie. Check out the mural in the back room.

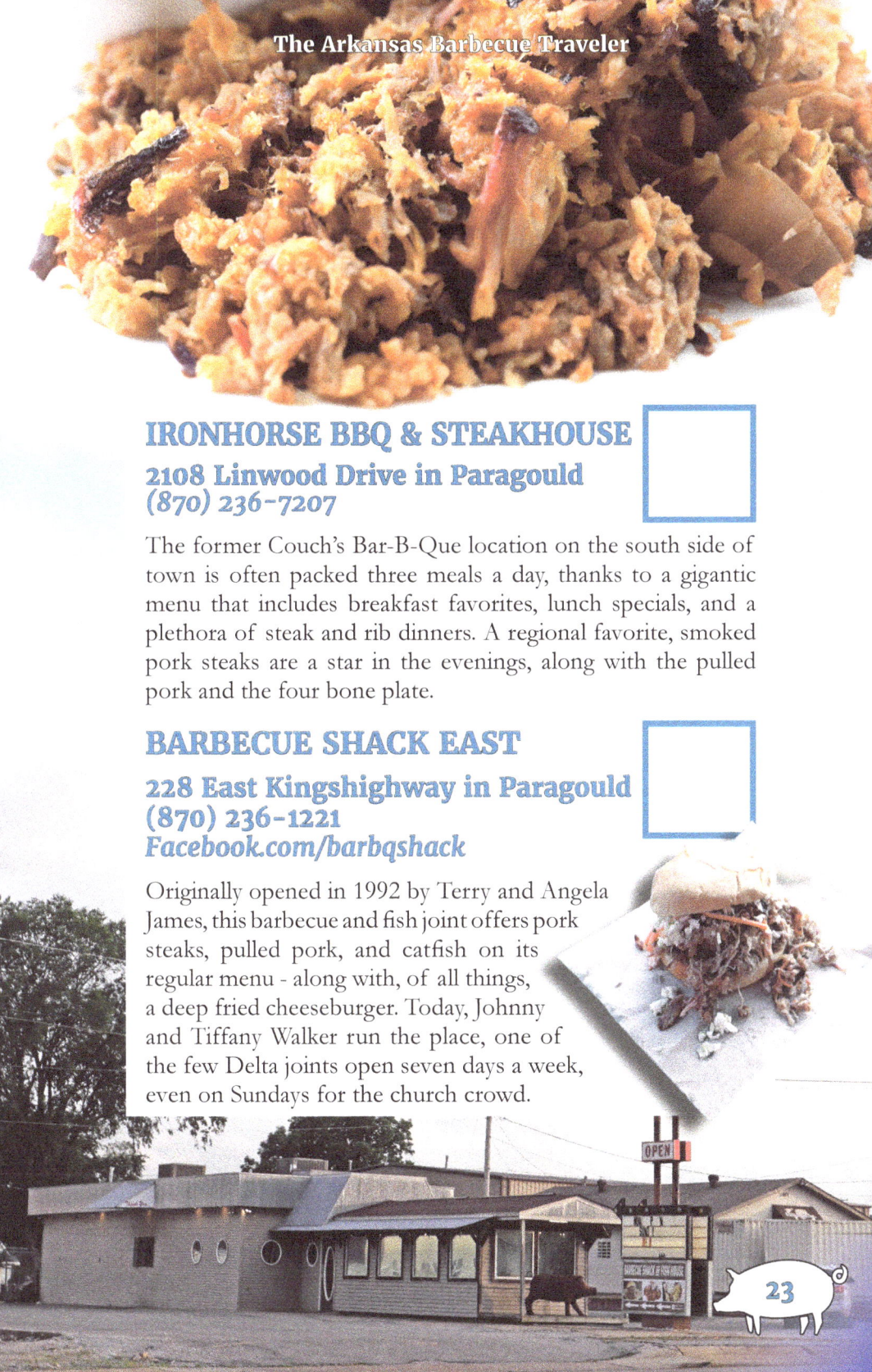

IRONHORSE BBQ & STEAKHOUSE
2108 Linwood Drive in Paragould
(870) 236-7207

The former Couch's Bar-B-Que location on the south side of town is often packed three meals a day, thanks to a gigantic menu that includes breakfast favorites, lunch specials, and a plethora of steak and rib dinners. A regional favorite, smoked pork steaks are a star in the evenings, along with the pulled pork and the four bone plate.

BARBECUE SHACK EAST
228 East Kingshighway in Paragould
(870) 236-1221
Facebook.com/barbqshack

Originally opened in 1992 by Terry and Angela James, this barbecue and fish joint offers pork steaks, pulled pork, and catfish on its regular menu - along with, of all things, a deep fried cheeseburger. Today, Johnny and Tiffany Walker run the place, one of the few Delta joints open seven days a week, even on Sundays for the church crowd.

GLADISH'S BBQ

**350 US Highway 49 in Paragould
(870) 205-4566**
Facebook.com/GladishBBQ

A tiny house that's also a drive-thru restaurant. Brandon Gladish is doing things his own way at his place right off US 49 in Paragould. He's been smoking, just like his dad did, all his life. After more than 20 years doing factory work, Gladish stepped into this new adventure in 2020. Unlike other Paragould establishments, which all specialize in smoking pork, Gladish is focused on brisket. Every brisket spends about 14 hours in a pellet hybrid smoker he built himself. It's offered in a whole host of ways, like the Tangler Sandwich, where the brisket is matched up with house-made pickles and French fried onions and a unique cherry chipotle sauce.

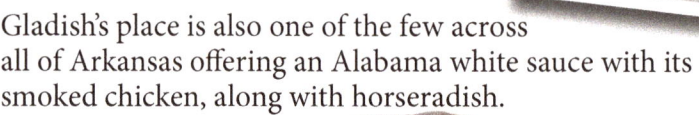

Gladish's place is also one of the few across all of Arkansas offering an Alabama white sauce with its smoked chicken, along with horseradish.

VAUGHN'S PIT STOP BBQ

201 West College Street in Bono and a mobile food truck, too
(870) 316-0702
Facebook.com/VaughnsPitstopBBQ

Pulled pork and pulled chicken smoked with hickory stars at this growing enterprise. Tyler and Megan Vaughn opened the original location in August 2018. Since then, the Vaughns have shared generously portioned sandwiches, plates, nachos and salads and gained a lot of good renown. Tyler, the grandson of J&N Bar-B-Que founder Jim Vaughn, also competes at George Ray's dragstrip over in Paragould. The name, hence, makes a lot of sense. The location you see here will soon be replaced by a new spot over on US Highway 63, as the couple goes brick-and-mortar. Their mobile food truck shows up at so many of the regional festivals in the area.

J&N BAR-B-QUE

3503 Dan Avenue in Jonesboro
(870) 972-9724
Facebook.com/BBQinJonesboro

Jim and Nora Vaughn started this barbecue landmark in an old truck stop alongside US Highway 63 in 1996, then moved it to its current location in 2001. Jim had worked in a garage but hurt his back, and decided to dive into one of his hobbies instead. He loved collecting and repairing tractors, and smoking Boston butts and chicken over charcoal and hickory - so he did both. Before he passed in 2021, Jim was known to smoke raccoon for local coon suppers! Nora cooked everything else, including the signature creamy potato salad and all the desserts. Today, granddaughter Samantha Wicker Golden and Emily Brice continue the tradition.

LEGENDS BBQ SMOKEHOUSE

1025 West Johnson Avenue in Jonesboro
(870) 931-3310
Facebook.com/LegendsBBQSmokehouse

Reginald and Ruthie Prunty opened the first black-owned Jonesboro nightclub back in the 1990s, a spot called Envision. At the time, Reginald also worked for Xerox and Ruthie ran catering operations at St. Bernard's Medical Center. Reginald had previously founded Jonesboro CityYouth Ministries, an after-school program for children, and the bar funded the barbecue for the kids. The Pruntys faced conflict in the community, but worked hard to keep their operation going. In 2017, the Pruntys remodeled and reopened as Legends BBQ Smokehouse and Lounge, offering barbecue, the bar, and an event space. Reginald Prunty's 45 years of smoking expertise shows in the excellent brisket, pulled pork, pulled chicken and wings served and in the exceptional spice rub the couple spent five years developing, that's not just tasty, but low in sodium as well.

DEMO'S SMOKE HOUSE BBQ

1851 South Church Street and
 4115 East Johnson Avenue in Jonesboro
(870) 935-6633 and (870) 203-9944
DemosSmokeHouse.com

Spencer and Channon Moore's longstanding operation in two different Jonesboro area locations focuses on hickory smoked and chopped pork, beef, and chicken. The place is best known for smoked ribs, chicken leg quarters and a thicker barbecue sauce than average, and there's always an apple fried pie waiting for you.

CANDY APPLES BBQ

Food Truck and Spices
(870) 790-0708
CandyApplesBBQ.com

This is a locally owned and operated sauce and spice manufacturing company based in Jonesboro, producing Arkansas Delta focused products used by both professional competitors and folks smoking meats at home.

H2QUE BBQ

Caterer and Food Truck in residence at Arkansas State University
(870) 219-9729
Facebook.com/H2Que

It's a curious combination - a food truck that's the go-to concession for barbecue at all Arkansas State University sports functions, that's also one of the biggest noisemakers on the food scene at each and every Arkansas State Fair. Patrick Hinson and family have managed to create something unique and wonderful - a barbecue concession that offers magnificently hickory smoked pulled pork and chicken in sandwiches and on nachos, along with other standards like smoked sausages and ribs - but which also stands out for crazy creations that stick. Hinson's Meat the Mac, a layered cup of mac and cheese, beans, cheese, and smoked meat, went from being a great new fair food to a unique standard at Red Wolf ballgames. Crazy items like the Pork Waffle and a smoked turkey leg stuffed with everything you can imagine got H2Que BBQQ on the map, but the overall quality of that smoked meat keeps it there. Be forewarned - the grape and tropical punch served up here is considerably sweeter than you're expecting.

Kat Robinson

LORADO SMOKEHOUSE AND GRILL

31 Arkansas Highway 168 north of Jonesboro
(870) 275-4654
LoradoGrill.com

Dale Pugsley's back woods grocery store originally opened in 2005 has evolved over time, first taken over in 2011 by Dale's son Randy and daughter-in-law Angela, who expanded the space, then passed to Randy's son and daughter-in-law, Brandon and Mika Pugsley, in 2022. Still a vibrant, working country grocery complete with deli counter and beer case, Lorado's western side is now a full-scale steakhouse, serving half pound burgers, fried catfish, and pork barbecue, namely pulled pork butt and racks of ribs. On Fridays and Saturdays, the stars are smoked pork steaks, a regional specialty, and a rubbed and smoked half chicken dinner. Pies, cakes, and milkshakes are how dinners wrap up here.

YESSUH BBQ & MORE CATERING

Food Truck
2401 East Parker Road in Jonesboro
YessuhBMC.com

Austin Lewis brings barbecue, burgers and fish to the table with his mobile operation, often setting up pre-order only sales when he's not catering all over Craighead County. Contact through Facebook or email *yessuhbmc@gmail.com*.

SOUTHERN BBQ HILLTOP

1804 North Old Greensboro Road in Jonesboro
(870) 790-2271
SouthernBBQHilltop.com

This brand new red-walled barbecue, burgers and wings shop opened in early 2024 with a full bar and an array of traditional barbecue sandwiches, nachos, and salads, plus plenty of bar food options.

The Arkansas Barbecue Traveler

QUE49 SMOKEHOUSE
1312 Red Wolf Boulevard in Jonesboro
(870) 333-5454
Que49Smokehouse.com

Opened in 2019 by father-daughter team Skip and Hannah Steele, this roadhouse-dressed operation shook up the status quo of Jonesboro barbecue, introducing true burnt ends, house smoked pork belly pastrami, smoked tri-tip, fire and ice pickles and much more to the restaurant scene. Skip's experience running dozens of restaurnats across the globe is evident here, with a precise operation where nothing is wasted. Brisket trimmings are turned for tallow to fry the fries. Hannah is in charge of this show, and she runs a tight ship of employees who act more like family. The smoke here is cherry wood, the condiments are pickles and pickled red onions, and ribs are the house specialty. Try the Reuben.

33

DADS' BBQ

Food Truck and Caterer
2010 Arkansas 18 in Lake City
(870) 351-6370

A common sight at local festivals and raceways, Dads' can also be spotted in Monette, Lake City, Leachville, Corning and parts all around, appearing wherever barbecue is desired. The specialties here are pork steaks, pulled pork and ribs, while customers do brag a lot on those baked beans loaded with smoked pork.

HOLY SMOKES BBQ

Food Truck in Manila
(870) 278-5935
Facebook.com/HolySmokesBBQ

This is a barbecue joint with a mission - to help others. A percentage of sales each month go to various organizations doing good work for others in northeast Arkansas. The meat here is pulled pork, served on sandwiches or nachos, and the homemade sides include apple baked beans. Look for special nighs for sausage rolls, ribs and more.

SMOKESTACK BBQ

717 North Boston Street in Manila
(870) 561-8282
SmokestackBBQ-Manila.com

Smokestack BBQ in Manila has become known for catfish dinners, buffets, breakfasts, and so much more - and yes, they still offer barbecue, too, like this pulled pork sandwich. Pulled pork is also available on salads and nachos or as a plate on its own. There are also rib dinners. And the kids will love the Famous 1000 Legger - a crazy new version of a chili cheese dog!

FAT DADDY'S
317 Greenwood Avenue in Lepanto
(870) 475-3537

Jim Stacks ran Fat Daddy's with his wife, Peggy, as a side job while also working as a dispatcher for Lepanto Police. He passed in 2022, but Peggy and their daughter Karen Brown still keep up the tradition, serving the extremely small menu - pork butt sandwiches and nachos, ribs, beans, coleslaw, and whole butts - and serving it early. When it's gone, it's gone. Cash or check only.

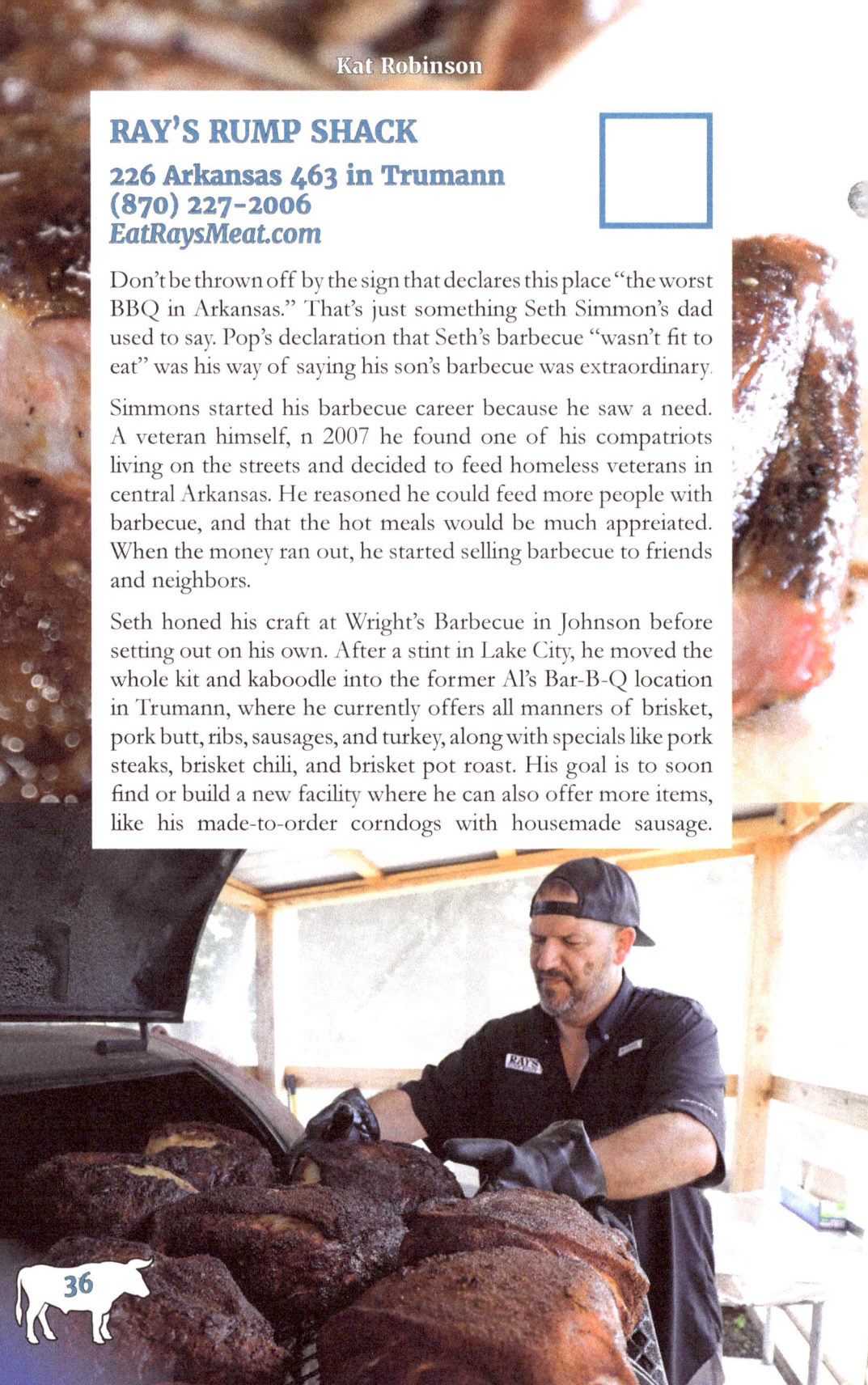

RAY'S RUMP SHACK

226 Arkansas 463 in Trumann
(870) 227-2006
EatRaysMeat.com

Don't be thrown off by the sign that declares this place "the worst BBQ in Arkansas." That's just something Seth Simmon's dad used to say. Pop's declaration that Seth's barbecue "wasn't fit to eat" was his way of saying his son's barbecue was extraordinary.

Simmons started his barbecue career because he saw a need. A veteran himself, n 2007 he found one of his compatriots living on the streets and decided to feed homeless veterans in central Arkansas. He reasoned he could feed more people with barbecue, and that the hot meals would be much appreiated. When the money ran out, he started selling barbecue to friends and neighbors.

Seth honed his craft at Wright's Barbecue in Johnson before setting out on his own. After a stint in Lake City, he moved the whole kit and kaboodle into the former Al's Bar-B-Q location in Trumann, where he currently offers all manners of brisket, pork butt, ribs, sausages, and turkey, along with specials like pork steaks, brisket chili, and brisket pot roast. His goal is to soon find or build a new facility where he can also offer more items, like his made-to-order corndogs with housemade sausage.

HOG WILD BAR-B-Q

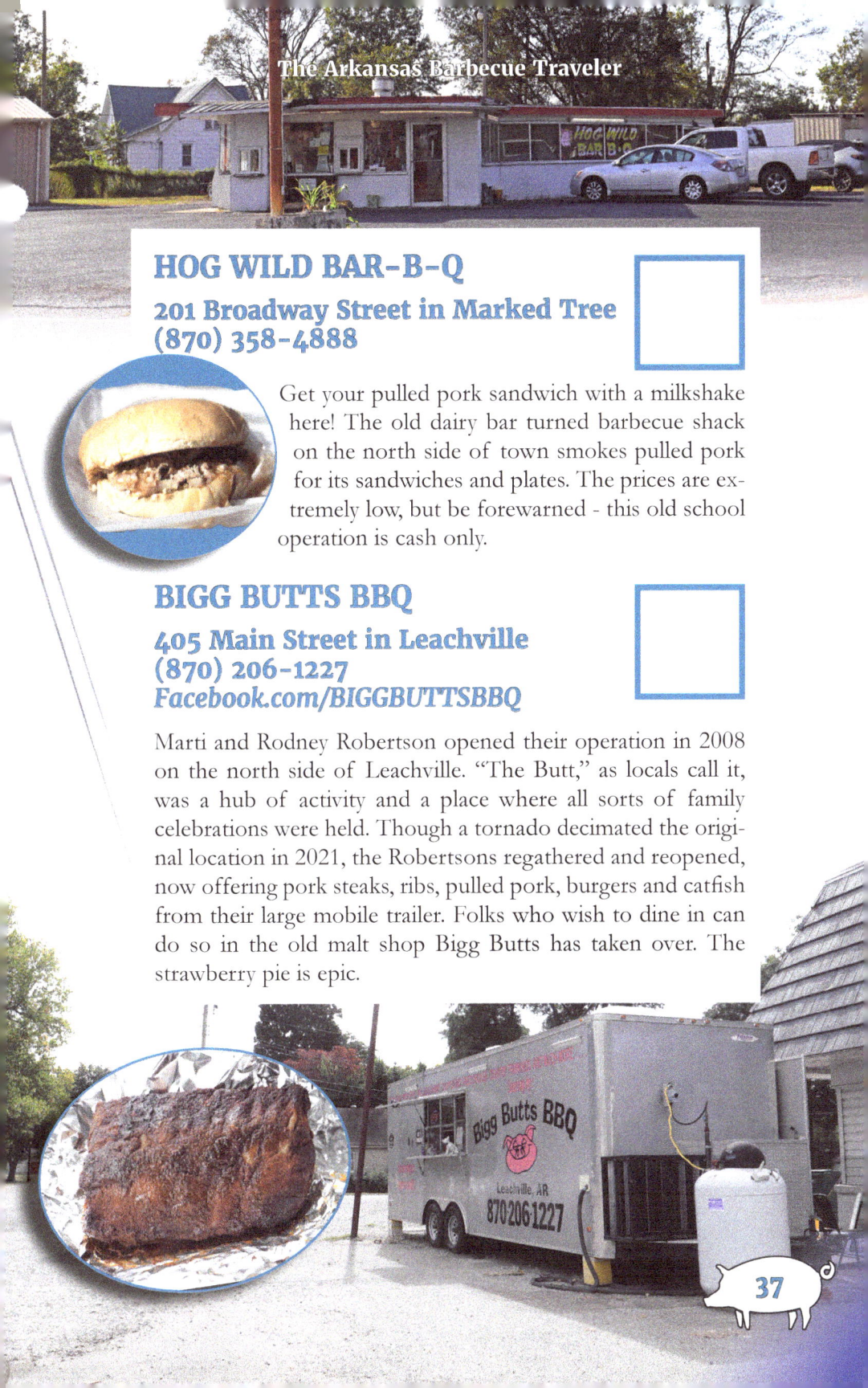

201 Broadway Street in Marked Tree
(870) 358-4888

Get your pulled pork sandwich with a milkshake here! The old dairy bar turned barbecue shack on the north side of town smokes pulled pork for its sandwiches and plates. The prices are extremely low, but be forewarned - this old school operation is cash only.

BIGG BUTTS BBQ

405 Main Street in Leachville
(870) 206-1227
Facebook.com/BIGGBUTTSBBQ

Marti and Rodney Robertson opened their operation in 2008 on the north side of Leachville. "The Butt," as locals call it, was a hub of activity and a place where all sorts of family celebrations were held. Though a tornado decimated the original location in 2021, the Robertsons regathered and reopened, now offering pork steaks, ribs, pulled pork, burgers and catfish from their large mobile trailer. Folks who wish to dine in can do so in the old malt shop Bigg Butts has taken over. The strawberry pie is epic.

PORK-N-STUFF

259 East Main Street in Piggott
(870) 634-6374
Facebook.com/PorknStuffPiggott

Brittany Owens may hail from the Kansas City area, but the barbecue she's serving up is honest to goodness north Delta delightful. She took over this place, originally opened in 2012, from her boss in 2021 and has worked real magic, providing a community favorite location to dine on the east side of town. The name comes from one of the waitresses, who when asked by customers what they had available, replied, "we got pork and stuff." The place is known for its exceptional ribs and pork steaks so tender you can cut them with a plastic fork. It's also known for the unusual way of letting the customers choose its decor, with signatures of happy patrons all over the place, even on the ceiling!

Owens met her husband when he was working with his dad's construction business near Kansas City. He'd stop in at the restaurant she had up there every day for lunch. The last day he was up there, he talked her into a date, it worked out, and they ended up marrying. Today, he owns a Piggott area tree service, which means she gets all the wood she needs for smoking.

KINGS BACKYARD BBQ

Caterer
559 North 10th Street in Blytheville
(870) 409-3322
Facebook.com/Brice.Leaks

Brice Leaks offers up barbecue pork and chicken, along with pig salads, nachos, and changing specials - like smoked salmon, lamb chops, turkey, pork burnt ends, and ribs.

Kat Robinson

DIXIE PIG

701 North Sixth Street in Blytheville
(870)-763-4636
Facebook.com/DixiePigBlytheville

Ernest Halsell's family moved from Pontotoc, Mississippi, where they had a restaurant, to come farm cotton. In 1923, he opened the Rustic Inn within a log cabin that had a sawdust floor. There, he offered two types of sandwiches and chips, along with sodas. Back then, he would cook what he could get - whether it was hogs or frogs! Halsell's flame roasted pork shoulders gained notoriety, and in 1950 he opened The Dixie Pig on Sixth Stret, where it remains today.

While the elder Halsell used mostly hickory, the restaurant now uses mostly lump charcoal. Ernest's grandson Bob Halsell continues the tradition. There are more items on the menu, like meat spaghetti, catfish, nachos and pig fries, but it all comes back to that roasted pork. That being said, I'd highly suggest adding those housemade onion rings to any order. Be sure to pick up a bottle of sauce while you're there.

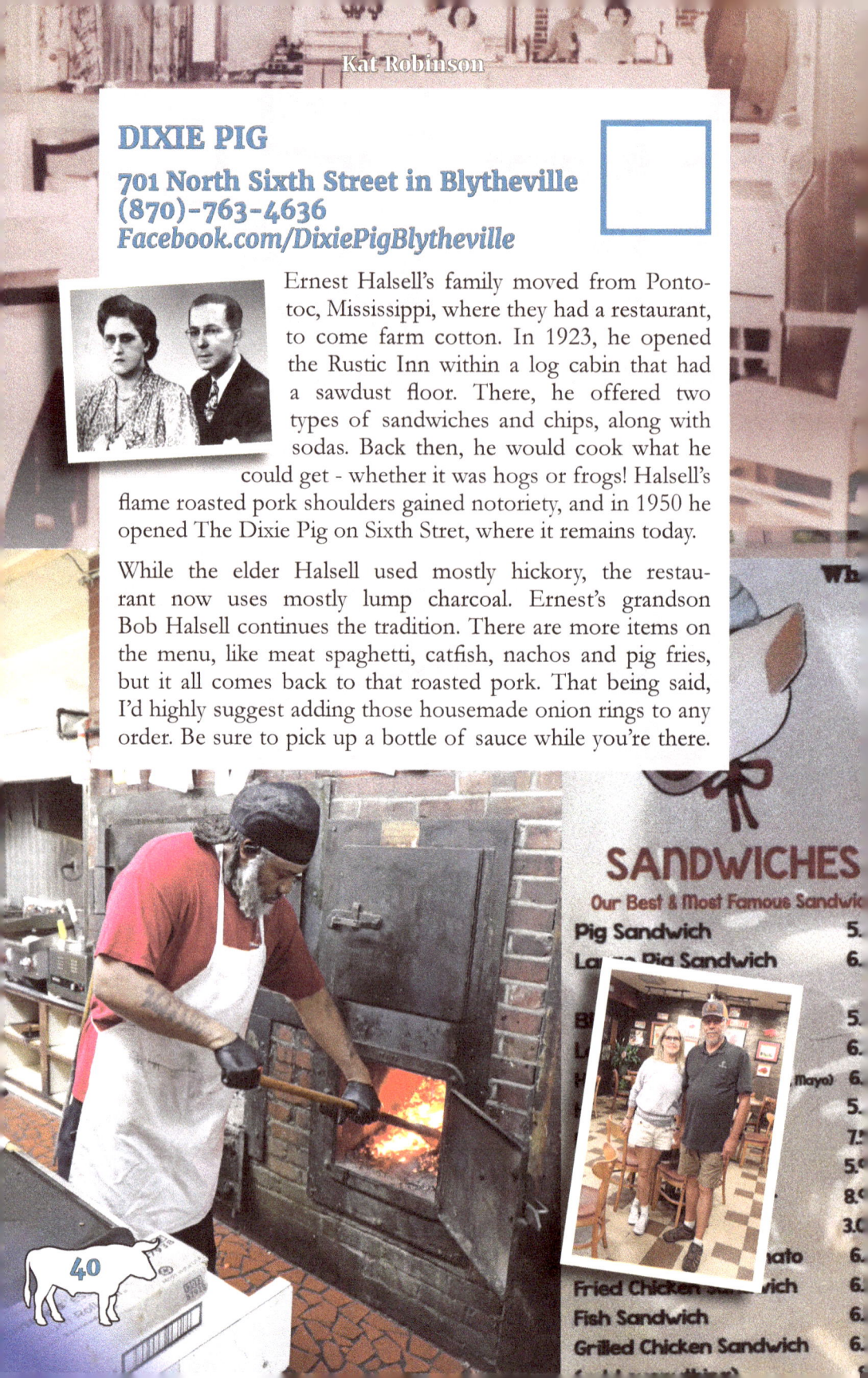

40

The Arkansas Barbecue Traveler

Kat Robinson

42

KREAM KASTLE
112 North Division Street in Blytheville
(870) 762-2366

Steven Johns originally opened the Kream Kastle as a milk bar back in 1953, serving malts, sundaes, and shakes. He added hot dogs, and then in 1955 he decided to bring on barbecue. The move cemented the restaurant as one of the pillars of the Blytheville barbecue community. Johns was also the first area business owner to drop the "Whites Only" signs in 1964.

Suzanne Johns Wallace, Steven's daughter, owns the Kream Kastle today with her husband Jeff Wallace, who runs the pit and chops that pork for pig sandwiches, pig nachos, pig plates, you name it. That pork comes from shoulders smoked with hickory charcoal for 12 to 13 hours. Jeff smokes up to 200 pounds a day.

The pig sandwich comes standard with Kream Kastle's peppery vinegar sauce and coleslaw. It's assembled on a seedless bun and heated on a press. A popular variation is to add chili and cheese instead of coleslaw.

Just be aware - the Kream Kastle is only open on weekdays and you better bring cash. Order at one of the call stations for quick service.

YANK'S FAMOUS BARBEQUE
141 East Main Street in Blytheville
(870) 762-2935

Yank's Famous BBQ recently grew into bigger digs, with a large dining room to accompany the order-at-the-window service it's offered for years. Saucy sandwiches and super specials reign supreme here, where pork ribs and pulled pork top the menu but are served side-by-side with chicken leg quarters, half chickens, brisket, and even fried fish. Check the white board before you order to see what you've already missed out on for the day - and try the hot sauce.

BENNY BOB'S BBQ
841 East Main Street in Blytheville
(870) 763-0505

Open since 1989, this strip mall joint offers its meat dry rubbed with a couple different sauces - thick and hickory smoky and thin and peppery. Pork and chicken are both available. The lemon icebox pie is not to be missed.

The Arkansas Barbecue Traveler

SOUTHERN UNORTHODOX
Food Truck in Blytheville
(870) 623-3469

Matthew Huffman grew up on the same street as the folks who run Kream Kastle and Dixie Pig. He's making a name for himself in a town best known for pig sandwiches by breaking out with brisket, smoked pork belly and whatever he feels compelled to create each day. His sister Jennifer often runs the register while he crafts crazy sandwiches like the Bubba Cole, a sandwich featuring slices of brisket, turkey and housemade pimento cheese. Look for the long black food trailer, usually parked in the used car lot east of the viaduct, or follow where he's at on Facebook.

Kat Robinson

HOG PEN BBQ

2874 South US 61 near Osceola
(870) 563-2283
Facebook.com/TheHogPenBarbecue

Jeff Lynch wants his customers to be happy. That's part of the reason why when you walk into Hog Pen BBQ, you'll see a plethora of condiments on the table - A1, ketchup, lemon juice, salt and pepper, Tabasco, Louisiana Hot Sauce, Tiger Sauce, Cavender's Greek Seasoning, other spice mixes and both hot and mild Hog Pen barbecue sauce. To him, it's up to you what you want to enjoy. Lynch was broke when his friend Cortez Kennedy and his brother came together and helped fund the restaurant. From its opening as a tiny drive-thru shack the day after Christmas 2007, it's blossomed into one of those great places where the locals come to eat and shoot the bull. Today, Jeff and his staff are at it six days a week, smoking pork steaks, butts, ribs, and chicken halves. He has a dish called Double BS in a Bowl, which is pulled pork in sauce over beans and coleslaw. You can get a smoked grilled chicken breast on a sandwich or a grilled bologna sandwich, and you can dress it how you like.

Kat Robinson

BOWLES BAR-B-QUE
512 West Keiser Avenue in Osceola
(870) 563-3500

Danny Ray and Sarah Staggs Parker have ran this adults-only barbecue lounge for decade. He passed in 2023, but Sarah keeps this place going. The barbecue here is pork, served loose meat (finely chopped) in sandwiches or on a plate. If you get a half pound, it comes in a large styrofoam beverage cup. Be aware - this place is 18 and older only and allows smoking.

VON'S TASTY WINGS & SOUL FOOD
302 South Poplar Street in Osceola
(870) 622-9360

Not just your average wing shack, Von's offers ribs and rib tips on the regular, along with smoked pulled pork shoulder, pork chops, smoked sausage and barbecue bologna alongside burgers, catfish, chicken livers and gizzards and, of couse, hot wings. From time to time you can also catch smoked ox tails, turkey necks, and neckbones on the specials board.

48

The Arkansas Barbecue Traveler

LITTLE PIGGY BBQ

500 Normal Avenue in Harrisburg
(870) 680-7923
Facebook.com/LittlePiggyBBQ1

There are a lot of crazy combination businesses that have barbecue joints as part of their operation, but I don't know another one that's also a garden center! Flowers, herbs, vegetables, and all the things you can image to grow them in your yard can be found here. Sit down at the counter and order pulled pork sandwiches or plates, or come on Friday for ribs. Try the pumpkin bread!

BIG O RIBS

211 North Main Street in Harrisburg
(870)578-0390
Facebook.com/OwensRibs

The restaurant itself may be small, but the patio at Big O's is often rockin'. Head cook and pitmaster Heath Owens brings expertise from the competition circut to downtown Harrisburg, showcasing ribs, pulled pork, sausage and bologna straight from the smoker. The beer is cold, and those ribs just come right out of the meat with a quick twist.

WOODY'S BAR-B-Q SAUCE CO.

Available online at
WoodysBBQSauceCompany.com

William "Woody" Wood and Ceceilia Wood ran a little barbecue truck at the intersection of US 71 and Arkansas 14 for decades. Their shop, Woody's Bar-B-Q, was a favorite stop for travelers and locals alike. The couple passed within days of each other in 2020. The sauces and spice rubs the couple created are now available from this company based in Weiner, and at locations all over Arkansas.

RAMSEY'S B.B.Q.

Food trailer and smoker
6512 Arkansas 14 (Intersection of Highways 49 & 14) in Waldenburg
(870) 579-4227

The folks who now make the Woody's sauces and rubs, also operate a food trailer at the same location. Tony, Suzy and Madelyn Ramsey offer smoked Boston butts whole or in sandwiches, on nachos, and on plates, along with ribs, pork chops and chicken. Ramsey's is all to-go, but there's plenty of room on the lot for picnics.

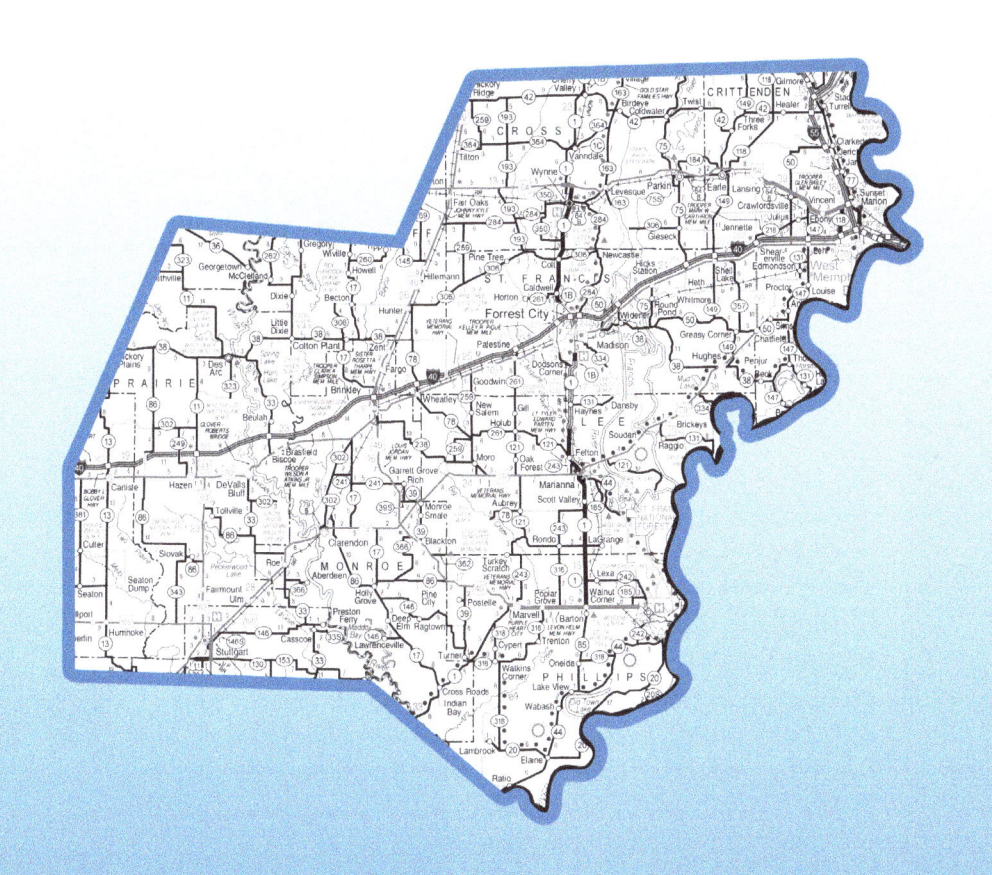

The Middle Delta

NICK'S BAR-B-Q AND CATFISH

1012 Bobby L. Glover Highway
  in Carlisle
(870) 552-3887
NicksBQ.com

Originally opened in 1972 by E.C. Ferguson, this longstanding favorite draws locals and folks traveling on I-40 through the area to its doors. Over time, the operation had gone through three different buildings, with this latest iteration a giant warren of high-ceiling rooms perfect for family gatherings, with a capacity of 200. Ferguson's grandson Clay Waliski essentially grew up in the restaurant, and manages this behemoth of a restaurant today. Smoked pork, brisket, chicken, sausage, and ribs are all on the menu, available in dishes like the sausage and cheese platter, the Garden Salad Plus with pulled pork, and a host of different combinations that include possibilities of having hot smoked barbecue right next to fried seafood on the same platter. Don't miss the pecan pie.

SCRBBQ

Regional food truck
(501) 912-2813

Susan and Richard Cunningham's operation covers a section of the state lacking in barbecue restaurants, such as the communities of Furlow, Hazen, Carlissle, and Lonoke. Their simple menu is just smoked and chopped pork, chicken and beef as a regular or jumbo sandwich, a barbecue Frito pie, half or full racks of St. Louis-style ribs, and a simple roster of sides.

SNO WHITE DAIRY BAR

405 Main Street in Des Arc
(870) 256-3306

On Fridays, this longstanding eatery pulls out the smoker for barbecue ribs served with baked beans, fries, coleslaw and a drink - a classic Arkansas barbecue set-up.

TREY'S DELI & GRILL

20093 US HIghway 70 West in Wheatley
(870) 945-6207

This little red shack offers pulled pork, brisket, and polish sausages alongside traditional deli sandwiches, breakfast and snowcones. Look for rib plate specials.

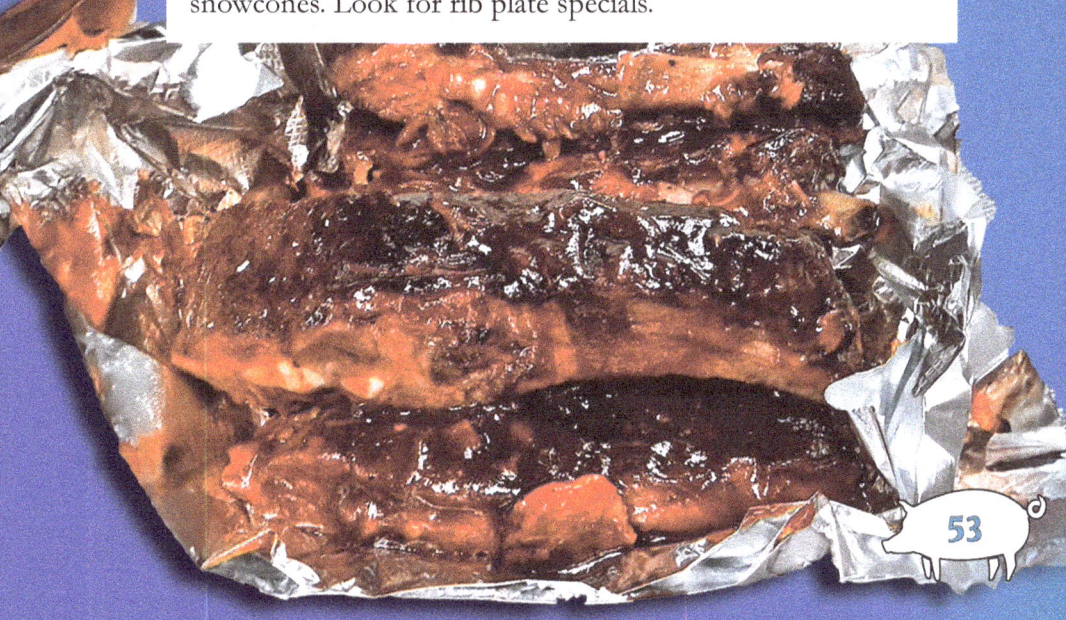

BURT'S BBQ

8089 US Highway 70 in Palestine
(870) 261-2498
Facebook.com/BurtBBQ1

When you walk into Burt Swiney's place the first time, chances are he will hand you a sample without even asking first. His barbecue tends to stand out in a region where pork is king. In this unassuming little converted carport tied to a kitchen and outdoor workshop, there are just a few tables. If Burt's not at the kitchen window, he's at one of those tables, wont to start telling you about the reclaimed ship wood used to line the ceiling. Burt spent a good chunk of his life as a truck driver, and experienced a lot of bad barbecue in those days. Knowing he could do better, he did just that, and this little place is where he sells it today. His brisket, touched with salt, pepper, brown sugar and just a hint of Crystal, is a worthy sandwich that doesn't require sauce - but he will suggest you try a little Miracle Whip on it. You should.

MIKE'S PARADISE GRILL & BBQ

**1320 North Division Street
  in Forrest City
(870) 633-0262
Facebook.com/Mikes.Paradise.BBQ**

For more than 30 years, this family-run beach-themed operation has offered pit-smoked barbecue, catfish, and hand-patted burgers. The barbecue here is pork, particularly chopped pork butt, racks of ribs, and smoked sausage. The outside may not look like much, but within, the walls are decorated with a vacation's worth of ocean dreams. Sauces range from medium heat to extra spicy, delineated by sandwich with colored toothpick.

DELTA Q + DELI

**1112 North Washington Street
  in Forrest City
(870) 633-1234
Facebook.com/FineSouthernSwine**

Delta Q started off as a pure barbecue shop but over the years has transitioned to a lunch-only deli with catering services. Today little of that original menu survives, though you can still get pulled pork and smoked bologna sandwiches, along with pulled pork egg rolls.

Kat Robinson

BETTY B'S SMOKEHOUSE BBQ
144 West Broadway in Forrest City
(870) 630-8221

Betty B's isn't large, but its menu is ample, with an emphasis on chicken and pork. Leg quarters, pork chops, whole wings, and rib tips star, along with chicken, pork, and turkey sandwiches and a mean Frito pie. Like many mid-Delta eateries closer to the eastern border, Betty B's offers spaghetti and smoked cabbage, in addition to the traditional beans, potato salad and coleslaw. It's all to-go, so be sure to grab a brownie or a slice of delectable lemon cake.

OLE SAWMILL CAFE

2299 North Washington Street in Forrest City
(870) 630-2299
OleSawmillCafeAr.com

Dating back to 1939 when it originally opened as the Liberty Bell Cafe, Ole Sawmill Cafe has become the region's best known country buffet, including chopped pork and pork ribs in its regular dinner service.

RIBS AND MORE

128 Highway 64 in Wynne
(870) 587-3131
Facebook.com/RibsAndMoreLLC

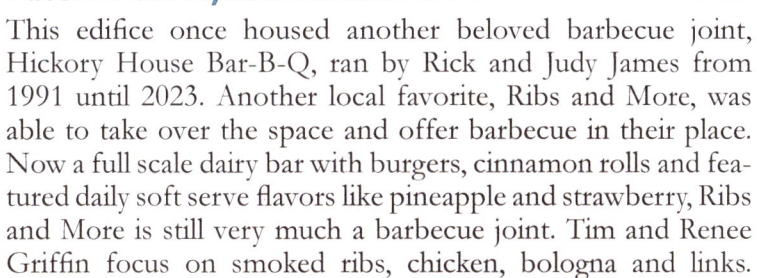

This edifice once housed another beloved barbecue joint, Hickory House Bar-B-Q, ran by Rick and Judy James from 1991 until 2023. Another local favorite, Ribs and More, was able to take over the space and offer barbecue in their place. Now a full scale dairy bar with burgers, cinnamon rolls and featured daily soft serve flavors like pineapple and strawberry, Ribs and More is still very much a barbecue joint. Tim and Renee Griffin focus on smoked ribs, chicken, bologna and links.

MOMMA LOUISE'S BBQ, BURGERS AND MORE

520 F Street in Wynne
(870) 362-6334
Facebook.com/WaitsBBQWynne

Once or twice a month, this food truck operation offers its menu, including pulled pork barbecue with coleslaw and sauce on a toasted bun.

GERONEE'S BBQ EXPRESS

5674 Highway 64 in Parkin
(870) 755-7832
Facebook.com/GeroneesBBQExpress

The building on the corner next to Parkin Archaeological State Park may not look like much from the outside, but pull up to the drive thru and peruse the menu handed to you for a selection of soul food and barbecue delights. Rib tips, chopped pork and smoked links come with two sides that include your choice of collard greens, candied sweet potatoes, fried cabbage, spaghetti, rice, and much more. Geronee's also smokes turkey necks, a soul food classic, and a generous number of other dishes. One of the few places left offering butter roll, that mid-Delta dessert specialty.

A&A CITY CAFE

101 Parkin Street in Parkin
(870) 755-2266

Family owned for generations, this humble eatery offers pulled pork sandwiches alongside its famous burgers and plate lunches. A community secret. Also known as Atkin's City Cafe.

CRAZY HORSE BBQ

909 Alabama Avenue in Earle
(870) 244-1011

Joe Hoard and Candace Cheers-Hoard have crafted a great new barbecue shop with plenty of space to enjoy your dine-in experience. The eatery - which features a horse smoking ribs as its logo instead of a pig- is known for its pulled pork sandwiches, ribs and rib tips. It also offers a brisket sandwich in the add-on section of the menu, and seasonal meats such as smoked turkey legs during November.

GLORY GRILL

1011 Second Street in Earle
(870) 792-4033
Facebook.com/TheGloryGrill

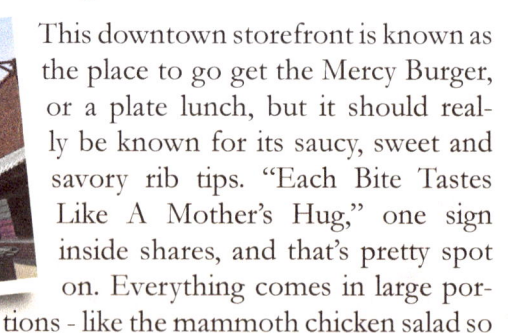

This downtown storefront is known as the place to go get the Mercy Burger, or a plate lunch, but it should really be known for its saucy, sweet and savory rib tips. "Each Bite Tastes Like A Mother's Hug," one sign inside shares, and that's pretty spot on. Everything comes in large portions - like the mammoth chicken salad so loaded you can barely see the iceberg lettuce. Get dessert - there's usually pecan cobbler, peach cobbler, and butter roll to enjoy.

TOPS BAR-B-Q

**3320 Interstate 55 in Marion
(870) 739-4085
TopsBarBQ.com**

There are 17 outlets for this Memphis-based franchise, but just the one in Arkansas. It bears letting you know that Tops offers smoked pork shouldeer, brisket, bologna and ribs on sandwiches with sauce and slaw, or as plates with two sides. What should be noted as unusual for our state is the mere existence of its breakfast, which in addition to traditional breakfast meats offers a breakfast bologna sandwich, a brisket and cream cheese sandwich with egg and cheese, and its original pork barbecue with white queso over an egg with barbecue sauce on a toasted bun.

BIG GUN'S PIT BBQ

**Regional Food Truck
(901) 395-1233
Facebook.com/BigGunsPitBBQ**

Based in Marion, this food truck operates in both Arkansas and Tennessee, offering smoked and chopped pork shoulder and chicken, half racks of ribs, thick sliced bologna and sliced beef brisket. Its signature sandwiches are served on buttered Texas toast with coleslaw.

Kat Robinson

STUMPY'S BACKYARD BBQ

2695 Arkansas Highway 77
Suite B in Marion
(870) 559-4451

One of the newer restaurants in this book, Stumpy's opened for business on October 14th, 2023. Kevin and Kelly Brawner started the place as a retirement job. Kevin's father and grandfather were both firefighters, as was he. Kelly's a nurse, and their daughter is a paramedic. Kevin was the firehouse cook, and both sets of their parents knew each other on the barbecue competition circuit, so it's always been in their blood. The couple bought a food truck a few years back, and eventually decided to retire and turn to barbecue full-time. They operte the restaurant with family.

The front room is all about the emergency responders in the family; the back, it's all about the sports Kevin is passionate about - mostly wrestling and racing. Belts, trophies, car doors, and framed photographs cover the walls. And on special occasions, a miniature wrestling ring is assembled, where the kids get to have a little fun.

The menu is packed with smoked meats - brisket, pulled pork, pulled chicken, ribs and more. From the pineapple slaw to the loaded mac and cheese to the Hawaiian Pork BBQ Sandwich with its pile of jalapenos, the menu is packed with plenty of choices.

62

KELLEY'S KICKIN' CHICKIN

1397 North Missouri Street in West Memphis
(870) 400-0013

Well known for 14 flavors of whole wings, Kelley's also offers smoked pork butt sandwiches, barbecue nachos, barbecue sandwiches, and smoked and fried bologna sandwiches alongside turnip greens, fried banana peppers, and a dozen other sides.

HOMETOWN GRILL

510 North Missouri Street in West Memphis
(870) 394-2621

A traditional neighborhood lunchroom, Hometown Grill offers several smoked meats, including West Memphis-popular smoked bologna, pulled pork butt, and bright red hot dogs alongside burgers, salads and daily lunch specials. The onion rings here are spot-on, and there's always a host of slices of various cakes by the register.

Kat Robinson

WILLIAMS BAR-B-Q
106 South 14th Street in West Memphis
(870) 735-0979

Since 1962, Mr. William's fine barbecue has delineated a fine West Memphis tradition, with all the particulars you would expect of an establishment of this sort. It is small, sure, with just a few tables. But the menu's humble offerings are satisfying - chopped pork butt, barbecue chicken, Polish sausage, burgers, catfish, smoked sausage, beef smoked sausages, and fried and smoked bologna - all offered with sides of baked beans, coleslaw or seasoned fries. The smoked and fried bologna comes either burger-dressed (lettuce, tomato, onion, and mayo or mustard) or barbecue style with sauce and coleslaw, and with its thick sweet sauce does a diner great. Sausages come hot dog style served on a long seedless bun. Go for the hot sauce - it has a lot of black peppery flavor.

The Arkansas Barbecue Traveler

RAY'S WORLD FAMOUS BAR-B-QUE

1805 North Missouri Street in West Memphis
(870) 732-2044
Facebook.com/RaysWorldFamous

If you're hungry and truckin' through West Memphis, tune to Channel 16 and ask for Ray's. The recently relocated barbecue joint is now drive-thru and delivery only. Ray's offers its pork, beef, bologna, Polish, ribs. and chickens "wet or dry," and with just a small handful of sides - beans, slaw, potato salad, fries, and barbecue spaghetti. A rarity in the Delta, Ray's offers massively thick beef ribs, each big enough for a meal in itself. The Super World Famous One Pounder is so big, Ray's sign declares "You'll need three hands to hold it!"

65

J&S GROCERY, GRILL and BAIT SHOP

24 US Highway 79 at the Heth exit (intersection with US Highway 70)
(870) 735-5648
Facebook.com/JandSGroandGrill

There's been a grocery of some sort or another in this lone building at the intersection since 1905. Today, it's a grocery, a grill, a bait shop, a deli, you name it - J&S happens to be a whole lot of things, and in addition to cooking killer breakfasts and burgers, smokes some great meat, too. Pulled pork sandwiches, plates and by-the-pound are on the regular menu; ribs, bologna and chicken are often ran as specials.

ROADSIDE BAR-B-QUE

196 Arkansas Highway 147 at Proctor
(870) 733-9208

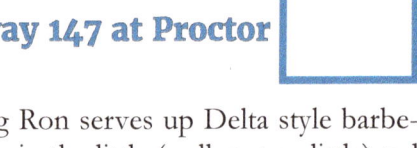

Big Ron serves up Delta style barbecue in the little (well, not so little) red shack with the smoker in the back. Folks have written all over the walls inside this establishment, with many leaving their decorated dollars to be posted on the wall. Ron smokes and chops pork, beef and chicken for sandwiches and plates, and also offers smoked bologna, Italian sausage, turkey legs, chicken halves and racks of ribs. Of note is the barbecue spaghetti, a side that's much more common in Memphis, but very popular here.

313 BLUES CAFE

313 South Broadway in Hughes
(870) 339-5025
Facebook.com/313BluesCafe

A soul food eatery in the eastern Delta, the 313 offers all sorts of comfort foods and Sunday dinners. Barbecue plates of pulled pork, smoked sausage and ribs come up on the specials rotation.

BONDS GROCERY and HIGHWATER LANDING

15235 Arkansas Highway 147 South in Horseshoe Lake
(870) 339-2464
Facebook.com/BondsGrocery

Throughout the year, this gas station/deli/convenience store throws meat on the smoker and serves up ribs, Boston butts, and all the sides - beans, coleslaw, potato salad and sweet-and-sour slaw. Check the Facebook for each feast, usuaally scheduled for major holiday weekends.

Kat Robinson

JONES BAR-B-Q DINER

219 West Louisiana in Marianna
(870) 295-3807
Facebook.com/JonesBarBQDiner

"It's steady hickory because it's tasty," Harold Jones told me when I asked one summer morning about the wood he used. It gets fired into coals in an old brick fireplace in the back room before being taken over to put in the smoker. Not much has changed at this place since he took over in 1964, and nothing worth noting has changed about the product since the Jones family name was attached to the eatery in 1943. Its roots stretch back to post-Civil War times, to The Hole in the Wall, a cafe on the Marianna square. It's the same barbecue prepared in the same way from butts smoked overnight that are fall-apart tender when they're pulled off, all ready to be served when the James Beard America's Classic winner opens the door at 7:30 a.m. Sometimes folks are waiting. Often, it's all gone before nine or ten. You have three choices for your pork - on a sandwich with slaw or without slaw or by the pound. That's it. It's just smoked pork with a thin vinegar sauce on white bread with slaw, and it's still (in 2024) just $4. Anything else you want, you're limited to bags of chips or a Coke from the fridge.

CYPRESS CORNER BAR-B-Q

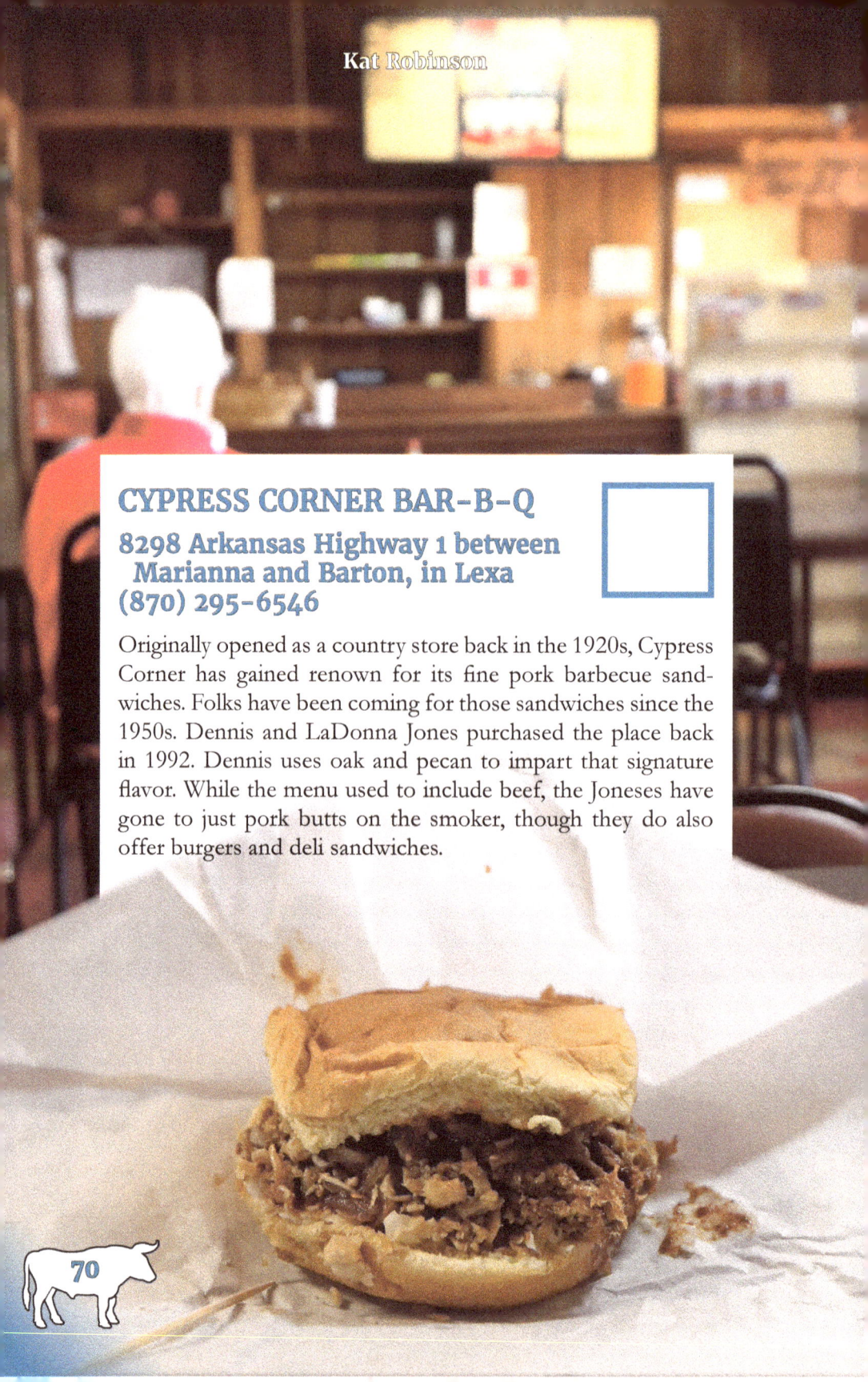

8298 Arkansas Highway 1 between Marianna and Barton, in Lexa (870) 295-6546

Originally opened as a country store back in the 1920s, Cypress Corner has gained renown for its fine pork barbecue sandwiches. Folks have been coming for those sandwiches since the 1950s. Dennis and LaDonna Jones purchased the place back in 1992. Dennis uses oak and pecan to impart that signature flavor. While the menu used to include beef, the Joneses have gone to just pork butts on the smoker, though they do also offer burgers and deli sandwiches.

DEE'S BBQ at
SOUTHLAND ROAD STORE & DINER
23 Phillips Road 230 in Lexa
(870) 572-3166

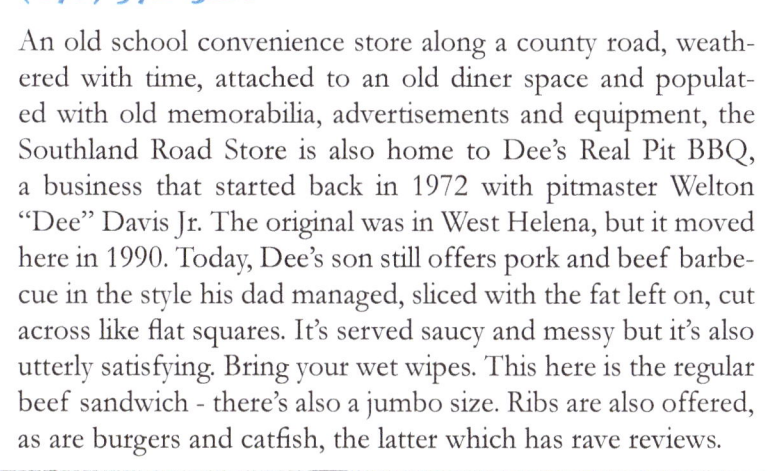

An old school convenience store along a county road, weathered with time, attached to an old diner space and populated with old memorabilia, advertisements and equipment, the Southland Road Store is also home to Dee's Real Pit BBQ, a business that started back in 1972 with pitmaster Welton "Dee" Davis Jr. The original was in West Helena, but it moved here in 1990. Today, Dee's son still offers pork and beef barbecue in the style his dad managed, sliced with the fat left on, cut across like flat squares. It's served saucy and messy but it's also utterly satisfying. Bring your wet wipes. This here is the regular beef sandwich - there's also a jumbo size. Ribs are also offered, as are burgers and catfish, the latter which has rave reviews.

BURGER SHACK
372 Sebastian Street in Helena-West Helena
(870) 572-2271

Barbecue sandwiches perfect to go with the Best Coke in Town await you at this local longstanding favorite.

HARVEY'S QUE

Regional Food Truck
205 Plaza in Helena-West Helena
(240) 216-9705
Facebook.com/HarveysQue

"Drag them feet, miss ya meat!" A heck of a slogan but appropriate for this meat-heavy food truck, which provides ribs and rib tips, Polish sausages, pulled pork and "sneaky links" off the smoker. Matthew Harvey's bright red trailer can be spotted all over the region, out to Marvell, Gould, Elaine, Bethlehem and home base in Helena-West Helena. Watch out for Leg Day - that is, turkey leg day!

DOWNTOWN BAR AND GRILL

520B Walnut Street
 in Helena-West Helena
(870) 714-2940

This popular downtown lunch spot offers smoked and chopped pork and chicken on sandwiches, nachos, and salads. The chicken comes mixed in its sauce in advance.

BISCUIT ROW BBQ

321 Phillips Street in Helena-West Helena
(870) 714-0184

Frank Clancy and Karen Stoner took a building on Phillips Street that was about to be torn down and revitalized it into a destination for dining. Smoking takes place in the old service station on the corner, while service happens at a counter indoors. In-between there's a patio, and who knows what else will be conjured. The barbecue hotspot has a strong focus on chicken thighs, the dark meat taking the flavor very well. There are also chicken wings, as well as sliced fall-apart brisket, pulled pork and ribs. The wood for the smoke comes from land Clancy's held for decades. Stoner's family recipe potato salad includes sweet pickles, which really makes it something special.

SMITTY SMOKE BBQ, RIBS & CATFISH

Food Truck in Helena-West Helena
(870) 995-5610
Facebook.com/SmittySmokeBBQ17

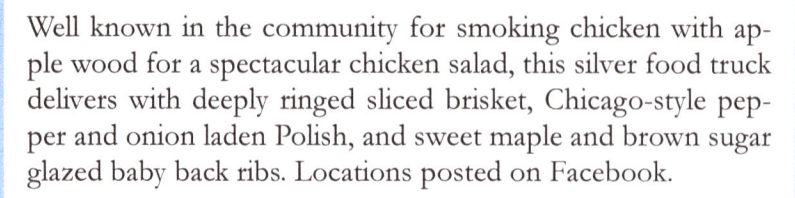

Well known in the community for smoking chicken with apple wood for a spectacular chicken salad, this silver food truck delivers with deeply ringed sliced brisket, Chicago-style pepper and onion laden Polish, and sweet maple and brown sugar glazed baby back ribs. Locations posted on Facebook.

DELTA QUE AND BREW

233 Cherry Street in Helena-West Helena
DeltaQueBrew.com
(870) 995-5150

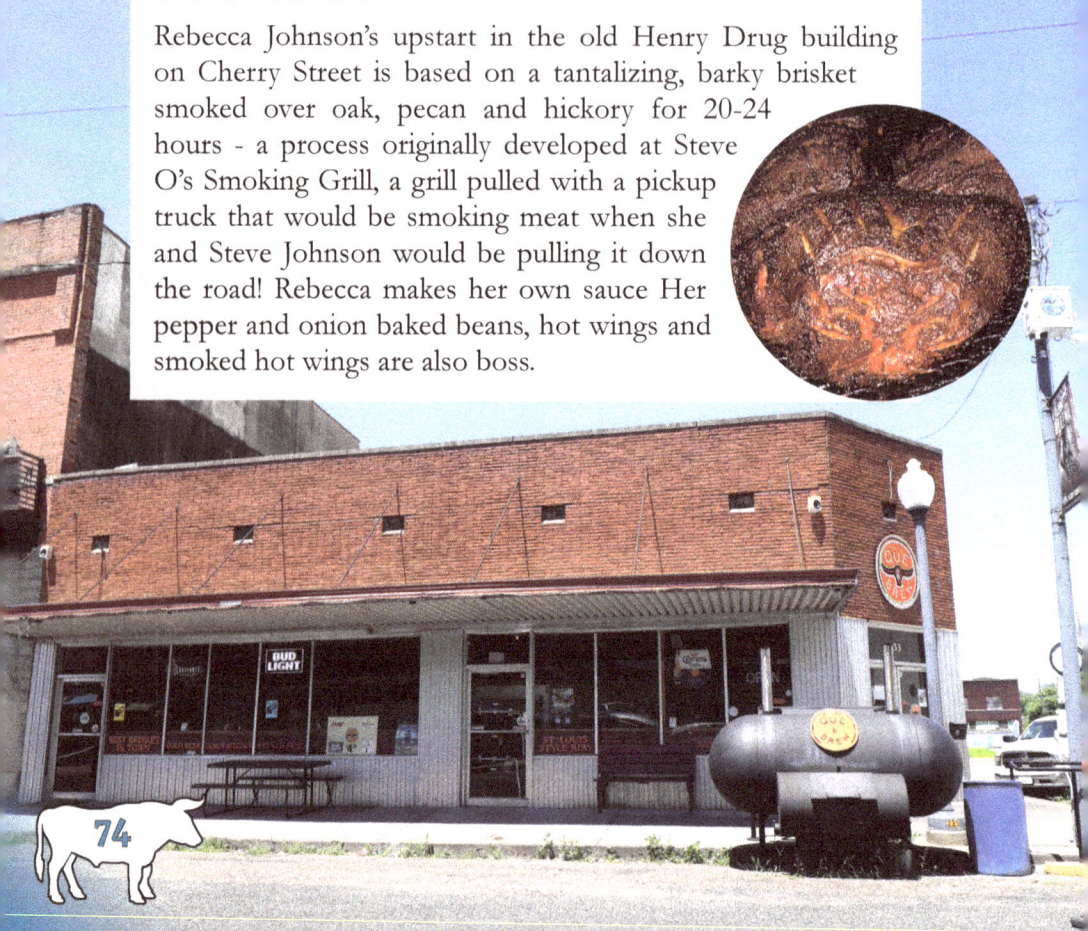

Rebecca Johnson's upstart in the old Henry Drug building on Cherry Street is based on a tantalizing, barky brisket smoked over oak, pecan and hickory for 20-24 hours - a process originally developed at Steve O's Smoking Grill, a grill pulled with a pickup truck that would be smoking meat when she and Steve Johnson would be pulling it down the road! Rebecca makes her own sauce Her pepper and onion baked beans, hot wings and smoked hot wings are also boss.

The Arkansas Barbecue Traveler

POPLAR GROVE BAR-B-Q
11166 US Highway 49 in Poplar Grove
(870) 638-9158

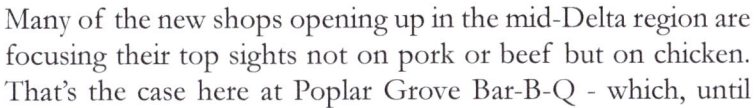

Many of the new shops opening up in the mid-Delta region are focusing their top sights not on pork or beef but on chicken. That's the case here at Poplar Grove Bar-B-Q - which, until recently, didn't even have a Google listing. The menu begins with chicken leg quarters and half chickens, exactly where I think it should start, after trying the half chicken dinner myself. I was on my way from place to place and didn't have time to dine in, but caught myself a couple miles down the road salivating at the scent. Beautifully smoked, herb rubbed chicken where the flavor went all the way into the breast and thigh, served with a thin lush sauce, so good I was sucking on the bones while sitting in a parking lot with no shame. It was so quick out of the smoker it had barely rested, and it was so hot it was hard to hold, but there was no resisting that bird. The creamy potato salad and the piquant sweet coleslaw are made by ladies who are friends of the proprietor. Ribs, pulled pork, and brisket are also available, and often homemade desserts on the counter for later.

LION'S DEN DRIVE IN

212 South Fifth Street in Clarendon
(870) 747-5221
Facebook.com/LionsDenDriveIn

For more than half a century, this dairy bar has served as the hub for Clarendon. It's even named after the local school mascot. Justin and Amber Beck bought the place from Carolyn Vent, who had owned and run the place since the 1970s. They added to the menu several items, including sandwiches, quesadillas and nachos featuring the pork butts they smoke each week. You can even call ahead and reserve a whole Boston butt to pick up on Saturday.

My dude Grav loves the Squealed Cheese, a grilled cheese sandwich with bacon, pulled pork and barbecue sauce with buttered and toasted bread. A good bet!

BENDI'S DINER

101 North Sixth Street in Clarendon
(870) 747-1447

One stop convenience - grab your breakfast or lunch while doing your laundry at the on-site laundry mat, or wash your car in the single stall at the back of Bendi's lot while you're waiting for your to-go order. That carwash is out back of the barbecue hut, where the pork for sandwiches and nachos is pit smoked daily. Check the menu board for daily sides, specials and flavors of fried pies.

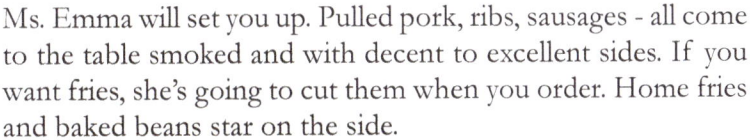

KIBB'S BAR-B-Q #1

436 West Second Street in Stuttgart
(870) 673-4261

Ms. Emma will set you up. Pulled pork, ribs, sausages - all come to the table smoked and with decent to excellent sides. If you want fries, she's going to cut them when you order. Home fries and baked beans star on the side.

Kat Robinson

KIBB'S BAR-B-Q #2
1102 East Harrison in Stuttgart
(870) 673-2072

If you're looking for your sign, you're going to find it here. Walker Kibble's unfinished wood building is covered with various signs promoting "Bar-B-Q Beef or Pork, Hot, Medium or Mild Sauce," "Bar-B-Q Ribs Large or Small," and "Today GOOOD for Bar-B-Q" all point out the obvious to anyone who's eaten here. That hickory smoked meat is always a hit, whether it's the thin sliced and layered bologna on a sandwich or a wax paper wrapped serving of rib tips. Beef sandwiches come two ways - with barbecue sauce and slaw or dressed like a burger. Both are just swell.

CRAIG BROS BAR-B-Q CAFE
15 West Walnut (US 70) in De Valls Bluff
(870) 998-2616

Lawrence and Wes Craig, a nephew-and-uncle team, opened Craig Brothers Cafe in 1947. Lawrence had been the cook on one of the many boats working the Mississippi, and he brought with him a lot of the technique he learned to create the flavor that's now one of those signature Arkansas essences found nowhere else. That sauce - I like the hotter version of it more than the mild - has some seriously unusual notes to it - something that comes across as nutmeg or cinnamon, touches that could be apple or green bell pepper - but it's a family secret. If you ask real nice, you can purchase a bottle to take home with you.

Today, Lawrence's son Robert Craig - who's also a deacon and internet radio host - operates this throwback establishment, changing none of what made the restaurant famous. You can still smell the smoker going more than a mile to the west and sometimes as far off as Interstate 40, and if you follow it, you can enjoy that sliced brisket or pork or an order of ribs, or a Polish sausage. There are burgers for those who make the decision not to savor that barbecue, and they're pretty decent, but if you're coming all this way, you're not coming for a burger. Just remember to bring cash.

THE SWAMP

223 North Main Street in England
(501) 842-1414
Facebook.com/SwampOfEngland

Brian and Tina Hawkins bought the restaurant building and opened it under their name in the fall of 2019. Brian had previously run another restaurant in the building for a previous owner, so they had some idea of what they were getting into. Brian puts a smoke of 16-20 hours on his butts and brisket, and also smokes a killer turkey. Chicken halves, gator sausage, all sorts of things come off that smoker. They all pair well with the Louisiana flavors imported into the menu - fried oyster and fried shrimp sandwiches and gumbo and such, and homemade beans, slaw, sauce - all around, just a delightful place to grab lunch. Just don't come between lunch and dinner - the doors are locked while the Hawkins prepare for the next rush.

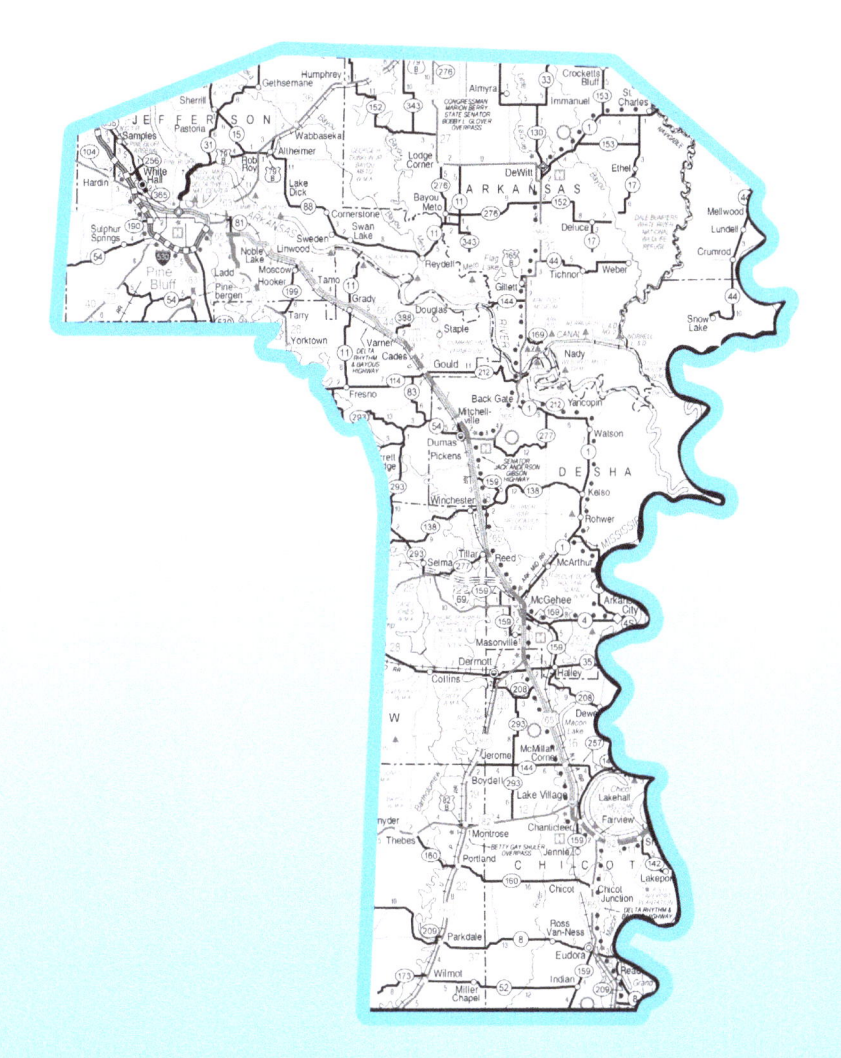

The Lower Delta

BUBBA FLAY
Food Truck/Caterer in Pine Bluff
(870) 413-3081

Neighborhood barbecue? Bubba's your guy. He pops up here and there all around Pine Bluff with his smoker and a little attitude. Ribs, turkey legs, pulled pork, he's got you covered when he's out and about. When he's not, he's fishing. Can't blame him there!

LIL D'S BBQ
412 East Harding in Pine Bluff
(870) 209-9377

Opened in April of 2019, Daryl and Evette Graydon have a problem I haven't encountered at other barbecue restaurants - a line of cars that can stretch for blocks each day. The restaurant, which primarily serves drive-thru customers, tends to swell out every single day. Folks call ahead to pick up "cotton ball soft" rib tips, Polish, pulled pork, St. Louis-style ribs, chicken, and brisket. If turkey wing flats are on the menu, get them.

KIBB'S BAR-B-Q

1400 South Blake Street in Pine Bluff
(870) 535-8400

KIBB'S BAR-B-Q #2

2117 University Drive in Pine Bluff
(870) 535-8400

Walter Kibble's family operates these two outposts of the Kibb's name, with all the good food you'd come to expect. Here, smoked bologna is quite popular, as are the rib tips. Sauce comes mild, medium or hot, and the hot is real hot.

T'S PLACE

3714 South Camden Road in Pine Bluff (Watson Chapel area)
(870) 879-9691

It started out a quarter a century ago as Anne's Country Cookin', but after Anne passed, it became T's Place in 2017. Each morning offers tri-fold omelets and big fat biscuits every morning at breakfast. When it comes to lunch or dinner, you can get a smoked pork sandwich with slaw covered in sauce or have it on a salad with tomato, egg, cheese and bacon.

Kat Robinson

LEGENDS RESTAURANT at SARACEN CASINO

1 Saracen Resort Drive in Pine Bluff (870) 686-9001
SaracenResort.com/dining

Chef Manley Clark's attention to detail is evident in his array of dishes featuring hickory and mesquite smoked pork butt, brisket, and baby back ribs. From a two pound loaded baked potato to a platter of brisket-topped nachos, and even a massive half pound burger with chuck, brisket and short rib, this is gorgeously large, tasty dining within a brand new casino and resort.

BRIGGS BBQ, COOKING & CATERING

Food Truck in Pine Bluff
(870) 718-9769
Facebook.com/B2C2BriggsBBQ

Briggs, or B2C2 as it's also known, is big around Pine Bluff, offering up legendary smoked St. Louis style ribs, pork butts, chicken and brisket. Clinton Briggs and his team bring not only extraordinary smoked meats but a cadre of magnificent desserts, from a large selection of homestyle cakes to massive pans of banana pudding.

POP'S PLACE

Food truck
2901 South Camden Road in Pine Bluff
(870) 550-6322
Facebook.com/ PopsPlaceWatsonChapel

A friendly, family-run enterprise selling sandwiches and breakfast biscuits. The simple menu includes a large brisket sandwich topped with large cut coleslaw and a sweet sauce. Look for the blue food truck.

BULLSDENGRILL

Mobile catering from White Hall
(501) 920-4784
Facebook.com/BullsDenGrill

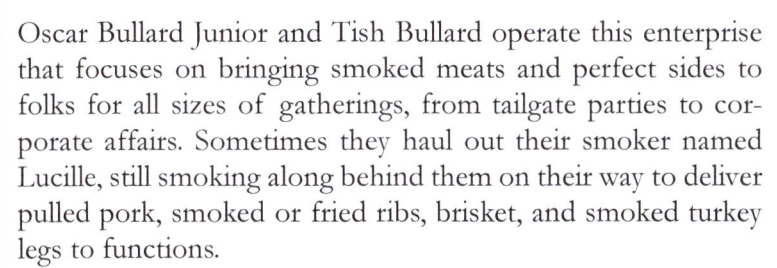

Oscar Bullard Junior and Tish Bullard operate this enterprise that focuses on bringing smoked meats and perfect sides to folks for all sizes of gatherings, from tailgate parties to corporate affairs. Sometimes they haul out their smoker named Lucille, still smoking along behind them on their way to deliver pulled pork, smoked or fried ribs, brisket, and smoked turkey legs to functions.

WRIGHT'S RANCH HOUSE
6220 Dollarway Road in White Hall
(870) 329-5359

A slightly smaller version of the one in Sheridan, this original country haven offers both smoked beef and pork, with its Piggy Pies and Hoggie Pies (on beans with slaw, sauce and nacho cheese). The ribs here are loin back pork ribs. Sausage links are also popular alongside the steaks, burgers and chicken fried pork (!) that grace the menu.

THE WOOD SHED BBQ & CATERING
9621 US Highway 270 in White Hall
(870) 247-7424
TheWoodShedBBQ.com

Bryan and Kassie Atwood have created this adorable countryfied stop out of an old dairy bar, expanding it and adding a massive smoker to handle its wide berth of smoked meats. Of note is The Lumberjack Sampler - chicken, sausage, pork and brisket as its own big plate. One of the few joints around still offering tamales alongside barbecue.

KI BBQ AND FISH

109 West Choctaw Street in Dumas
(870) 382-0056
Facebook.com/KiBBQandFish

A spotless joint in downtown Dumas, this place is best known for its fish - some say that catfish is the best in the state - but it's also a barbecue joint where saucy pork ribs reign supreme. Look out for turkey leg day.

BIG BOYS BBQ

437 US Highway 65 in Dumas
(870) 382-0822

Saucy tips and ribs have put this place on the map, but I found the beautifully spiced and smoked half a chicken to really shine on this menu. Polish, pork butt, brisket are all smoked here. The menu is small but also has burgers and fish dinners, and the dessert is always banana pudding.

HOOT'S BBQ

2008 US Highway 65 in McGehee
(870) 222-1234

Suzie Powell continues to operate and manage this oversized barbecue hall that's become the center of nightlife in McGehee. The spacious dining rooms, banquet room and bar inside this reclaimed cattle sale barn are decorated with memarabilia she and her husband David found while touring the United States in their RV after retirement. The couple started Hoot's after returning home from those travels. The brisket here is, in my opinion, the best in southeast Arkansas and one of the top in the state. The chicken is also high on my list, and those onion rings are mighty fine.

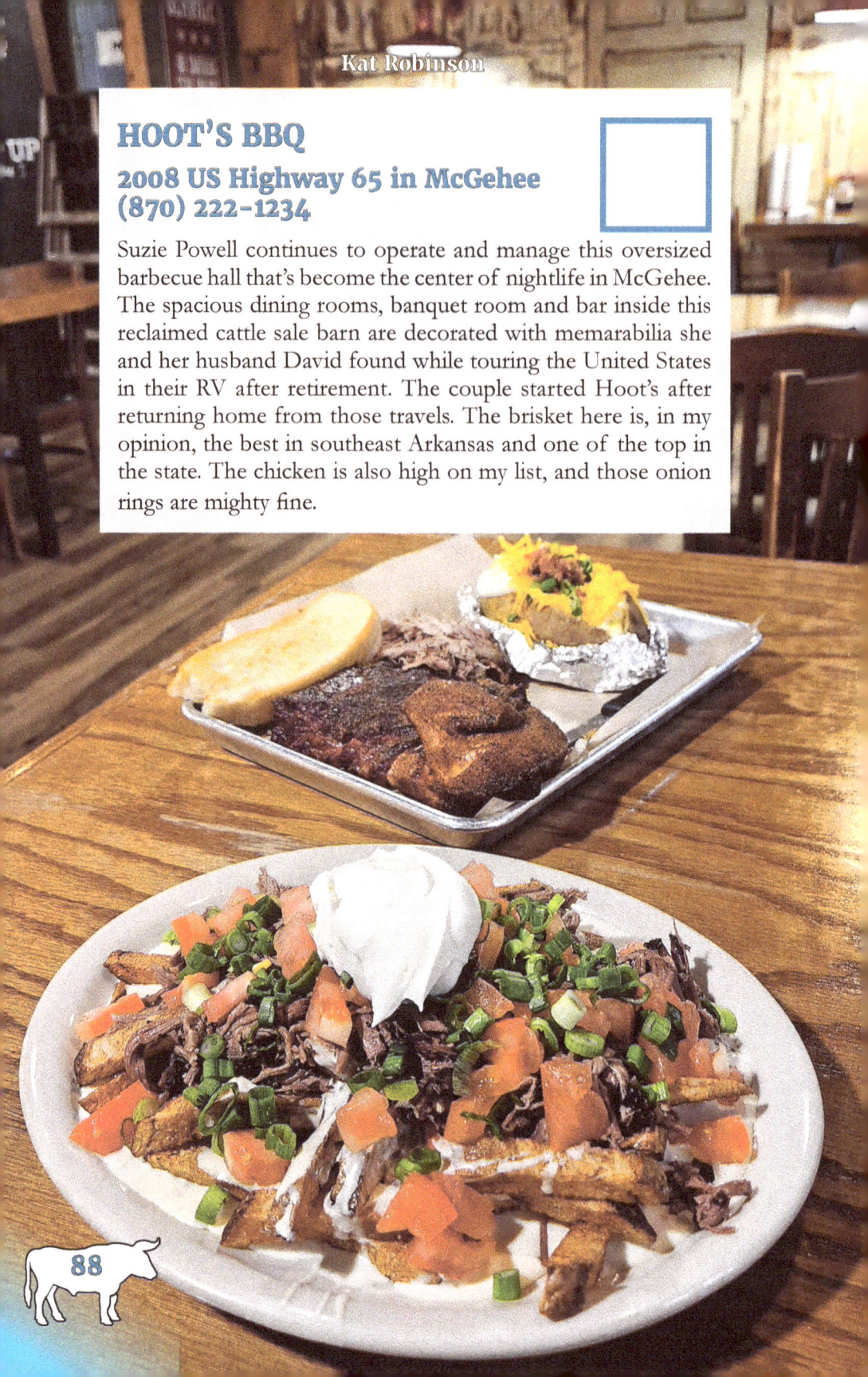

DERMOTT BBQ

105 East Iowa Street in Dermott
(870) 538-3131

Nature abhors a vacuum. The owners of Dermott Bar-B-Q and Deli closed shop in May 2024, but the space was soon back open two months later. In adition to ribs, brisket and pulled pork plates, the place has a smoked pork melt that's much talked about.

RIVER BEND BBQ, SEAFOOD AND STEAKS

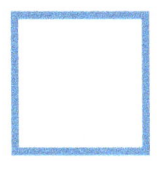

1024 US Highway 65 in Lake Village
(870) 632-0766

Opened in July 2024 in the former JJ's Cafe on Lake Village's main drag, this hotspot tends to sell out several times a month. While catfish and gulf seafood are the stars of the menu, barbecue pork ribs and pulled pork are also popular, **the ribs served saucy and the pork shredded fine.**

Lower Arkansas

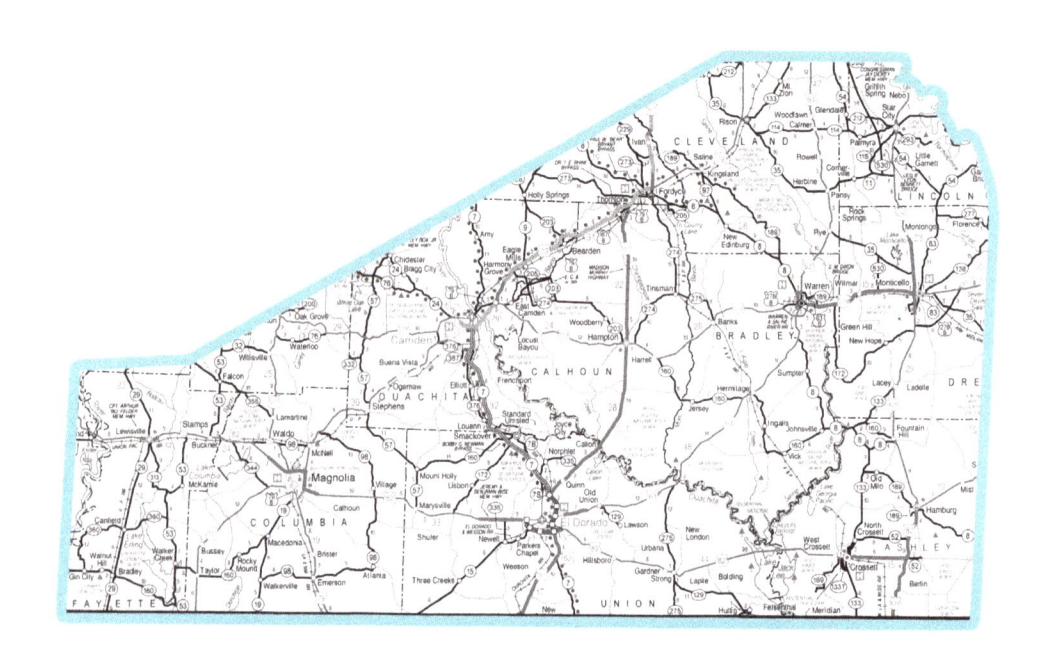

L&Y CARWASH AND BARBECUE

1034 Arkansa Highway 133 in Crossett
(870) 831-1862
Facebook.com/GreatBBQCrossett

Barbecue at a carwash? More like a carwash at a barbecue. The family that opened their barbecue joint in this gas station kept having folks walk in and tell them they needed to open a carwash. Peer pressure won out. Now you can have your smoked ribs, sausage or chicken dinner while your car receives a complete detail and wash - a good one, as I can personally attest!

RAY'S

**207 US Highway 425 in Monticello
(870) 367-3292
RaysHamburgers.com**

Since 1964, Ray's has been a local institution, offering a broad menu to generations. Originally opened by C.L. Ray, the tiny dairy bar expanded to accommodate an entire city's worth of hungry eaters. Chris Ray continues the tradition, offering the restaurant's vast menu, which includes his grandfather's famed smoked pork and beef, served chopped or sliced on sandwiches or thickly sliced for plate dinners.

BUBBIE'S

157 North Park Drive in Monticello
(870) 367-0600
Facebook.com/BubbiesinMonticello

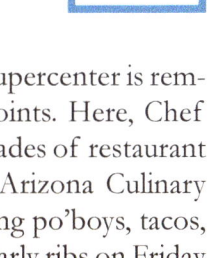

This friendly spot out front of the Walmart Supercenter is reminiscent of a host of college town burger joints. Here, Chef Brian Alexander has taken more than two decades of restaurant experience and a culinary degree from the Arizona Culinary Institute to craft a comfortable menu featuring po'boys, tacos, salads, spuds, burgers, and barbecue - particularly ribs on Friday and Saturday and brisket and pork sandwiches. The barbecue here is more Lower Arkansas style, where the meat is kept moist and soft until ready to serve.

THE BUCK STOP MEAT STORE

822 Barkada Road in Monticello
(870) 460-9337

Double smoked hams are one of the specialties at this full service meat market and deer processing storefront. Smoked prime rib and turkeys are also often available, as are particularly Arkansas specialties like double-smoked deer bologna . Smoking supplies are also on-hand if you want to pick up fresh meat from this store and take it home for your own use.

3 HEETHENS BBQ
249 US Highway 425 in Monticello
(870) 377-0319

Justin Linely says it's divine providence that he's now serving barbecue from a truck under a carport along US 425 in Monticello. Linely had spent around three decades working as a welder. He'd had a pretty tough day, and he prayed for a sign to tell him it was time to hang it up. He walked out on his back porch under overcast skies, and the sun just came out momentarily and blinded him before going back behind the clouds. He took that sign, quit his job, moved back to his hometown of Monticello and bought the barbecue trailer. He opened 3 Heethens in the summer of 2022 and has been going strong ever since. Justin smokes with local red oak. Hi s specialties are pulled pork, jumbo smoked cheeseburger, rib tips and beef sausage links. He's usually open on Fridays and Saturdays.

ENDSLEY'S BURGER SHACK

109 Carla Lane in Monticello
(870) 281-5793

Pork loin? Larry Endsley knows how to smoke the tar out of it. After starting out by the old Breaker Drive In, this orange food trailer is now in its permanent home on Carla. It's become a destination for folks wanting a smoked loin sandwich, quarter pound smoked franks, Polish, smoked sausage, butts and briskets.

TWISTIN COPPER KITCHEN

Regional food truck
(870) 692-4384

Matthew Jones has this operation all over south Arkansas, with stops in Rison, White Hall, Pine Bluff and Star City. Brisket heads the barbecue menu, along with pulled pork and Cajun sausage. Smoked meats are also served on nachos and mac and cheese here.

JACKSON'S HOLY SMOKES BBQ

1003 North Lincoln Avenue in Star City
(870) 628-1454
Facebook.com/JacksonsHolySmokesBBQ

Just north of Star City sits this residential barbecue joint that features all the meats, incluuding a rather succulent and moist chicken breast. The Jacksons started with a converted camper, then over time moved their operation from food truck to brick-and-mortar in March of 2023. Check Facebook for specials, including scrumptious cakes and pies.

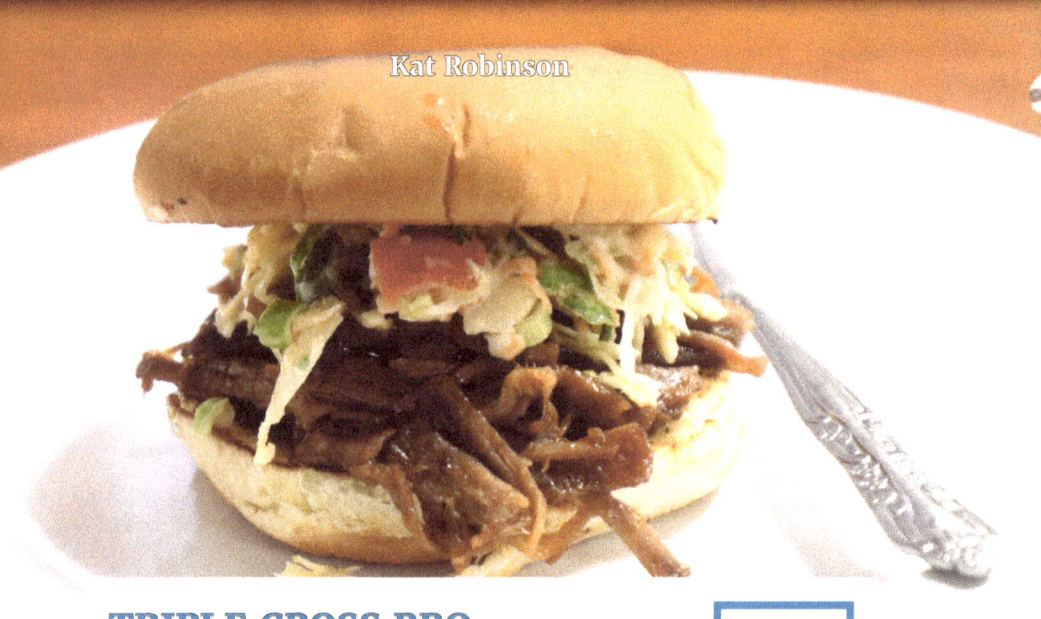

TRIPLE CROSS BBQ

730 Arkansas Highway 35 in Rison
(870) 325-2267

This is the regular barbecue beef sandwich at Triple Cross BBQ in Rison. It's based on long, slow-smoked brisket that's rendered down to the soft, almost pot roast consistency common to sandwich barbecue in Lower Arkansas. It's topped with a homemade bell pepper and cabbage slaw and it's served on a seedless bun. Triple Cross started off in Fordyce in 2013 before moving to Rison for a brand new brick and mortar in 2021. It's a place where fellowship is common and the desserts and the fried pies come in a beautiful array of flavors.

MONA JO'S KITCHEN & GRILL

700 North Edgar Street in Fordyce
(501) 521-4318
Facebook.com/
MonaJosKitchenandGrill

"High quality comfort food with a touch of soul" is how this grill is advertised, and for good reason. The dry rub ribs fall off the bone, and the pulled pork sandwiches come with both slaw and a nice thick sauce.

RED'S RESTAURANT

**1935 US Highway 79 in Fordyce
(870) 352-7803
Facebook.com/RedsRestaurantFordyce**

Red's does a lot of things - home cooking, catfish cooked multiple ways, burgers - but man, this beef barbecue has a wonderful smoke flavor, the coleslaw is sweet and chopped small, and that massive side of sauce is really, really thick. And if you're not in the mood for barbecue, I highly recommend the small blackened catfish dinner, complete with green tomato relish, lemon, onion and hushpuppies, like all good Arkansas catfish is served. Be sure to ask what pies are available when you order so you can secure your slice.

Kat Robinson

ROBERTSON SMOKEHOUSE

215 West Central Street in Warren
(870) 226-2271
Facebook.com/RobertsonSmokehouse

Cody and Jana Robertson's massive smoker handles all sorts of meats over hardwood smoke at this rustic-built barbecue shack. Brisket, smoked chicken legs, pulled pork, ribs, and sausage, all served wth one of three sauces - hot, Carolina gold and sweet. Holiday orders with turkeys and hams are available.

WILLIE'S PLACE

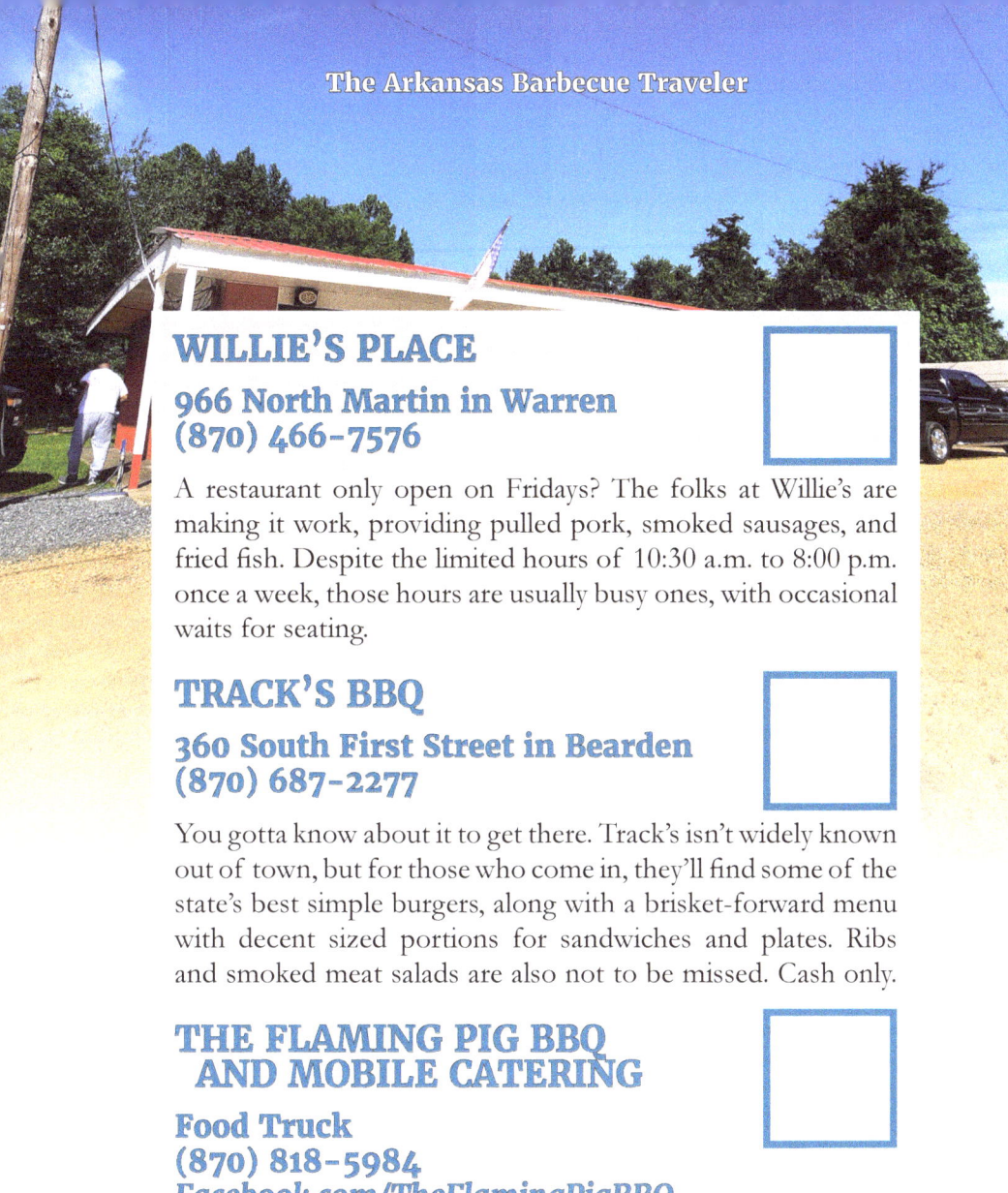

966 North Martin in Warren
(870) 466-7576

A restaurant only open on Fridays? The folks at Willie's are making it work, providing pulled pork, smoked sausages, and fried fish. Despite the limited hours of 10:30 a.m. to 8:00 p.m. once a week, those hours are usually busy ones, with occasional waits for seating.

TRACK'S BBQ

360 South First Street in Bearden
(870) 687-2277

You gotta know about it to get there. Track's isn't widely known out of town, but for those who come in, they'll find some of the state's best simple burgers, along with a brisket-forward menu with decent sized portions for sandwiches and plates. Ribs and smoked meat salads are also not to be missed. Cash only.

THE FLAMING PIG BBQ AND MOBILE CATERING

Food Truck
(870) 818-5984
Facebook.com/TheFlamingPigBBQ

Clifton and Angela Humphries run a bright red food trailer that's always on the move. Trying to track down this barbecue can be a challenge, especially during festival seasons in the spring and fall - but it's worth it. Brisket burnt ends, pulled pork grilled cheese, even smoked hot dogs can be found on this menu.

BULLDOG DRIVE IN

206 Third Street in Hampton
(870) 798-4525

This place offers classic drive-in fare like burgers, chicken strips, fried pickles and the like - with nice smoky pork barbecue for sandwiches and nachos.

MORTUARY BBQ AND GRILL

Food truck in Lower Arkansas
(501) 697-2905
Facebook.com/MortuaryBBQ

Dexter Samual opened his memorably named food truck in 2016. While operating out of Hampton, he ranges out to El Dorado and further to serve his unusually themed food truck dishes like the QuesaKilla, the Undertaker, Tombstone Potatoes and Casket Chips - all served with your choice of pulled pork, chicken, or brisket, depending on what he's smoking that day. Be looking for his large black trailer - he's dying to see you.

HICKORY HUT

665 Bradley Ferry Roand in Camden
(870) 837-2541
Facebook.com/HickoryHutBbq

Beef, pork, ribs, turkey and sausages smoked with, you guessed it, hickory - all part of the regular fare at this intersection barbecue shack. Vinegar coleslaw, corn on the cob, and homemade potato salad and baked beans round out most of the menu here - and there's always peach cobbler for dessert.

TJ's PLACE

1385 California Avenue in Camden
(870) 837-1707

One of those great little cash-only operations that has barely changed since the 1980s, where you can still get hand-squeezed lemonade and fried pies. While burgers and fish are the specialties, TJ's also offers barbecue pork plates and sandwiches.

OLD HICKORY SAUCE COMPANY

801 South Broadway Street in Smackover
(870) 725-2190
OldHickorySauceCompany.com

Remember the Old Hickory Restaurant from back in the day in El Dorado? That restaurant opened in 1944, and though it's been closed for decades, the sauce persists thanks to this company. You can find it on the shelves at Brookshires stores throughout the region or order straight off the website.

SMOKIN JOE'S PIT STOP BBQ

809 Pershing Highway in Smackover
(870) 944-5002

Burnt ends are not common in Lower Arkansas. This place offers them both in brisket and in pork belly - and that's just at the start of its extravaganza. With a meat-driven menu that features hot links, smoked sausage, chicken halves, baby back ribs and pulled pork, carnivores will be satisfied here.

Kat Robinson

HOWELL's BBQ
2011 Junction City Road in El Dorado
(870) 864-9800

Originally started in Waldo, Lynnwood and Barbara Howell moved into the Cranky Frank's BBQ location on Junction City Road around 2012 and expanded their offerings, quickly stepping into their spot as a force in El Dorado area barbecue. Brisket stars here, and it's served with your choice of sauce. The meat on its own needs no sauce, being juicy and extremely tender. However, that spicy Babbs BBQ sauce will take your breath away. On my first bite I found myself suddenly unable to speak, the capsaicin had grabbed hold of my vocal cords and rendered me mute. You better believe I finished that sandwich! In addition to great ribs, turkey, sausages and chicken, the Howells serve up both beef and pork tamales and offer homemade cakes, cheesecake, and banana pudding for dessert.

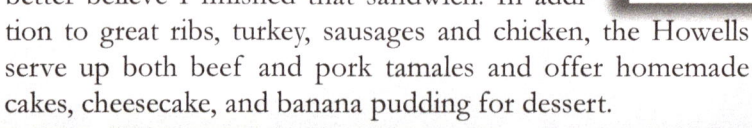

BROWN'S SOUTHERN SMOKE BBQ

1304 East Hillsboro in El Dorado
(616) 729-7570
Facebook.com/BrownsSouthernSmoke

Harold Brown's family owned operation may be carry-out and catering only, but it's gotten rave reviews for the generous portions and excellent flavors. Harold believes in working in the community and helping others out, and it's not uncommon to see Brown's on the scene at various charity gatherings here and there. The operation recently moved to this Hillsboro shop. Check the Facebook for specials and call your order in ahead.

CANDLEY'S COOKIN' #1 AND #2

Two food trucks
1205 West Hillsboro in El Dorado
(870) 310-5520
Facebook.com/CandleysCookin

Shelia McGhee and Valerie Lumsey love to feed people - and it shows. The sisters run two food trucks serving soul food to El Dorado. They're carrying on a tradition began by Reverend James Candley, who would smoke meats and bake cakes to feed folks who needed it. The menu varies but often includes brisket, ribs, turkey legs and even smoked oxtails.

Kat Robinson

JJ's BBQ

1000 East Main Street in El Dorado
(870) 862-1777
JJsBBQ.com

Joe and Joyce Gallea opened JJ's in 1990 with their own concoctions of sauce and rub, focusing on pork, turkey, brisket, and cured hams to put into their smoker. This is the sort of place you might envision when thinking of classic barbecue restaurants - the entire facility is covered with memorabilia, articles about the locals, various signs and such... all great to read and enjoy as you dive into a plate of ribs or that smoky, pliant chicken. Cakes made daily, or you can always enjoy a Flywheel fried pie for dessert.

BIG BEAR BBQ

Food Truck
2411 Edgewood Street in El Dorado
(870) 312-2065
Facebook.com/BigBearBBQARK

This mobile traler is where you'll find a plethora of smoked meats ready to go for a quick order of satisfying, savory delights like burnt ends, brisket, chicken thighs, ribs and brisket. Big Bear has a signature dish that's a meal in itself - a cheese-filled jalapeno wrapped in sausage and bacon that's smoked to doneness and served with sauce. Memorable and craveworthy.

MAD 2 ME BBQ SHACK

Food Truck in El Dorado
(870) 639-0448
Facebook.com/Mad.To.Me.BBQ.Shack

Opened in April 2024, Susan Morgan Smith is knocking it out of the park with her array of smoked meats. One of Arkansas's pitmistresses, she's smoking up a variety of meats, including boudin (not common at Arkansas barbecue joints), brisket burnt ends, sausage, pulled pork and ribs. This pit boss queen also understands other needs, and offers a sugar free barbecue sauce for those who want sauce but have to watch that glucose. Mad 2 Me BBQ Shack also has spicy coleslaw and offers pulled pork sliders for a quick, easy bite.

PAULEY'S PIT STOP
1173 Urbana Road east of El Dorado
(870) 260-2919

Dewayne and Theresa Pauley are making their sausage, smoking it, and serving it to the bends and ends at this tiny shop east of town. It's the flavors - like mango habanero, green onion, even Cajun boudin - that really make these sausages stand out. Daily specials often include other smoked meats, like brisket, ribs and smoked pork butt. Everything's served Cajun and Creole style, so that smoked brisket may come to you on a po'boy roll!

McDONALD'S GROCERY & DELI
526 North Main Street in Junction City
(870) 924-4839

A full deli and meat market with daily specials and a hot case. Smoked sausages almost always available. Turkey, brisket and ribs also common.

CRAYTON'S BBQ
Food Truck in Magnolia
(870) 299-3433

O.B. and Harriett Crayton have spent decades cooking. He learned how to cook because his ex-wife was terrible about it. It's been three decades, and he's doing much better now. Crayton's started out as a brick-and-mortar, but in 2021 they started up a new enterprise with a mobile food truck. Look for smoked brisket, ribs, turkey necks and pig's feet, to go along with Harriett's collard greens, potato salad, baked beans, yams, mac and cheese and hot water cornbread. Be sure to grab a slice of cake or some peach cobbler when you go.

THE BACKYARD BARBECUE COMPANY

1407 East Main Street in Magnolia
(870) 234-7890

David and Susan Greer and their family ran this bastion of barbecue for 35 years, but decided in 2024 it was time to pass it on to the next owner. Justin Cross, who grew up in Magnolia and who also owns a truck stop and liquor store in town, bought the place and, for the most part, has kept it same as it ever was. The ribs are the star here, and they're still slow smoked with only hickory. The brisket is served Lower Arkanas moist, and in case you worried, Ms. Glenda Jones is still making the pies.

HART'S BACKROAD GRUB

102 East McKissack in Waldo
(870) 904-9516
Facebook.com/HartsBackroadGrub

One of the few places in Arkansas using mesquite to smoke meat, Hart's offers an Angus beef brisket that is remarkably tender and with great flavor all the way through. So good, in fact, that I ended up eating all of the brisket in the container above while driving - and finished before I realized there was sauce in the box this came in - then went back when I passed by the next day for more! Juicy pulled pork, ribs, and sausages are also menu favorites.

A POOR MAN'S HEAVEN

Food Truck in the Stamps area
(903) 599-2362

Kelvin Howell's operation moves about a bit, as does his menu, but rib tips and ribs and whatever else he creates on Saturdays will make you happy.

JUICY PIG BBQ

117 South Bay Street in Buckner
(870) 953-9781
Facebook.com/JPWellWorthIT

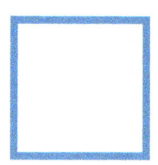

Kevin and Brenda Wood's operation about a block off US Highway 82 is kown for its ribs and its loaded baked potatoes - including one stuffed with pulled pork, baked beans, and cheese. Brisket and sausage from the smoker are popular, as are juicy steaks and a full breakfat menu. Get your cherry Kool-Aid fix when you stop in.

Kat Robinson

C & C MEAT PACKING COMPANY

1197 US Highway 82 in Stamps
(870) 533-2251
CandCPackagingInc.com

Father and son team Lloyd Nix and Harlis Camp opened C & N Packing House in 1959. The name was changed when Nix sold his interest to his daughter, Sarah. Camp's sons Randy and Kenny took over in 1979, and ran the old meat market and grocery until selling to Caleb Bennett and Adam Turner. Little has changed. Fresh meat is still cut and packaged at one counter, while a second counter to the left is where you can order fresh deli sandwiches, burgers, and barbecue. Walk in and order sandwiches with sliced or chopped beef, pork loin or pulled pork, turkey or link sausage, or get any as a dinner. Peach cobbler for dessert!

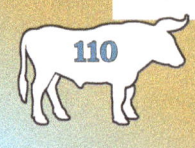

The Arkansas Barbecue Traveler

BURGE'S HICKORY SMOKED TURKEYS AND HAMS

**526 Spruce Street in Lewisville
(870) 921-4292
SmokedTurkeys.com**

Alden Burge's original dairy bar still operates across the street from the massive smokehouse where thousands of turkeys and hams are smoked each year. Burge started smoking turkeys in his backyard in 1953, and his neighbors soon had him smoking for them, too. He'd smoke chickens for Friday night football games. In 1962, he and his family bought this place and opened it, selling his barbecue alongside burgers and ice cream. Today the place is known for those smoked meats - and for great catfish as well. You can order all these smoked meats online or even drive over and pick them upi yourself, and enjoy a smoked turkey or ham sandwich, or get a barbecue plate with fresh smoked sliced or chipped beef, pulled pork, or hot links.

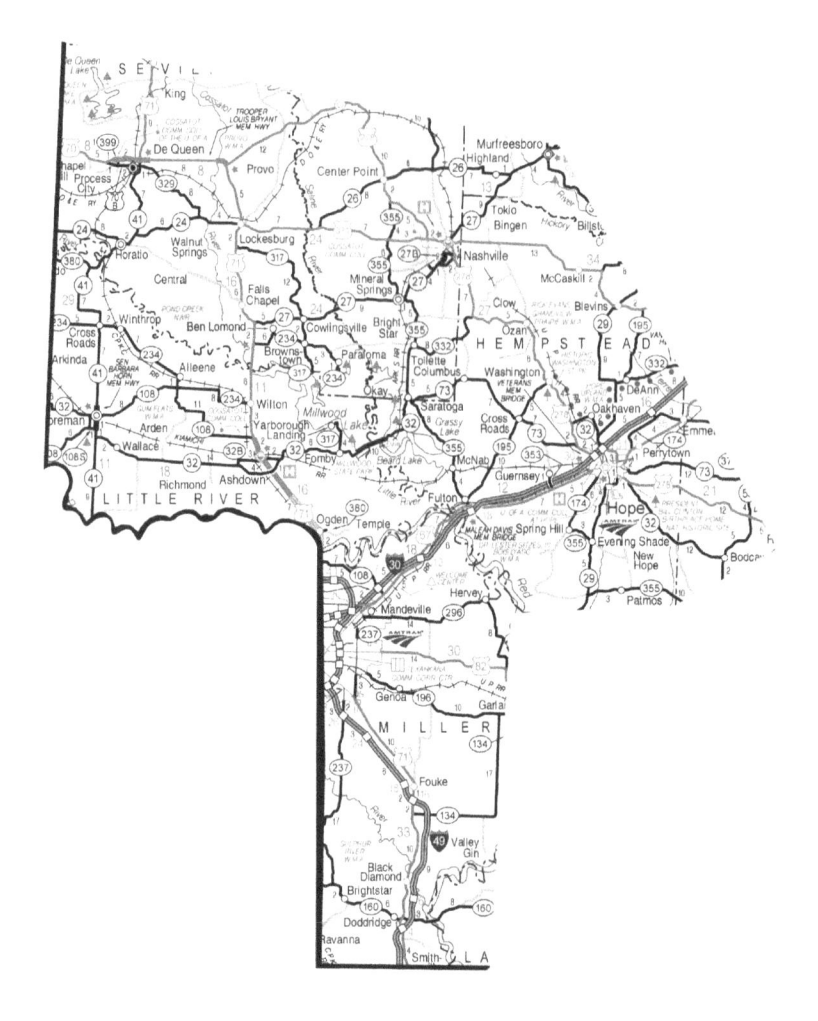

Southwest Arkansas

NAAMAN'S WORLD CHAMPIONSHIP BBQ

5200 North State Line Avenue in Texarkana
(903) 826-2827
NaamansBBQ.com

Darby Neaves began smoking meats when he was a teenager, and has spent the past 40 years perfecting his craft. He opened his first food truck in 2012 in Ashdown, before moving to brick-and-mortar on the Texas side of State Line Avenue in Texarkana. In 2019, he converted the old Pizza Inn across the street into a massive edifice for barbecue lovers. Today, Naaman's offers a full selection of smoked meats, along with chicken fried ribeye and The Blasphemer - my favorite sandwich there, brisket with coleslaw and Naaman's mustard sauce. Ask for your dessert to go.

MR. J'S BBQ

6104 Mount Olive Drive in Texarkana
(870) 648-1065

Originally opened in 1976, this family operation offers smoked ribs, brisket, sausage and chicken on the last Saturday of every month. Enjoy a frozen margarita with your pull-apart ribs.

BIG JAKE'S BBQ

1521 Arkansas Boulevard in Texarkana
(870) 774-0099
170 North Constitution Avenue in Ashdown
(870) 898-2227
BigJakesBBQ.net

Matthew Palmer began working in barbecue restaurants when he was 16. When he was 23, he had the opportunity to buy the first Big Jake's BBQ in New Boston, Texas. He has expanded to six locations. The restaurants - named for the famed John Wayne movie - sport quality touches. While you can get smoked beef, pork, sausage, and turkey with your order, when you dine in you can grab your own bread, enjoy a hot bean pot, and choose a fresh hot fried pie to go with it all.

BIG GILLEY'S SMOKEHOUSE & DINER

290 South Dupree in Ashdown
(870) 648-7888
Facebook.com/BigGilleysSmokehouse

Matt Gilley started out his barbecue food truck in 2018. The former welder from Ashdown spent years creating his method of smoking and seasoning before starting his own barbecue joint. In 2001, he bought Herb's Creamland, incorporated its menu with his own, and fused together a barbecue joint with breakfast. Then in 2023, he broke the barbecue back out, buying the old Jim's Place building off US 71 and opening his smokehouse as a sit-down restaurant there.

Matt's smoker handles a lot of meat - and a couple of the best ways to try it is by grabbing a Big Ugly Tater or a pile of Big Ugly Fries. These are dishes where the potato or fries is covered in beans, bacon, cheese, green onions, and your choice of smoked meats. You can get it with sour cream and jalapenos if you wish - it's a dish big enough for a meal in itself.

RAGIN CAJUN LOUISIANA KITCHEN

Regional food truck
(318) 517-8619
Facebook.com/RaginCajunLA

Ranging from Shreveport to Dallas to Little Rock, this Cajun food truck brings the ribs right along with the Texas brisket and Swamp Nachos. Available for events throughout the area, for catering, and for generally pigging out at.

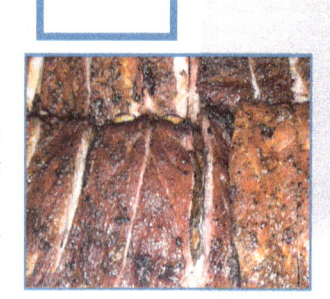

PAPA MIKE'S BBQ

113 North Bell Street in Foreman
(870) 571-6747

Mike McCombs started this tiny barbecue shack in 2022. It features sliced and chopped brisket, chopped pork, hot links and jerked chicken - and also soft serve ice cream.

The Arkansas Barbecue Traveler

PRIME COUNTRY MEAT MARKET

**223 Main Street in Horatio
(870) 832-4805
Facebook.com/PrimeCountryMeatMarket**

It started out with a processing facility, then a meat market. Then in 2023, Prime Country Meat Market started offering all sorts of on-site smoked meats, particularly on Friday and Saturday nights, with a varying menu that covers everything from brisket and ribs to prime rib, tri-tip, and even pork belly cinnamon rolls. Worth the drive out to the southwest corner of the state.

KRISTY'S COOK SHACK

Food truck
227 US Highway 71 in North De Queen
(870) 582-5113

This trailer on the north side of De Queen offers pulled pork in sandwiches, nachos, and fries.

OUTLAW BBQ

Food truck
880 East Collin Raye Drive in De Queen
(479) 216-5893
Facebook.com/OutlawBBQ2021

Outlaw BBQ is a big barbecue powerhouse in a tiny white food trailer serving up pork, chicken and beef dinners and sandwiches. My dude Grav is splendidly satiated with the pulled pork here, with its great flavor and bark bits throughout, not really needing any sauce at all. I dig the brisket, which similarly maintains a great flavor throughout. Check Facebook for opening times.

G & G DELI

207 De Queen Avenue in De Queen
(870) 982-9937

Since 2021, two sisters and their daughters have been offering hickory and oak smoked barbecue at this delicatessen on sandwiches and plates. The Gilmores and the Goodmans offer brisket, pulled pork, ribs, chicken, turkey and sausage links as well as cakes and pies on the regular. Banana pudding is also a popular dessert.

TRISH'S SMOKIN' BAR-B-Q

1501 US Highway 371 in Nashville
(870) 451-9701
Facebook.com/TrishsBBQ

There's not much to Trish's on the outside - it's just a walk-up window with a menu on the windowsill. But Trish's has some of the most tender smoked beef I've had in a long time. Like, dissolvingly soft. It makes for a good sandwich - but I have to warn you, with that coleslaw and tender beef it's a mess. But a good mess! Trish Lingo also has pork loin, hot links, ribs and pulled pork. Be sure to ask for the daily dessert.

Kat Robinson

SMOKIN RICK'S HICKORY HOUSE
815 South Main Street is Nashville
(870) 200-9722

Originally opened in 1977, Smokin' Rick's is a pick-up or sit-down restaurant, depending on which end you approach it from. In the front, or on the street side if you will, is a pick-up window for to-go orders. On the back end, there's a huge dining room where a community meets to eat. Rick Rowe took over this place in 2011 - then he bought the Hickory House in 2015 and merged the two businesses and both menus together. Pulled pork, pulled chicken, brisket and ribs are all smoked daily - but you better get there early, since Rick's is only open 6 a.m. to 2 p.m. each day, except Sunday.

BIGMAC'S BARBEECUE

2703 North Hazel Street in Hope
(870) 722-8011

Big Mac's Barbeeque (Hope). Margaret McLaughlin's booming startup on the north side of town has quickly become Hope's barbecue mecca. With pitmaster Doug Ozment working the smoker, the eatery's quickly racked up all the local awards for best restaurant, boss, and waitress, and keeps folks coming in the door with smoked brisket, ribs, turkey, sausage and pulled pork. If that wasn't enough, catfish is also available, and you can get your fries, potatoes, nachos and mac and cheese loaded up with barbecue any time.

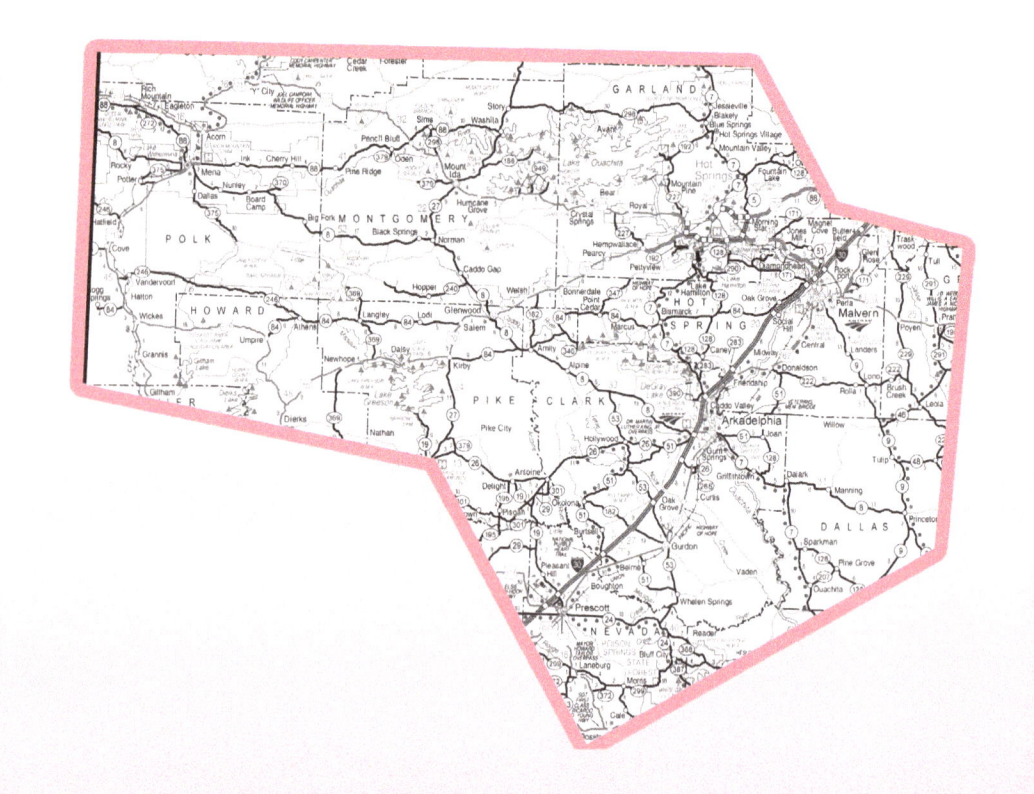

The Ouachitas

NORMAN'S 44 RESTAURANT
1643 US Highway 371 West in Prescott
(870) 887-2269

A trucker's delight! Smoked pork ribs and sandwiches are a dinner selection for this oversized roadside diner, which also offers breakfast any time, hot and not-hot sandwiches, and a special charge if you want to come fill your thermos with coffee.

TRINA'S DINER: A TOUCH OF SOUL
221 Holly Street in Prescott
(870) 796-8014

Catrina Tidwell has been in the kitchen since she was eight years old. She takes a lifetime of cooking experience behind the counter at this soul food diner, where she offers specials each day alongside casseroles, beans, sandwiches, and wings - and ribs are offered on the regular.

WALK BABY LOVE BBQ
Food truck
1414 North 10th Street in Arkadelphia
(870) 210-0979
Facebook.com/WalkBabyLoveBBQ

It's only good vibes at this busy barbecue trailer. Hosea Walker's family operation opened in 2022 and hit the ground running. Here you'll find saucy wet ribs, juicy brisket, and smoky wings along with whatever the occasion calls for - sometimes it's homemade chili, sometimes catfish, but always some great smoked meats.

Kat Robinson

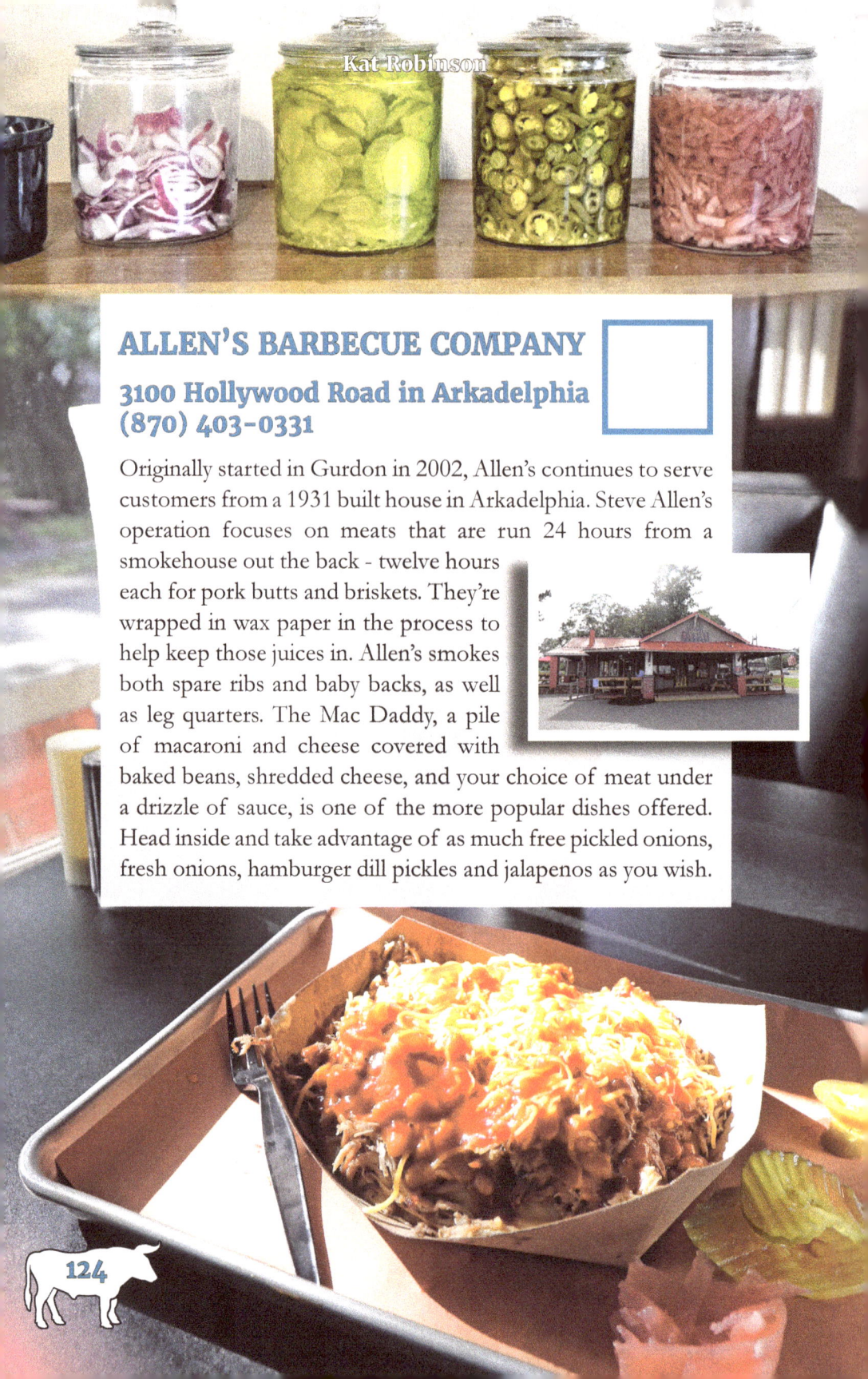

ALLEN'S BARBECUE COMPANY
3100 Hollywood Road in Arkadelphia (870) 403-0331

Originally started in Gurdon in 2002, Allen's continues to serve customers from a 1931 built house in Arkadelphia. Steve Allen's operation focuses on meats that are run 24 hours from a smokehouse out the back - twelve hours each for pork butts and briskets. They're wrapped in wax paper in the process to help keep those juices in. Allen's smokes both spare ribs and baby backs, as well as leg quarters. The Mac Daddy, a pile of macaroni and cheese covered with baked beans, shredded cheese, and your choice of meat under a drizzle of sauce, is one of the more popular dishes offered. Head inside and take advantage of as much free pickled onions, fresh onions, hamburger dill pickles and jalapenos as you wish.

SAVORY AVERY

1029 North 10th Street in Arkadelphia
(870) 403-6177
Facebook.com/SavoryAveryBBQ

Sgt. Rover Avery's family has put in serious time in the U.S. Army. He's retired after 31 years of service, including time in the Cold War, Operation Desert Storm, Guantanamo Bay, and Iraq, where he was in more than 100 missions. Both of his sons are currently serving, his daugher is in JROTC, and his wife served - as an Army wife and mom, holding down the homefromt while working as an English teacher.

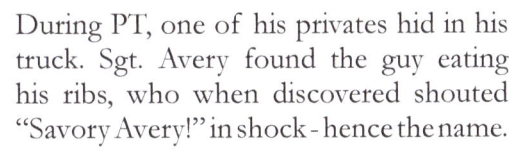

During PT, one of his privates hid in his truck. Sgt. Avery found the guy eating his ribs, who when discovered shouted "Savory Avery!" in shock - hence the name.

The barbecue really got going one day when Sgt. Avery's First Sergeant didn't want to feed his soldiers. His wife, Holly, stepped up and provided the barbecue for his troops.

The family's operation began in 2010 in Bismarck before bringing a food truck to Arkadelphia in 2021. They recently moved into this permanent location over in the Caddo Valley area. The barbecue, is of course, star here, and that tender, pulled apart brisket is a marvelous delicacy. I see why that private stole those ribs.

OUACHITA VALLEY MEATS

**2859 Walnut Street in Arkadelphia
(870) 800-6328
OuachitaValleyMeats.com**

This farm-to-table butcher shop run by Luke Huneycutt and Jeff Liggins, the seventh generation of farmers in the Huneycutt family, operates as both a butcher shop and a restaurant. Opened in February 2023, this place offers its meats deli style in various sandwiches and by the pound. Daily lunch specials vary. This is also a great place to pick up meat you'd like to smoke yourself.

FAT BOYS FINE FOOD

**130 Valley Street in Arkadelphia
(870) 246-6552**

Sheila and Tony Bell's barn along US Highway 67 in Caddo Valle plays host to lots of family gatherings and travelers off Interstate 30. Its focus is on hickory pit smoked hand-rubbed brisket, smoked pork, sausages and St. Louis style ribs. Meats come chopped instead of pulled, and if you order a sandwich it comes with the coleslaw on the side.

SWEETPEA'S SMOKEHOUSE

2897 Highway 70 West in Kirby
(870) 398-4004
Facebook.com/Sweetpeas.FastFoodStyle

Micah Niederhofer and Melissa Golden opened this small town smokehouse back in 2014. Today, their business thrives, not just in their rustic wooden restaurant but also with local catering. Their chopped brisket, spare ribs, chicken leg quarters and smoked sausages are often on the table. Sweetpea's is one of the very few places in Arkansas serving their smoked meats at breakfast. You can get brisket, pulled pork or smoked sausage links in your breakfast omelets and burritos or over hashbrowns

GLENWOOD FISH NEST

164 US Highway 70 in Glenwood
(870) 356-3875
Facebook.com/FishNestGetHooked

A longstanding family favorite, the Fish Nest offers smoked pork ribs on its buffet each and every Thursday night.

BIG D'S STATION and HEY HAWGZ BBQ

2414 US Highway 71 in Mena
(479) 385-5114

Gas station barbecue? Don't knock it 'til you try it. Mena has two gas stations with excellent barbecue. At Big D's, you can grab a Fat Boy sausage, pulled pork, or brisket on a sandwich or plate anytime - or grab a rack of ribs. Get your gas, your gear and get, all at one place. There ar a few tables available if you'd like to dine on-site.

COUNTRY EXPRESS OF MENA

1146 US Highway 71 in Mena
(479) 394-7310

Just up the road a little, Country Express offers ribs, smoked beef and pork in a similar facility - but this one has a full scale restaurant service area packed within. Not only can you enjoy a sit-down dinner of barbecue inside, you can also pick up a pre-packaged sandwich from the hotbox. Mobile catering also available. Specials daily. Chopped meat sandwiches here are chopped finer than I've ever encountered elsewhere.

BEARDED GUY BBQ AND EATS
414 Mena Street in Mena
(479) 208-5928

This family-run operation on the northwest side of downtown Mena opened in September 2003 and has become an instant hit. A menu with great brisket, pulled pork and chicken leg quarters, the stars on this menu may be The Mess, fries covered in pulled pork with cheese, beans, jalapenos, green onions and moonshine barbecue sauce. The chicken is succulently sublime.

BIG FORK MALL
5988 Arkansas 8 East near Mena
(479) 394-8010

Cheryl and Stony Edwards run this restaurant, gas station, convenience store and souvenir shop with omelets, pancakes, burgers, sandwiches - and at select times, smoked dinners with pork, brisket, or ribs.

BIGFOOT'S BACKWOODS BBQ FOOD TRUCK
877 Polk County Road 61 near Mena
Facebook.com/bigfoot.s.texas.style.bbq

Opened in 2024, this trailer splits times from being back out in the woods and right in Mena (usually at Southern Paws). St. Louis style ribs, sliced brisket, chicken leg quarters and whatever else is interesting that day. Often pairs up and offers other items, like Jillian O'Bannon's pastries from The Gingered Baker. Look for Bigfoot Bait - the pork burnt ends.

BIG T'S GENERAL STORE
1090 Arkansas Highway 88 West in Oden
(870) 490-2061

Fuel up and grab a bite when you're coming through. Have ribs, some brisket or pulled pork and perhaps an ice cream cone or slice of pizza while you're at it.

270 DINER
514 US Highway 270 in Mt Ida
(870) 867-0141

How many places do you know that offer barbecue alongside doughnuts? You can get pulled pork nachos, tacos, and sandwiches as well as diner breakfasts, fritters, bearclaws and doughnuts.

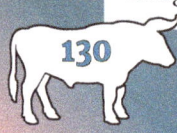

BURL'S COUNTRY SMOKEHOUSE

10176 Albert Pike Road in Royal
(501) 991-3875
Facebook.com/Outlaw316

A classc Arkansas roadside attraction opened in 1981, this rustic throwback is a photo op, a gift shop, and a smokehouse producing several types of traditionally smoked meats. You can pick up cured and smoked bone-in hams, salamis, pastrami, corned beef, turkey, canadian bacon, bologna, pork loin and brisket, by the pound or as a sandwich served cold or hot. You can also get a whole smoked chicken or turkey, get nachos topped with smoked meat, dine on a rib dinner, or, if you're lucky, enjoy a bean pot seasoned with the meat cured and smoked on site. Smoked jerky and sausages also available.

CLAMPIT'S COUNTRY KITCHEN

5398 North Arkansas Highway 7 in Hot Springs Village
(501) 204-5030
ClampitsCountryKitchen.com

Joey Clampit's butcher shop north of the entrance to Hot Springs Village on Scenic Highway Seven is a three-fer - it's a full meat market, a small grocery, and a restaurant where smoked meats are always on the menu. Clampit's smoked brisket, pork, chicken, sausage and ribs are offered on the daily. He's earned renown for his housemade smoked sausages, and like rural butcheries tend to do in Arkansas, does deer processing for hunters by appointment as well. He also does a number of jerky presentations, including chicken jerky. Smoked turkeys and hams are also common here during the holidays, but order yours in advance because they go quick.

HOME PLATE CAFE & BAKERY

5110 North Arkansas Highway 7 in Hot Springs Village
(501) 984-6969
HomePlateCafeandBakery.com

Originally opened by father-and-son team Dale and Zack Summit, now owned by Martin and Tonya Porterfield, this is a family restaurant that's evolved with the needs of its clientele in the burgeoning community of Hot Springs Village. The Porterfields hired in Jason Hunt, who brought his skills as a pastry chef to the table. Hunt had a previous career in business before going back to school to pursue his culinary dreams. He's worked his way up to general manager, and evolved the schedule and the menu at Home Plate Cafe to include Thursday barbecue nights as part of the regular rotation. The menu includes baby back ribs, half and quarter chickens, brisket, a selection of sandwiches including pulled pork, sliced or chopped brisket, and a barbecue melt with your choice of meat.

OUACHITA BAR AND GRILL

915 Central Avenue in Hot Springs
(501) 359-3884
Facebook.com/OuachitaBarandGrill

Rob and Tiah Koller saw a need for barbecue in a part of a barbecue-laden city - in the center of Hot Springs. In January of 2024, they opened a lot wiith a food truck, and over the course of its first eight months crafted a big deck, a big indoor dining room, kitchen storage, and an atmosphere akin to an adult playground. With a big social media presence and a crafting of its brand through an introductory period with chefs Michael Dampier and Corey Coleman, OBG has quickly made a name for itself in a city that already has several big names in barbecue. In addition to brisket, smoked chicken and pulled pork, OBG has added alligator sausage to the rotation to really spark interest. When you go, enjoy fried pork rinds while you await your dinner.

Kat Robinson

The Arkansas Barbecue Traveler

MCCLARD'S Bar-B-q
505 Albert Pike Road in Hot Springs
(501) 623-9665
McClards.com

One of the oldest restaurants left in the state of Arkansas, McClard's has been serving barbecue since 1928. It was originally the Westside Tourist Camp, a motorcourt hotel, gas station and diner ran by members of the McClard family. That diner served smoked goat, and when a traveler who couldn't pay for his stay offered instead a secret recipe for what he called "the world's greatest hot sauce" - history was made. Alex and Alice McClard ended up focusing their work on the barbecue joint that eventually bore their name, smoking goat and pork hams. Over time, goat fell out of favor, and briskets were added, along with chickens that were only offered on Wednesdays.

Ribs weren't on the original menu. Phillip McClard, the last member of the McClard family left in the operation after the restaurant was purchased by Lee Beasley in 2020, told me pigs back in the 20s and 30s were built differently. The ribs had little meat on them, and so they were thrown to the dogs to keep them happy while the family prepared meals.

The restaurant, as it approaches its century mark, has changed little. A new sweet thick sauce is now on the tables, but otherwise the menu's the same, and you can still dine under the photos of the famous folks - like President Bill Clinton and actor F. Murray Abraham - as you enjoy your meat.

SMOKIN' IN STYLE

**2278 Albert Pike Road in Hot Springs
(501) 767-9797
SmokinNStyle.com**

It's been a quarter century since Daniel Johnson first started with a barrel smoker - and it hasn't let off since. Johnson, who found after that 1999 purchase that he had a real knack for smoking, went all in creating rubs, sauces and baked beans. After five years of growing through catering gigs and food trailers, he decided in 2004 to go into a brick-and-mortar. He ended up hiring his brother Joe to help him manage what has become a behemoth of a shop on Hot Springs' western side.

The restaurant has something for everyone who loves meat, whether it's on its own, served with sides, or starring on a baked potato or a Frito barbecue pie. Plate dinners featuring pork, chicken, beef, turkey, ribs and sausages practically fly across the counter throughout rushes - all but one of these photos was taken within 15 minutes one afternoon. Smokin' in Style can handle both quantity - and quality - quite well.

The Arkansas Barbecue Traveler

137

BUBBA BREWS ON LAKE HAMILTON
1252 Airport Road in Hot Springs
(501) 547-3186

A brewery with barbecue? Sounds great. Sounds even better when you discover it's on Lake Hamilton with one of the Spa City's best patios. Here, pork butt, bologna, ham and ribs are fatured amidst all the items on a very thick sports bar menu, Ask for a good beer pairing - and get set up with a select choice that will only enhance the lakeside experience. Take your time here.

JEFFERSON'S MOBILE GRILLING
Food truck in Central Arkansas
(501) 944-7360
Facebook.com/ @JeffersonsMobileGrilling

Richard "Rico" Jefferson gets around this state. While often working out of Hot Springs, Jefferson takes his food truck all over. He's commonly seen in Little Rock and Plumerville. Jefferson's specialties included turkey legs stuffed with everything from mac and cheese to shrimp and sausage Alfredo. He also smokes ribs and rib tips, pulled pork and chopped chicken for sandwiches, and brisket for sandwiches and nachos. The grilled cabbage is underrated. Get your lemonade in one of several flavors.

THE BLITZED PIG
4330 Central Avenue in Hot Springs
(501) 525-1616
Facebook.com/Theblitzedpig

Live music and barbecue are meant for each other. At this bar tucked into a corner of one of Hot Springs's south side shopping centers, this is a good place to get ribs or a pulled pork sandwich late on a Friday or Saturday night.

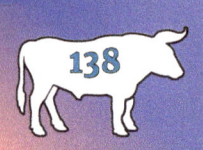

The Arkansas Barbecue Traveler

DRIP DROP BBQ SHOP

173 Marion Anderson Road in Hot Springs
(501) 547-1561
Facebook.com/DripDropBBQShop

Terrence Culclager grew up in a family of farmers, and has known how to cook since about the time he learned how to walk. He's always smoked ribs and brisket, and with the support of his wife, Brittany Estes, he got into the food truck business.

Colclager had a customer come to him that loved his barbecue so much, he wanted to help him get his own restaurant. That lead to the opening of The Drip Drop BBQ Shop

It's not your typical barbecue shop.

It's also Culclager's playground, where he experiments with all sorts of ideas, like his smoked sausage fried noodles - a new take on ramen, where he stir fries sausage and noodles, throws in a fried egg and sauces it for a unique barbecue experience. His brisket burrito filled with fries, beans, coleslaw, nacho cheese sauce and barbecue sauce is griddle-fried and wrapped in its own Cheddar cheese cracker, topped with sour cream, cilantro, peppers, onions and tomatoes, and is hefty enough the three of us in my family can eat it for dinner and still have leftovers.

RIB CAGE BBQ

5429 Central Avenue in Hot Springs
(501) 520-4030
Facebook.com/RibCageHS

Originally opened in a building in Bismarck in 2010, Angela and Jason Looney brought their business to Hot Springs in 2014 with this little red food trailer on the south side of town. When they started out in this spot, there wasn't much, but the city has grown outwards to meet them. Running the pit for this eatery is Jason's retirement job - after years working in his dad's shop. Angela still works in estate planning, but on Thursdays, Fridays, and Saturdays they're out here from 11 a.m. until they sell out. Sometimes that's before noon. With juicy brisket that's been smoked over oak for 14-16 hours and craveable pull-apart ribs, it's no surprise they find themselves running out so early.

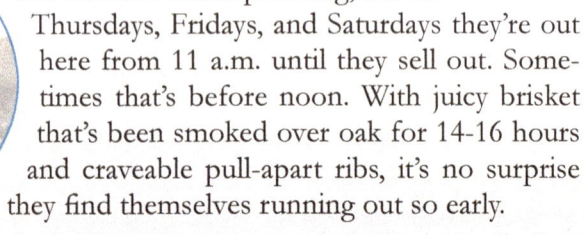

RED OAK FILLING STATION

**2169 Carpenter Dam Road in Hot Springs
(501) 701-8051
RedOakFillinStation.com**

Bill and Courtnie Maness re-opened the Red Oak Filling Station in 2018, originally a convenience store with a deli case that sold fishing supplies. They cleaned, redecorated, added tables and booths and fired up the smoker. Today, you can order brisket, sausage, pulled pork and St. Louis-style ribs separately or even all on the same plate. There's also the hickory smoked ribeye, with just the right touch of smoke.

ROLLING PIT BBQ

**Food truck
5962 Central Avenue
(501) 276-1887**

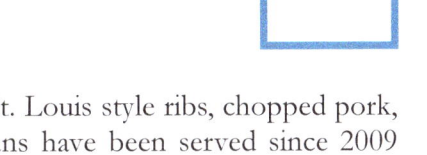

Mike Gardner's hickory pit St. Louis style ribs, chopped pork, sliced beef and smoked beans have been served since 2009 from this diminutive trailer along south Highway 7. That sweet honey vinegar sauce will have you sucking the bone on those ribs.

STUBBY'S HIK'RY PIT Bar-B-Q

3024 Central Avenue in Hot Springs (501) 624-1552
Stubbys.com

Stubby's is a culinary landmark, situated across the street from Oaklawn Racing Park. Back in 1952, Richard Stubblefield Sr. started slow smoking pork, beef and chicken with hickory at his restaurant at 1000 Park Avenue. Stubblefield sold to the Dunkels from New York in 1977. The Dunkels opened a second location in 1978 along Central Avenue - which remains the restaurant's key location today.

Chris Dunkel continues the tradition, overseeing a thick menu that all goes well with Stubby's thick, sweet sauce. While meat is smoked low and slow on a rotisserie that sits in the center of the kitchen, those meats aren't cut until ordered. The pot-o-beans and the baked potato are both great sides, as are the deviled eggs, but if you can manage it even after you've sopped up sauce with your white bread, it's woth finishing with some housemade peach cobbler.

The Arkansas Barbecue Traveler

3 J'S WINGS AND MORE

**2212 Martin Luther King Boulevard in Rockport
(501) 732-2621**

This family food truck operation often offers plain and stuffed smoked turkey legs, chicken, and ribs alongside 10 flavors of wings and a pork chop sandwich. Weekdays only.

MR. WHISKERS

**4195 Malvern Avenue east of Hot Springs,
(501) 262-3474
GreatCatfish.com**

Scott Irwin's fish shack has made its mark as being one of the state's best catfish destinations. But in addition to fried catfish, shrimp and chicken and a selection of burgers, Mr. Whiskers offers pulled pork sandwiches and racks of ribs with beautifully ringed and barked surfaces.

CRAIG'S BAR-B-QUE

814 East Page Avenue in Malvern
(501) 337-1199

A longtime Malvern staple known for its jumbo barbecue sandwiches, Craig's delivers with pork, beef and ham. The thick ribs are also featured on sandwiches and smoked plates. Tips, Polish, and chicken also smoked here - but be warned, when the barbecue has run out for the day, it's likely the restaurant will be closed, despite also offering fish dinners.

HWY 270 GRILL

14223 US Highway 270 in Poyen
(501) 601-5305
Hwy270Grill.com

Daniel Ellison's much-needed community restaurant opened in 2020. The Missouri-born restarateur offers a menu based on crowd pleasers, including the meats he smokes on site - beef, pork, and chicken. Plates come with coleslaw, baked beans and a slice of Texas toast. The barbecue topped nachos are a local favorite.

MAMA K'S

4593 Arkansas Highway 9 in Leola
(501) 332-7200

A good old fashioned home cooking place where the specials change by the day. Sliced brisket and smoked ribs are in the rotation - or you can get a pulled pork sandwich any lunchtime.

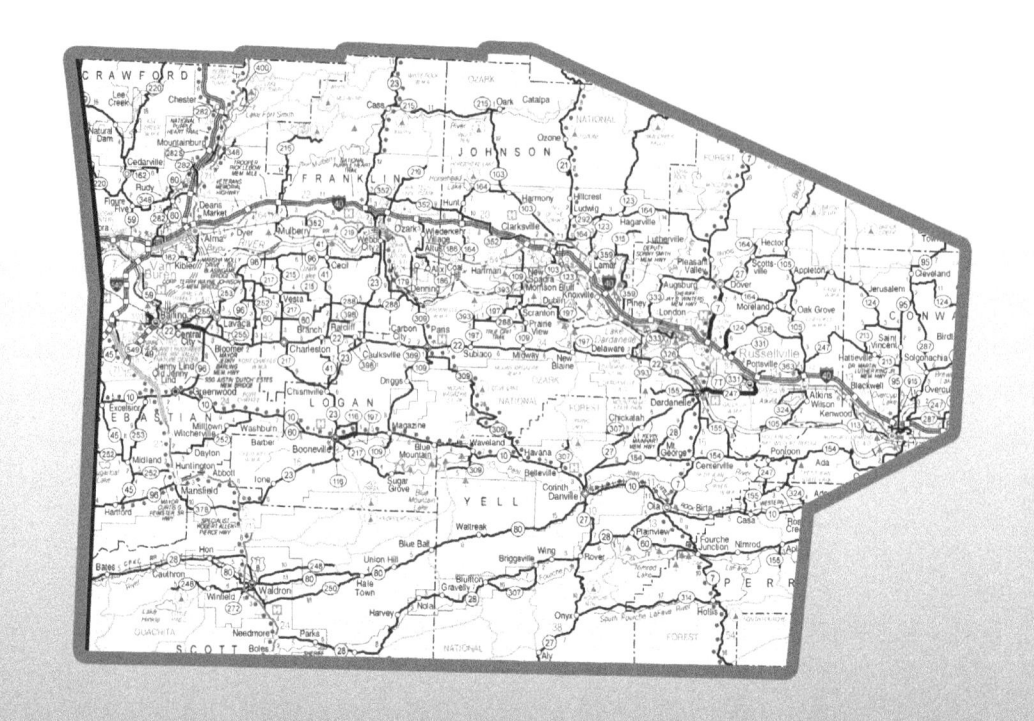

The River Valley

The Arkansas Barbecue Traveler

SALTY DALTY'S BBQ

1205 Arkansas Highway 9 in Morrilton
(501) 289-1018
SaltyDaltyBBQ.com

Dalton Stanley has a mission - to craft some extraordinary meats. He approaches smoking with science, with a perfect temperature and seasoning for brining every brisket, cuts of meat that have been specifically trimmed, before placing the cold brisket in a precicely heated and prepared smoker. Every slice is cut only on order. The result is a magnificent brisket with exceptional bark and tenderness. Dalton is also making marvelous all-beef sausages, smoking chickens to pull for sandwiches, and - when it's available - offering a smoked chocolate pecan cobbler. His inspired brisket elote is a meal in itself. Pork-free.

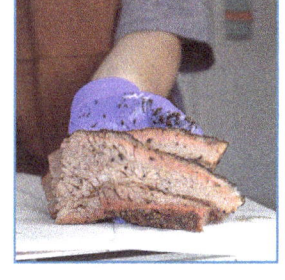

147

GC'S BBQ CATERING

1515 East Harding Street in Morrilton
(501) 306-2287

Pulled pork, ribs, brisket and chicken are the regular menu at this food truck during weekday lunches - but what sets it appart is its biscuit-driven breakfasts - biscuitts served with sausage or chocolate gravy, bacon or sausage or an egg - and breakfast burritos that you can have with brisket. Get yours and a chocolate milk and you're ready to get going on the day.

NOONER'S DINER

1601 North Oak Street in Morrilton
(501) 208-9897

The former Morrilton Drive Inn Restaurant offers a menu that includes pulled pork for sandwiches and salads. Soft serve ice cream and a full burger and hand-pulled chicken tenders also enhance the offerings.

CLEVELAND CORNER STORE

3953 Arkansas Highway 95 in Cleveland (Jerusalem address)
(501) 242-9351
Facebook.com/ClevelandCornerStore

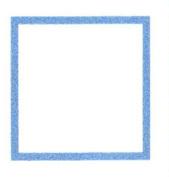

A convenience store for locals and hunters in the area, this place serves various smoked items for its daily lunch special. Pulled pork, ribs, bologna, meatloaf - the variety changes daily. Breakfast is also pretty good.

CHURCH STREET GROCERY

703 West Church Street in Morrilton
(501) 354-4694

A local secret even some of the locals don't know - this is Matt and Corrine Keeton'a corner grocery tucked into a neighborhood on the back side of the tracks that offers daily lunch specials at a pull-up window. Wednesdays are rib days, and Thursdays are for hickory sliced brisket - both served with sauce, side, and salad. Pulled pork lunch plates, sandwiches, and salads are available every lunchtime. Call your order in ahead of pick-up. Ask about the daily desserts.

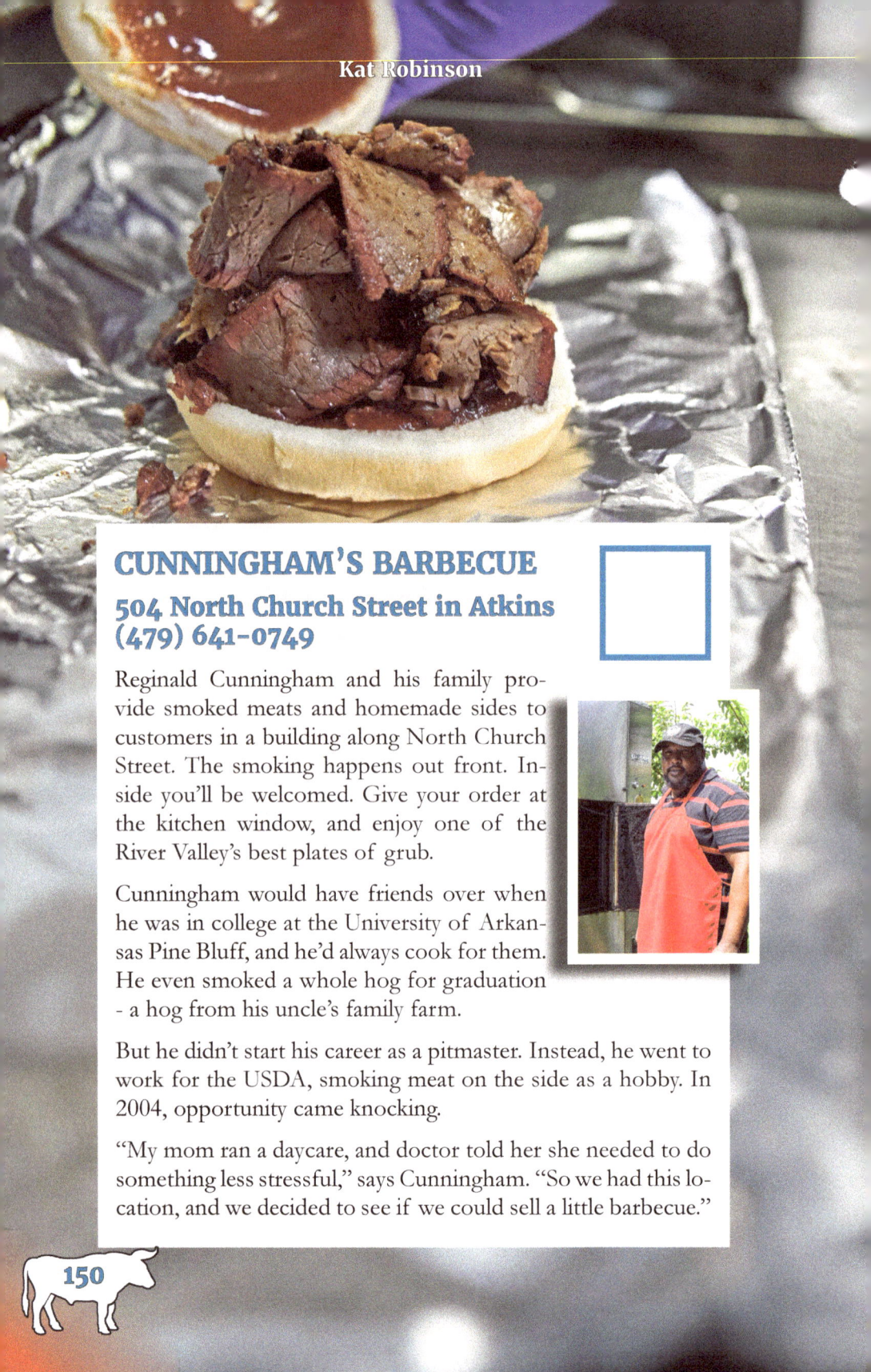

CUNNINGHAM'S BARBECUE
504 North Church Street in Atkins
(479) 641-0749

Reginald Cunningham and his family provide smoked meats and homemade sides to customers in a building along North Church Street. The smoking happens out front. Inside you'll be welcomed. Give your order at the kitchen window, and enjoy one of the River Valley's best plates of grub.

Cunningham would have friends over when he was in college at the University of Arkansas Pine Bluff, and he'd always cook for them. He even smoked a whole hog for graduation - a hog from his uncle's family farm.

But he didn't start his career as a pitmaster. Instead, he went to work for the USDA, smoking meat on the side as a hobby. In 2004, opportunity came knocking.

"My mom ran a daycare, and doctor told her she needed to do something less stressful," says Cunningham. "So we had this location, and we decided to see if we could sell a little barbecue."

The Arkansas Barbecue Traveler

While he's kept the day job, he runs the barbecue operation on Fridays and Saturdays. He'll put on briskets and butts for nine hours over hickory, then smokes ribs and chicken after. Members of the Cunningham family come together for the rest - the baked beans and coleslaw offered on the side, the potato salad his mom and sisters make up from scratch the Wednesday morning, the sweet barbecue sauce they've conjured to go with Reginald's meats, all woman made. His mom makes the pies: sweet potato, pecan, and oatmeal. The bread pudding is made from each week's leftover hamburger buns, the eggs from the family's own chickens. Dad, brothers, sons, cousins, and his wife are all involved.

Then there's The Mess. "We take a layer of meat," Cunningham shares. "Then a layer of beans and another layer of meat and then on top of the meat we put some BBQ sauce, and then the potato salad. It's like messing around with the food on your plate and thinking 'oh, that's not bad!' He's right. It's good.

151

RIDGEWOOD BROTHERS BBQ

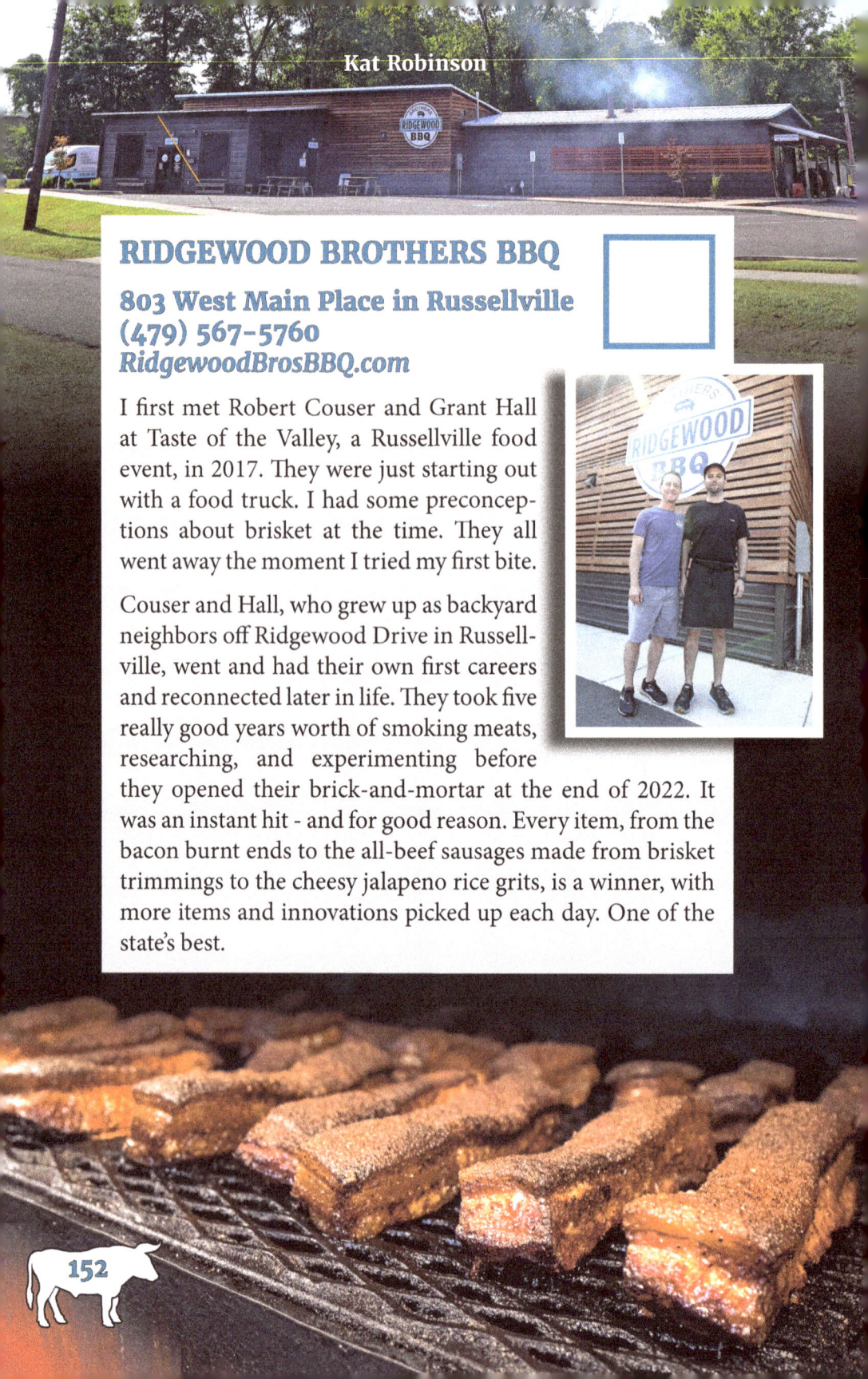

803 West Main Place in Russellville
(479) 567-5760
RidgewoodBrosBBQ.com

I first met Robert Couser and Grant Hall at Taste of the Valley, a Russellville food event, in 2017. They were just starting out with a food truck. I had some preconceptions about brisket at the time. They all went away the moment I tried my first bite.

Couser and Hall, who grew up as backyard neighbors off Ridgewood Drive in Russellville, went and had their own first careers and reconnected later in life. They took five really good years worth of smoking meats, researching, and experimenting before they opened their brick-and-mortar at the end of 2022. It was an instant hit - and for good reason. Every item, from the bacon burnt ends to the all-beef sausages made from brisket trimmings to the cheesy jalapeno rice grits, is a winner, with more items and innovations picked up each day. One of the state's best.

The Arkansas Barbecue Traveler

SMOKEHOUSE DELI

**1000 West Main Street
in Russellville
(479) 968-7290**
Facebook.com/TheSmokehouseRuss

This last outpost in the Ozark Mountain Smokehouse family still offers smoked meats and cheeses along with a selection of sandwiches, desserts and specials. The smoked cheddar is one of my favorite things.

FAT DADDY'S BAR-B-QUE

**104 North Denver Avenue
 in Russellville - (479) 967-0420
7206 US Highway 64 B
 in Russellville -(479) 967-1273**
FatDaddysBarbeque.com

The original Fat Daddy's was in Blackwell, but in 2006 the folks at Darrells' Hillside (a gas station on US 64 West towards London) got permission and started their own. Today there are two locations - the second being in historic downtown Russellville. Father and son team Gordon and Jon Shirron offer brown sugar glazed pork loin back ribs, brisket fajitas, and an oversized barbecue burrito stuffed with meat, French fried onions, coleslaw and cheesy taters.

NAUGHTY BBQ
108 Scenic Highway 7 in Ola
(479) 858-1720

Naughty BBQ was once in Dardanelle, but a short time back moved to the much-restaurant-starved Ola and set up shop. Nikki and Brian have combined the convenience of a food truck with a brick-and-mortar dining room across their parking lot - which opens up the eatery to dine-in customers who want to sit and relax while they're eating rather than taking to-go. The brisket dinner is a solid choice, with peppery slices of slow smoked brisket and a couple of decent sides. Seasonal February-October in Ola, catering November - January.

Kat Robinson

REID'S HOMETOWN BBQ
42 West Main Street in Booneville
(479) 675-2159
ReidsHometownBBQ.com

Steve Reid began his operation in 2016, with the help of his family. After medical issues took the former Booneville policeman out of commission, the women in his life stepped in, and when he was back up to snuff they kept on. While his daughters run the kitchen and front of the house, Steve concentrates on keeping the smoker full. Exceptional barbeue and dishes, including his own caseless housemade sausage that comes in large patties.

The Arkansas Barbecue Traveler

BACK STREET BBQ AND MORE

**502 Northway Alley in Charleston
(479) 467-7918**

Originally Main Street BBQ, a recent move to a spot off the main drag prompted the name change here. David and Alicia Meeh bought the restaurant in 2016 and, after a successful run there, moved it in 2024. The menu includes some massive sausages and this, the Hangry Artie Bird, which is a smoked chicken sandwich with sauteed veggies and sauce. A surprising delight.

CHARBROILER RESTAURANT

**58 US Highway 71 Bypass South
in Waldron
(479) 637-3163
Facebook.com/Charbroiler**

Originally opened in 1990. While the name implies flame roasted steaks, this eatery offers brisket and pulled pork on sandwiches, plus dinner plates with baby back ribs, smoked turkey, smoked sausage, brisket or pulled pork.

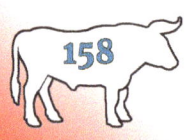

ROLLIN' SMOKE BBQ

Food truck serving Fort Smith and Greenwood
(479) 252-4436

Pitmaster Brad Huff has been perfecting his craft in hickory-smoking meats and creating the sauces and sides to go with it, over the course of the past 20 years. Despite severe vision loss, Brad was able to open his food truck in February 2024 to almost immediate popular approval. Brad tackles brisket, pulled pork, and sausage and offers an unusual garlic slaw and smoked pickle potato salad. He uses fresh buns from Harvest Moon Bakery out of Fort Smith for a gourmet touch.

SIMPLY SMOKED
620 West Center Street in Greenwood
(479) 883-7444
Facebook.com/SimplySMKD

Jeremy Lensing and John Valencia opened up a joint operation in June 2024, combining John's brand new J&D Meat Market and Jeremy's Simply Smoked barbecue shop in one space. While John specializes in all sorts of cuts of beef and pork and handmade sausages of half a dozen different flavor varieties, Jeremy has set up a small dining room and a to-go counter where his brisket and pulled pork can shine. Barbecue nachos are recommended - as are the sandwiches, which are served on onion rolls. It works for the smoke here, no sauce needed.

TITLETOWN FEED HOUSE
Food truck
1600 West Center Street in Greenwood
(479) 460-9502

Steve and Casey Lunsford operate this food truck at 10 Eats on the Spur, a court in Greenwood, where their black trailer anchors the eateries there. The pair are smoking and pulling pork, brisket, and chicken, as well as ribs and their famed side, Corey's Cowboy potatoes - which are peppers, onions, squash and smoked sausage in their potatoes that are smoked along with the meats. Check and see if they have a slice of their smoked apple pie when you go.

The Arkansas Barbecue Traveler

LINKS AT CHAFFEE CROSSING

11707 Custer Boulevard in Fort Smith
(479) 226-3126
Facebook.com/LinksAtChaffeeCrossing

Kim Flanagan runs the front, and Terry Flanagan is in the back working the smoker and delivering juicy brisket, ribs, pulled pork and cheese for epic mac and cheese. Great smoked meats are brought to the table with sides made from longstanding family recipes . Kim did factory work and Terry worked for the gas company before both retired to take over the concession on the golf course at Fort Chaffee in 2018. This is one of those spots you have to know about to get there, being tucked back off the highway a fair bit, but well worth it.

161

BRUCE TERRI DRIVE IN AND CATERING

1102 Fort Street in Barling
(479) 452-8171
Facebook.com/BruceTerriCater

This Barling standard is on its third generation. Originally opened in 1961 as a two-window walk-up dairy bar, the place was moved to its current location in 1969. It was at the time owned by Bill and Peggy Shopfner - and it's named for their kids, Bruce and Terri. Chuck and Terri took it over in 1987, and continue to run it today with their son Kyrk. Burgers, pork ribs, pulled pork sandwiches, and soft-serve ice cream are popular in the store. Chuck and Kyrk take the show on the road a lot, catering to some of the area's largest crowds - sometimes up to 5000 people at a time!

The menu is extensive, the customer base loyal, and the most commonly ordered meal is the Combo Plate, where you can enjoy both a pulled pork sandwich and a couple of ribs on the same order. A twist cone will suit you fine for dessert.

The Arkansas Barbecue Traveler

ARTS BBQ & BURGERS

8203 Rogers Avenue in Fort Smith
(479) 452-2550
ArtsBBQandBurgers.com

Art Porter opened his restaurant in the 1960s. It's moved around a bit, but ended up settling here on Rogers. Wade York began working at Art's in 1992, and a decade and a half later he and his wife bought it. He added the "and Burgers" to the name, and over time has brought more items to the menu, like crispy fried catfish, pork chops, steaks, and pork steaks (uncommon in this region). Of interest, especially to those watching their carbs - the stuffed smoked poblano peppers, which see time in the smoke before being stuffed with smoked meat of your choice and a lot of cheese, and being put back into the smoker again. Decadent. Also, get the onion rings - they're some of the best in the River Valley.

Kat Robinson

PIG BARN BBQ

9101 US Highway 71 in Fort Smith
(479) 322-9565
Facebook.com/PigBarnBBQ

David Waits left factory work to start up his barnyard themed food truck on the south side of Fort Smith. With juicy brisket, tender chicken and smoky pulled pork, he can't go wrong. Folks come for the good stuff but also for the ridiculous Brisket Cheddar Honey Bun Sandwich, an ample portion of shredded brisket covered in melted cheddar and barbecue sauce between two whole jumbo honeybuns. Outrageous - but he'll sell a half dozen every day.

PIG-N-PEPPER

1400 US HIghway 71B in Fort Smith (479) 434-5900.

This place tends to roam, opening in a new location for a few years before evaporating and appearing elsewhere. When you can find them, they do a good job with ribs, beef, pork, and chicken. Look for all-you-can-eat nights to really get a bang for your buck.

JERRY NEEL'S BAR-B-Q, CATFISH, & CATERING

1823 Phoenix Avenue in Fort Smith (479) 646-8085
Facebook.com/JerryNeelsBBQ

Arkadelphia-born Jerry Neel landed in Fort Smith in the 1960s to operate food services for Borg Warner (later Whirlpool) for more than 30 years. In 1977, he started his side hustle, opening up this place on Phoenix. Today, his son Jake mans the operation, and many other family members remain involved. The sides are still all homemade, and the meats rotate through the smoker on a 24 hour basis. The brisket here is the pinkest I've ever seen anywhere.

Kat Robinson

SILVER'S NC BBQ

70 South 7th Street in Fort Smith
(479) 739-6629
Facebook.com/SilversNorthCarolinaBBQ

As far as I've been able to find, this is the only restaurant in Arkansas serving eastrn Carolina style barbecue, utilizing a thin vinegar pepper sauce. Slow cooked pork shoulder for sandwiches, chicken halves and quarters, and Indian fry bread on the menu.

BIG DADDY D'S BBQ & D'S SWEET TREATS ENTERPRISES

3802 Midland Boulevard in Fort Smith
(479) 285-7960

Beans and coleslaw are both popular barbecue sides, but how often do you get beans ON your sandwich? Both are on the Big Daddy here, whether brisket or pork. Watch for ribs on Thursday and burnt ends Thursday and Friday.

NEUMEIER'S RIB ROOM

424 Garrison Avenue in Fort Smith
(479) 494-7427
Facebook.com/TheRibRoom

The Neumeier name has been a staple in Fort Smith's food scene since the days of the old Chickusine. Here, a massive hickory-fueled pit it how things get done. The dry-rubbed ribs are legendary enough to have folks returning, and the sliced pork loin and smoked bologna sandwiches are epic. But I find it's the delectably smoked chicken wings that have me darkening the door most often. This rock 'n roll clad eatery is certainly a date night destination for the barbecue enthusiast.

AL'S REAL PIT BAR-B-Q
3956 North O Street in Fort Smith
(479) 783-6986

Arkansas Delta barbecue, in Fort Smith. How? Thank Al Moody. He opened his original Al's Bar-B-Q in Trumann in 1972. He moved his family to Fort Smith a few years later so his kids could attend a certain private school, but kept the location open and commuted each week, staying in the back of the restaurant. His wife, Melva, managed family life in Fort Smith.

He started slowing down in the 90s, and decided to open a restaurant closer to home, a restaurant he'd run with his daughter, Dayna Jones. She still runs the place today. This restaurant, unlike the full-scale place he had in Trumann, would be a drive-thru only, a desire that came from a desire to simplify the operation and maybe work a few less hours.

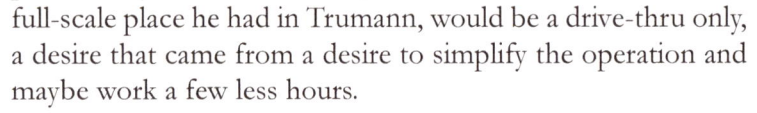

The original Al's closed in 2019. Today, it's home to another barbecue restaurant, Ray's Rump Shack. Jones keeps the Fort Smtih location going, along with her daughter, Emily Hernandez. The pair make sure everything stays as it always has. The primary meat is pork, and the ladies here smoke excellent pork butts and ribs. They added brisket, because Fort Smith's tastes lean heavily towards beef. They also keep the same sort of fries Al had at Trumann, a specially cut and battered skin-on chunk of potato, seasoned flour battered and deep fried. Irresistible.

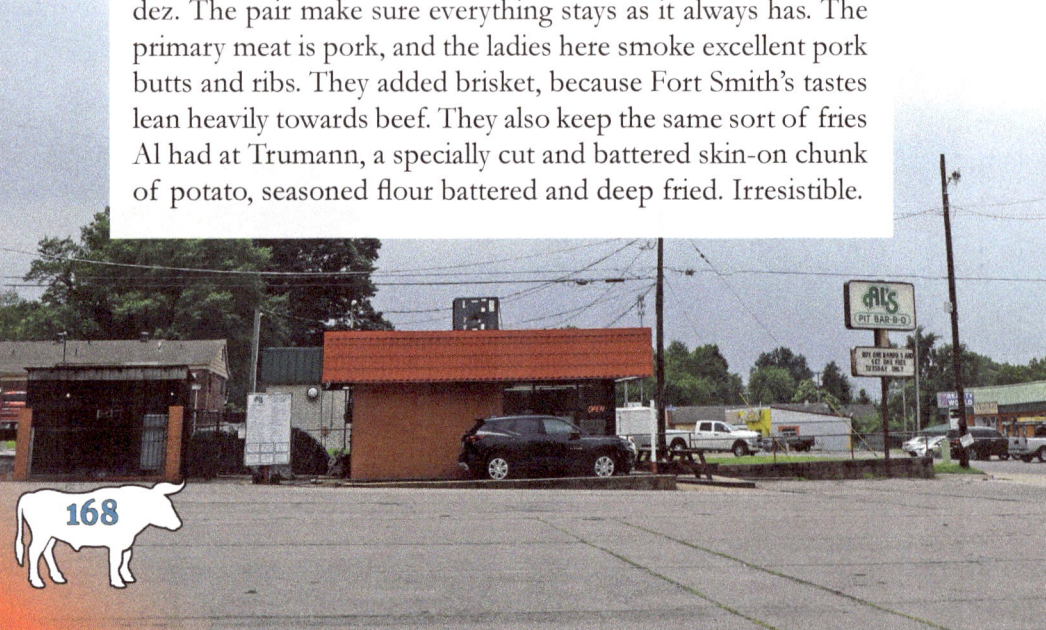

The Arkansas Barbecue Traveler

169

THE VAULT 1905 SPORTS GRILL

**624 Main Street in Van Buren
(479) 262-2468
TheVault1905.com**

Based at Hinkle Corner, where Citizens Bank had John Blevins build a facility back in 1905, this eatery mixes ambiance with expertly prepared and presented classic dishes. Its pulled chicken and pulled pork sandwiches come with diced onion and fresh mozzarella - a little unusual, for sure. Baby back pork ribs are also available for dinner.

BUTCHER BOYS MEAT MARKET & DELI

**1220 Main Street in Van Buren
(479) 474-6800
ButcherBoysMarket.com**

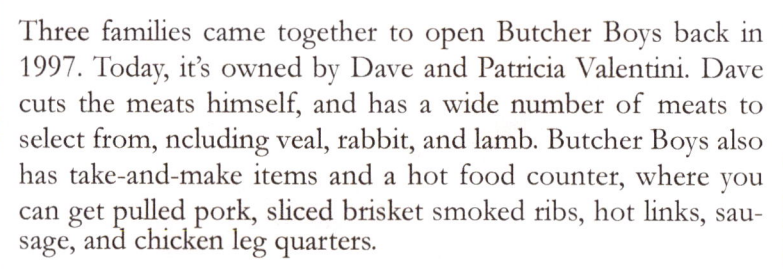

Three families came together to open Butcher Boys back in 1997. Today, it's owned by Dave and Patricia Valentini. Dave cuts the meats himself, and has a wide number of meats to select from, ncluding veal, rabbit, and lamb. Butcher Boys also has take-and-make items and a hot food counter, where you can get pulled pork, sliced brisket smoked ribs, hot links, sausage, and chicken leg quarters.

The Arkansas Barbecue Traveler

JC'S BAR-B-Q PLACE

2502 Alma Highway in Van Buren
(479) 262-2544
JCsBarBQ.com

Jerry Crutcher's dad had a barbecue joint down in Mount Holly. He started his up as a retirement job after decades in maintenance. His wife, Glenda, and their daughter Haley Nicholson operate this shop in the old Mug and Jug dairy bar location on US 64. His specialty is brisket - which ties their pulled pork sandwich as the shop's best sellers. Ribs, burnt ends, smoked chicken, and burgers all round out the menu. Look out for the Chachos - smoked meat on fresh fried tortilla chips with chipotle ranch sauce, barbecue sauce, and cheese. And get a fried pie while you're at it.

STU'S CLEAN COOKIN'

402c Main Street in Van Buren
5430 Phoenix Avenue in Fort Smith
Several other locations statewide
(479) 926-5807
CleanCookin.com

I really wish I could be listing The Meat Station here - it was, for less than a year, one of the five best places to get brisket in the state of Arkansas. I don't say that lightly. However, the lease on the building wasn't renewed. We're lucky we can still enjoy that extraordinary brisket and other great smoked meats through Stu's Clean Cookin' - a meal prep operation also ran by Stuart Rowland, a former full-time mechanic who researched nutrition and started cooking his own meals to lose weight. Stu's Clean Cookin' offers his smoked chicken, gunpowder brisket, smoked pulled pork and racks of ribs for pick-up.

SMOKY B'S BBQ & WING KRAZE

Food Truck
(479) 208-1775
Facebook.com/SmokyBsBBQ

A fun food truck run by Brandon and Taylor Gann, who smoke brisket and pork to go along with their wings and fries menu - the fries being the "kraze" part of the name, since you can choose to douse them in any of more than two dozen types of wing sauce.

RUB 'EM TENDER BBQ

5910 Alma Highway in Van Buren
(479) 279-0384
Intersection 96 And 255 in Lavaca
(479) 739-1534
Facebook.com/RubEmTenderBBQ

Chuck Geske turned his Army food service experience into a pair of enduring barbecue restaurants. The Wisconsin native was married to a woman from Arkansas; sadly, she died in a car accident in 1998 shortly after he retired, leaving him with two children to raise. He worked for 14 years operating in kitchens in retirement communities. In 2009, he took the leap and opened Rub 'Em Tender in a food truck in Lavaca. Eventually he would take that operation to a brick-and-mortar, and later a second location along US 64 in the area locals call "Van Alma." Smoked brisket, pulled pork, smoked chicken and sausage and hot links and ribs are all on the menu, as is a sandwich called the Screamin' Nieman, a hot link and pulled pork sandwich. I prefer the Beef and Cheddar, which is chopped brisket and shredded cheese mixed together and toasted on Texas toast, a hearty choice. The pork belly special is also popular when offered.

SURVIVOR-QUE

**Regional food truck
1402 West Commercial Street in Ozark
(479) 209-0593
Facebook.com/SurvivorQueLLC**

Janetta Mason is a full time nurse. She runs this barbecue food truck on Thursdays and Fridays, usually in Ozark. Janetta survived cancer, hence the name. She started in competition barbecue in 2016 before plunging into the food truck scene in 2018. Survivor-Que's specialties are brisket and pulled pork, with chicken halves being another popular item. They often offer burnt ends, too. The grilled mac and cheese burrito with brisket is crazy good.

SARGENT'S SUNOCO GAS & BBQ

**445 US Highway 71 in Alma
(479) 632-5020**

Simple and worthy of its stature, this smoked then fried bologna sandwich comes from a gas station. If you haven't dropped in to try the barbecue at Sargent's Sunoco in Alma, you should - Wednesday through Saturday, poke your head in, ask for a barbecue menu, and get set up with a tasty bite for the road. There are also sausages, pork butt, briskets and ribs coming off the smoker out back. Get gas and get your order quick.

BOAR'S HEAD CAFE
inside Workman's I-40 Travel Center
3202 Pence Lane in Ozark
(479) 667-3619

OZARK MOUNTAIN GRILL
inside Workman's Travel Center
8265 AR-282 in Alma, AR
(479) 632-0026
WorkmansTravelCenters.com

These two locations both offer counters where you can purchase fresh smoked meats and fried items to take with you on the road. These restaurants cater to over the road truck drivers looking for a quick meal to go. Up for grabs - smoked turkey legs, hot links, ribs, pulled pork and brisket. Hickory smoking occurs on site daily to keep up with demand.

Kat Robinson

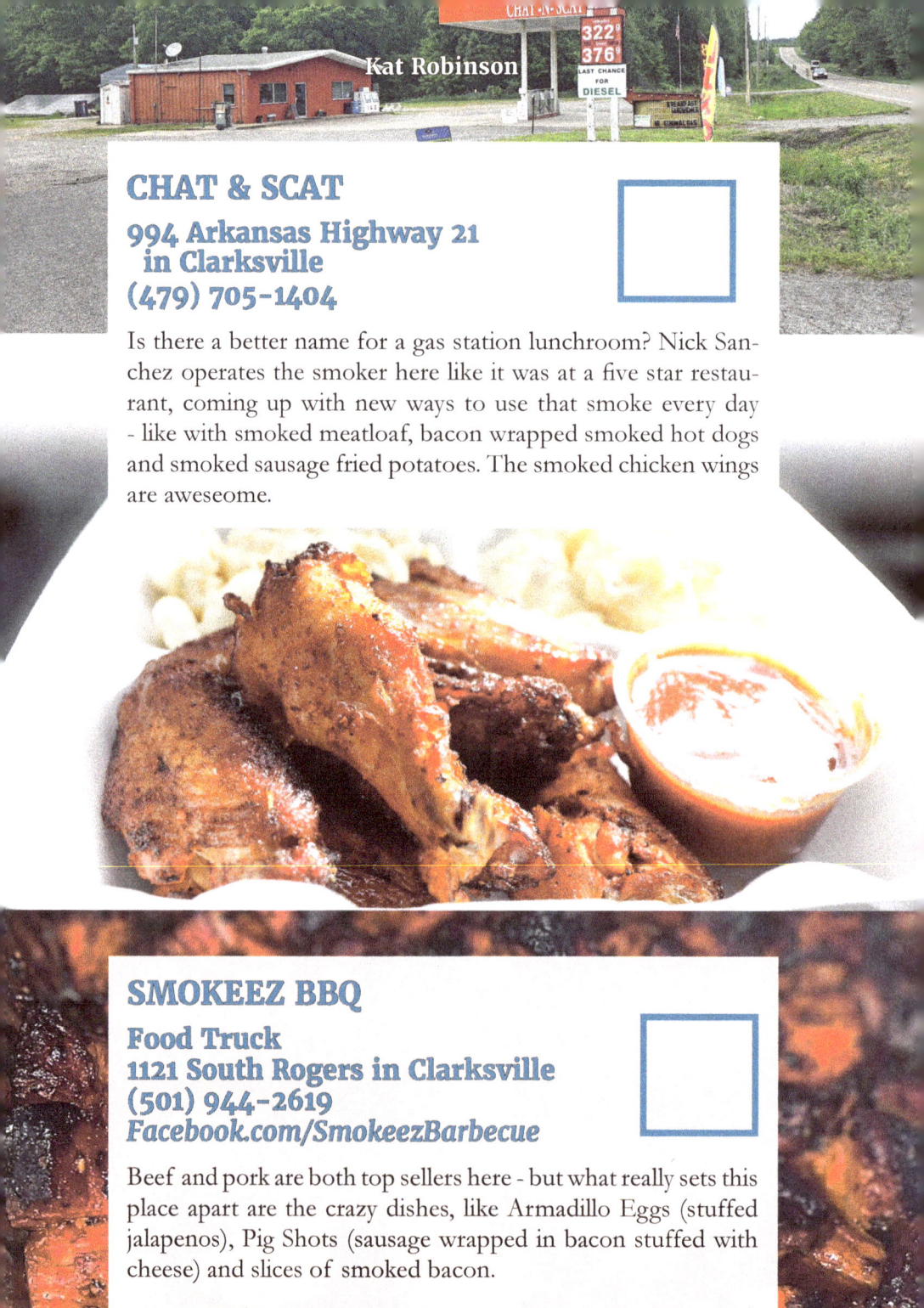

CHAT & SCAT

**994 Arkansas Highway 21 in Clarksville
(479) 705-1404**

Is there a better name for a gas station lunchroom? Nick Sanchez operates the smoker here like it was at a five star restaurant, coming up with new ways to use that smoke every day - like with smoked meatloaf, bacon wrapped smoked hot dogs and smoked sausage fried potatoes. The smoked chicken wings are aweseome.

SMOKEEZ BBQ

**Food Truck
1121 South Rogers in Clarksville
(501) 944-2619
Facebook.com/SmokeezBarbecue**

Beef and pork are both top sellers here - but what really sets this place apart are the crazy dishes, like Armadillo Eggs (stuffed jalapenos), Pig Shots (sausage wrapped in bacon stuffed with cheese) and slices of smoked bacon.

The Arkansas Barbecue Traveler

GRUMPY'S BURGER BARN

Food Truck in Ozone
(479) 214-4485

Randall Atkins, the former owner of the famed and distant Catalpa Cafe, now runs this truck near the original locaiton for the longstanding but now gone Ozone Burger Barn. He's smoking beef and pork for pulled pork samdwiches with homemade slaw and melted cheese, and sliced brisket sandwiches served with pepper jack. You can also get your smoked meat on his Barn Tacos.

BIG POPPA'S BBQ

249 West Main in Lamar
(479) 885-3816

Chicken, pork, ribs and brisket are all popular at this Highway 64 stop best known for its 10 Pound Hot Dog Challenge - which utilizes a specially made Petit Jean Meats hot dog and must be ordered in advance.

The restaurant business is fickle, and it is difficult. This page would have been used for the famed Rivertowne BBQ in Ozark. Sadly, the restaurant closed right as this book was coming to completion.

But hey - here's a space to write a few notes.

Northwest Arkansas

Kat Robinson

The Arkansas Barbecue Traveler

BEAU'S BAYOU SMOKEHOUSE

243 West Main in Farmington
(479) 871-5373
Facebook.com/BeausBayouSmokehouse

Beau McManus combines his south Mississippi upbringing and his training in Florida kitchens with Arkansas Ozark cuisine to create a thick menu of smoked meats and sides at his one-man concession in a gas station parking lot. Sausages, brisket, pulled pork and ribs are all accented with his unique sides, like an addictive blue cheese coleslaw, new potatoes cooked in Cajun boil, and a too-good-to-be-true mac and cheese. On top of all that, he makes cheesecakes in different flavors that you'll come back for time and again.

181

CENTRAL BBQ

417 MLK Jr. Boulevard #200 in Fayetteville
(479) 435-9543
EatCBQ.com/pages/Fayetteville

The sole Arkansas outlet of the famed Memphis barbecue franchise, serving slow smoked long-marinated Memphis style ribs, a sausage and cheese plate, sandwiches and more.

SMOKE N WILLIE

321 North Main Avenue in Greenland (Fayetteville Address)
(479) 396-2831

The Kennedy's young food truck space has a gazebo and lots of land around for expansion - which, considering the menu they're putting out, will be needed. They have all the traditional smoked meats, plus fun things like the Jalapeno Popper sandwich - which has pulled pork and a special dressing made from jalapenos and cheese, that tastes just like a stuffed jalapeno popper. Fun messages on every box.

RONDA'S ROADHOUSE

504 East 15th Street in Fayetteville
(479) 935-3240
Facebook.com/RondasRoadhouse

A locals-know joint where smoked ham is popular any time of day, along with pulled pork, sliced brisket, and hot links. Ribs on Fridays, smoked bologna and hot links available with breakfast.

FIRE AND LIGHTNING CATERING / TYLER'S CRAFT BBQ

(479) 409-7423 or (479) 601-6128
FireandLightningNWA.com

James Tyler has brought years of knowledge from his Texas hometown to northwest Arkansas. Unlike traditional pitmasters in the area, Tyler's barbecue scope ranges far and wide with meats prepared in various styles for particular cuisines. His range encompasses Tex-Mex, soul food, even Spanish and western European cooking. He's working with Chef Thor Maher, former chef at Cafe Rue Orleans and Ella's, to create extraordinary catering experiences.

Kat Robinson

PENGUIN ED'S HISTORIC B&B AND PENGUIN ED'S BBQ

230 South East Avenue in Fayetteville
(479) 521-3663
2773 East Mission Boulevard in Fayetteville
(479) 587-8646
PenguinEds.com

It all started with a barbecue stand under a tent beside the highway. Through a little white trailer and onto one brick and mortar, and another, Penguin Ed's built a reputation for itself. The "penguin" in the name comes from the little papier-mâché penguins Ed Knight would make. The little enterprise that began in 1993 took on the responsibility of running the historic B&B BBQ, which had been open since 1962. Ed and Diane Knight have signed on to keep going that joint the Basset family had led, keeping the decor there and items like the fried pickles. Today, smoked brisket, Polish and ham, hot links, pulled pork and chicken are offered at both place, alongside battered crinkle-cut fries, brown beans, and fried pies at the B&B, while cheezy tators, wings and cookies fill the menu at the Mission Boulevard location.

184

The Arkansas Barbecue Traveler

SOUTH SIDE SMOKE SHACK

3130 South School Avenue in Fayetteville
(479) 435-9543

The first time I chatted with Anthony Breathitt, he was smoking port butts - not for sale, but to take out and feed the homeless with the Salvation Army. His one-man operation is sometimes mobile, sometimes set up at the south end of town, no advertisements, just people pulling up to see what he's smoked that particular day. Lamb, chicken, tri-tip, salmon, brisket - Tony has a real knack for smoking meats to perfection. Pull up and find out - you really cannot go wrong here.

Kat Robinson

WES'S BBQ BURGER PLUS

**14 South University Avenue
 in Fayetteville
(479) 521-5901
WesBBQBurgerPlus.com**

You won't find Wes's BBQ Burgers Plus on the main drag, or even on a main road, in Fayetteville. But folks in the know can tell you about this wood paneled barbecue joint just off the U of A campus, where pork, beef, chicken, and sausage sandwiches have been served since the 1980s. Opened in 1985, little has changed about this place run by Wesley and Mary Whitmore. It stands as the oldest black-created business in operation in town, with a steady client base and some excellent smoked meats - beef, pork, chicken, ribs, and Polish - offered on sandwiches and plates alongside two handfuls of burger options and such. The sauce is thick and the buns are seeded.

The Arkansas Barbecue Traveler

LUCKY LUKE'S BBQ

**1220 Garland Avenue #1
in Fayetteville
(479) 521-7550
GetLuckyAtLukes.com**

Brian Smith gets ribs. He and his wife Sara started Lucky Luke's in Springdale in 2001 - the place is named after their son. They took over the old Fat Toney's Bar-B-Que in Fayetteville in 2002, and that's where the Smiths keep those ribs coming to the table. They are the prime item to order - but if you skip a basket of wings, you've made a critical error - these award-winning smoked wings are crispy edged and magnificent.

GIRLS GONE BBQ

2630 East Citizens Dr #20 in Fayetteville
(479) 879-8222
GirlsGoneBBQ.com

Dana Neely left the Arkansas Delta and the South behind to make it on her own in Seattle. She came back with her own barbecue operation, Girls Gone BBQ, in 2020 - offering some of the most notable Delta-style barbecue in the region - but instead of bringing it back to the Delta, she set up shop in Fayetteville.

If that weren't enough, this innovator has stepped up the barbecue game by venturing where few pitmasters have dared to tread, - creating smoked alternatives to traditional meats. Her smoked soy curl sandwiches have the flavor and mouthfeel of pulled pork, and can be offered in a completely vegan-friendly sandwich. Paired with apple Arkan-slaw and a whole pickled okra, you have all the flavor of Delta barbecue that's accessible to everyone. Yet her smoked brisket and sliced and sauced chicken can stand up against any other joint's meaty offerings. From smoked and seared duck breast to cornbread with smoked serrano rye honey, Delta Dog with house-made sausage to 'Nana Puddin' to pepper jack mac-and-cheese, Dana's a wizard, and her conjured flavors are unmatched.

The Arkansas Barbecue Traveler

SASSY'S RED HOUSE

708 North College Avenue in Fayetteville
(479) 856-6366

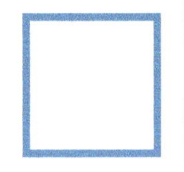

SASSYS BBQ AND GRILLE

1290 Steamboat Drive in Fayetteville
(479) 435-6996
SassysBBQ.co

Allen Brummett's gang knows how to smoke a brisket right, and that's good enough reason to go to Sassy's in the first place. But it's the sauce that started it all out. Back in 1986, Sharon and Bill Jones developed that original sauce based on his grandfather's, Jasper Jones, back in 1895. You can still get that small-batch sauce through the Sassy Jones Sauce Company.

The first of the two restaurants opened in the spring of 2009 and quickly became famous for its smoked ribs, wings, and brisket, along with chicken, pulled pork and sausages, and standout choices like mushroom fries, tacos and an utterly epic possum pie. Its fried pickles have appeared on Food Network's website, and its nachos have become a local favorite. Just all around good and tasty.

The Arkansas Barbecue Traveler

FLAVORSMITH'S CRAFT BARBECUE
50 East Township Street in Fayetteville
(479) 879-1902

Billy Ray Smith's newly opened joint at the location of Fayetteville's beloved The Beer Keg has quickly gained notice and traction in a city already well-stocked with barbecue joints. His tiny shop and smokehouse knocks out briskets, jalapeno cheese sausages, ribs, pulled pork and turkey at a satisfyingly quick rate to keep up with the sudden demand. You absolutely must try the banana pudding.

Kat Robinson

HERMAN'S RIBHOUSE
2901 North College Avenue in Fayetteville
(479) 442-9671

Herman's Ribhouse has become the place for University of Arkansas coaches, heads of industry, and hungry diners to all rub elbows over the years. Nick and Carrie Wright continue the traditions of this classic eatery that Herman Tuck opened way back in 1964. Nick worked his way up from a start as a dishwasher at the restaurant to grill cook, manager, and eventual owner, and keeps the traditions and menu alive with smoked baby back pork ribs, Spanish omelets, Herman's garlic chicken, and Bigun's half pound hamburger patty topped with grilled "gear" (sauteed ham, peppers and onions) and cheese. But he's made his own mark on the place, with one of the best Philly cheesesteaks I've had in ages and outright righteous steaks. Whether it's the classic smoked bologna Crabbie Patty sandwich or the barbecue half chicken, you'll be in good shape. Just don't expect room for dessert - all you're going to get is a Tootsie Roll Pop, and that's all that's offered or needed.

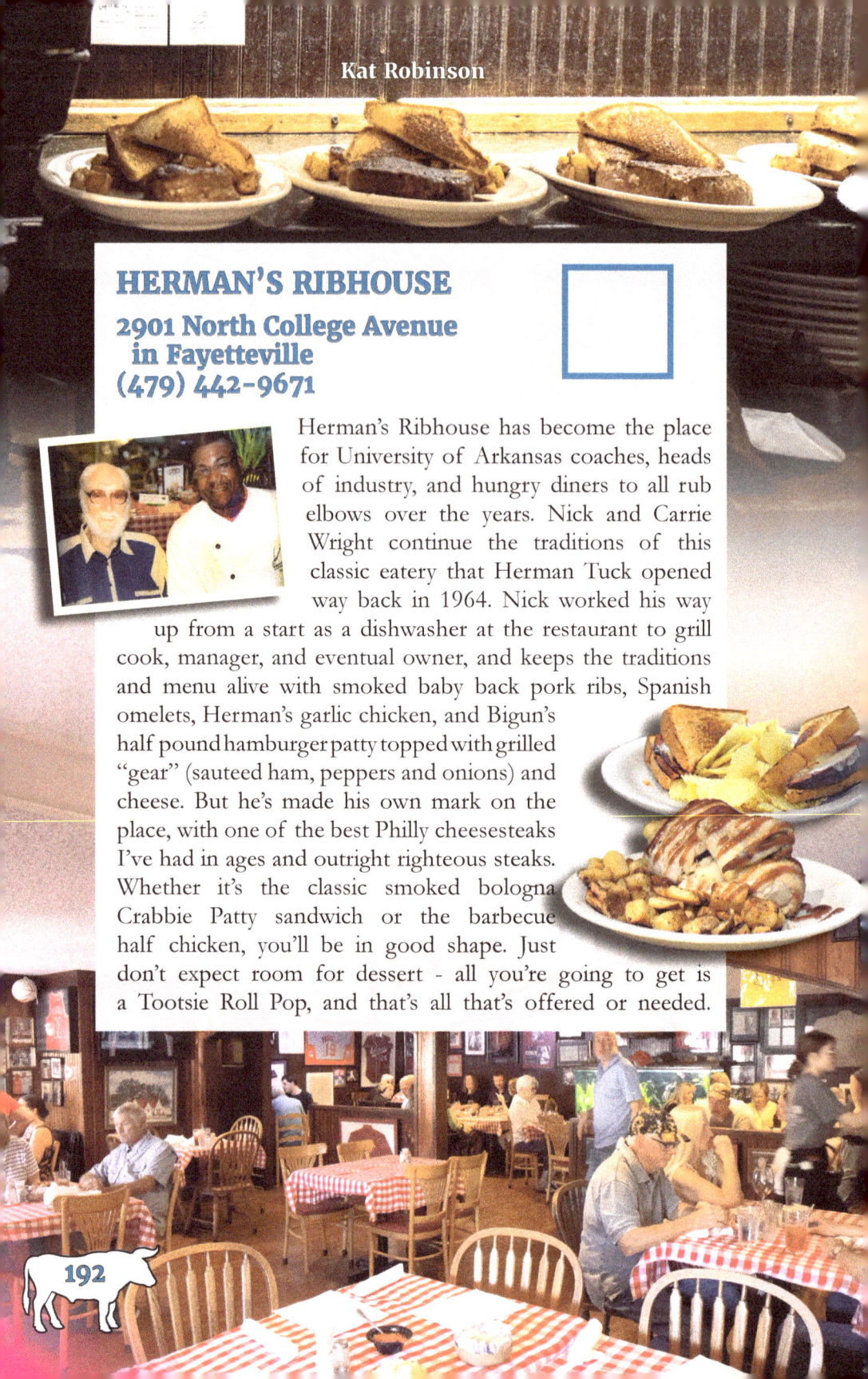

The Arkansas Barbecue Traveler

G's MEATY BUNS

2421 North Center Street in Elkins (Fayetteville address)
(479) 435-4838
Facebook.com/GsMeatyBuns

"More meat than your buns can handle," is a heck of a motto to pick up, but apt for this Elkins operation, which began as a food truck back in 2017. George Torres and Veronica Arellano-Torres are keen on making sure folks get the best bang for their buck, with oversized portions of smoked meats. Beginning with sliced and chopped brisket and pulled pork served on a bun (hence the name), the Torreses have expanded the menu and taken over the former Nellie B's space in a shopping strip that allows them a large kitchen and even larger community space to enjoy. From seriously large and overloaded stuffed potatoes to smoked burgers and even tacos, G's is following through on making sure Elkins gets on and stays on the barbecue map.

CITY PARK

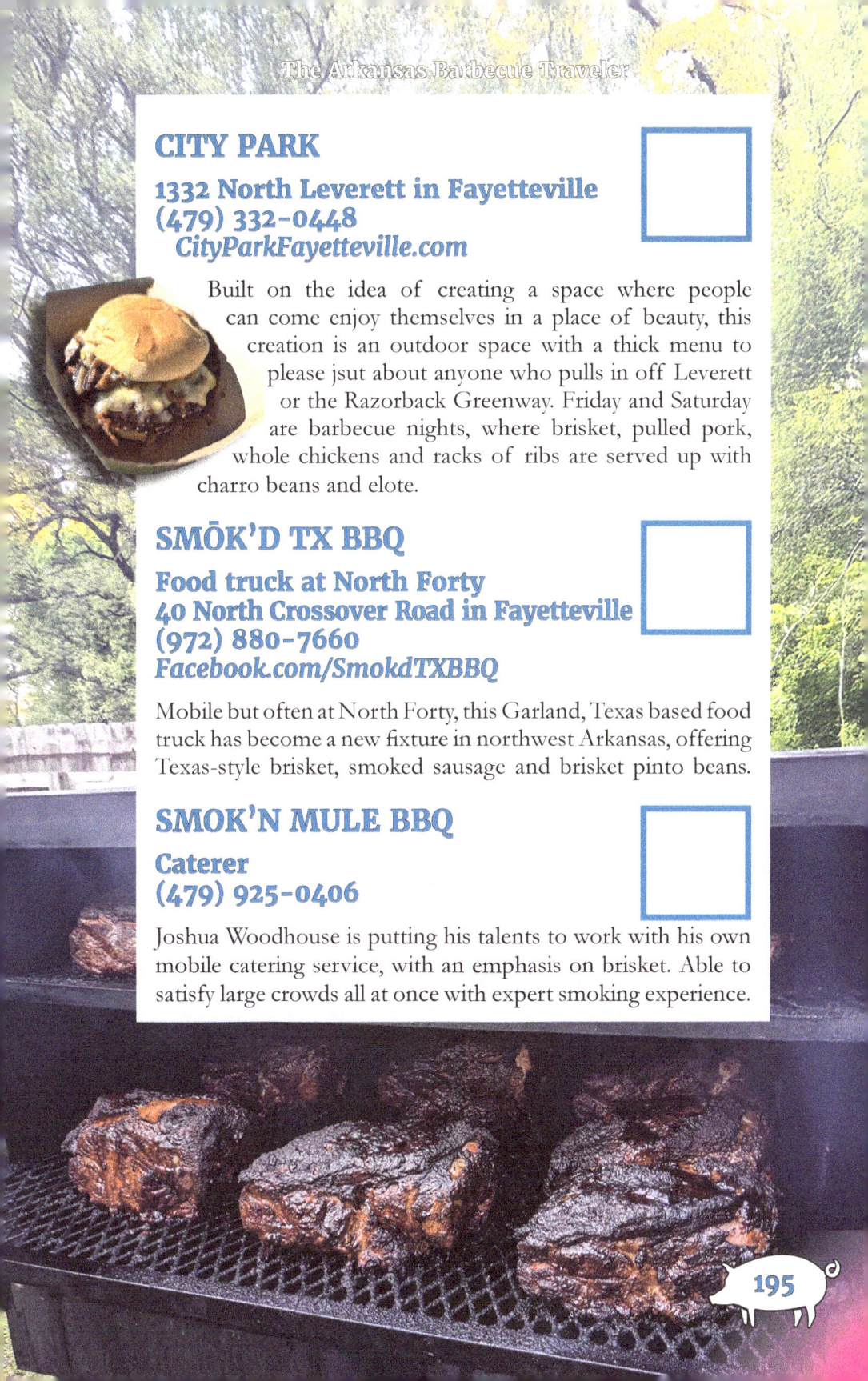

**1332 North Leverett in Fayetteville
(479) 332-0448
CityParkFayetteville.com**

Built on the idea of creating a space where people can come enjoy themselves in a place of beauty, this creation is an outdoor space with a thick menu to please jsut about anyone who pulls in off Leverett or the Razorback Greenway. Friday and Saturday are barbecue nights, where brisket, pulled pork, whole chickens and racks of ribs are served up with charro beans and elote.

SMŌK'D TX BBQ

**Food truck at North Forty
40 North Crossover Road in Fayetteville
(972) 880-7660
Facebook.com/SmokdTXBBQ**

Mobile but often at North Forty, this Garland, Texas based food truck has become a new fixture in northwest Arkansas, offering Texas-style brisket, smoked sausage and brisket pinto beans.

SMOK'N MULE BBQ

**Caterer
(479) 925-0406**

Joshua Woodhouse is putting his talents to work with his own mobile catering service, with an emphasis on brisket. Able to satisfy large crowds all at once with expert smoking experience.

Kat Robinson

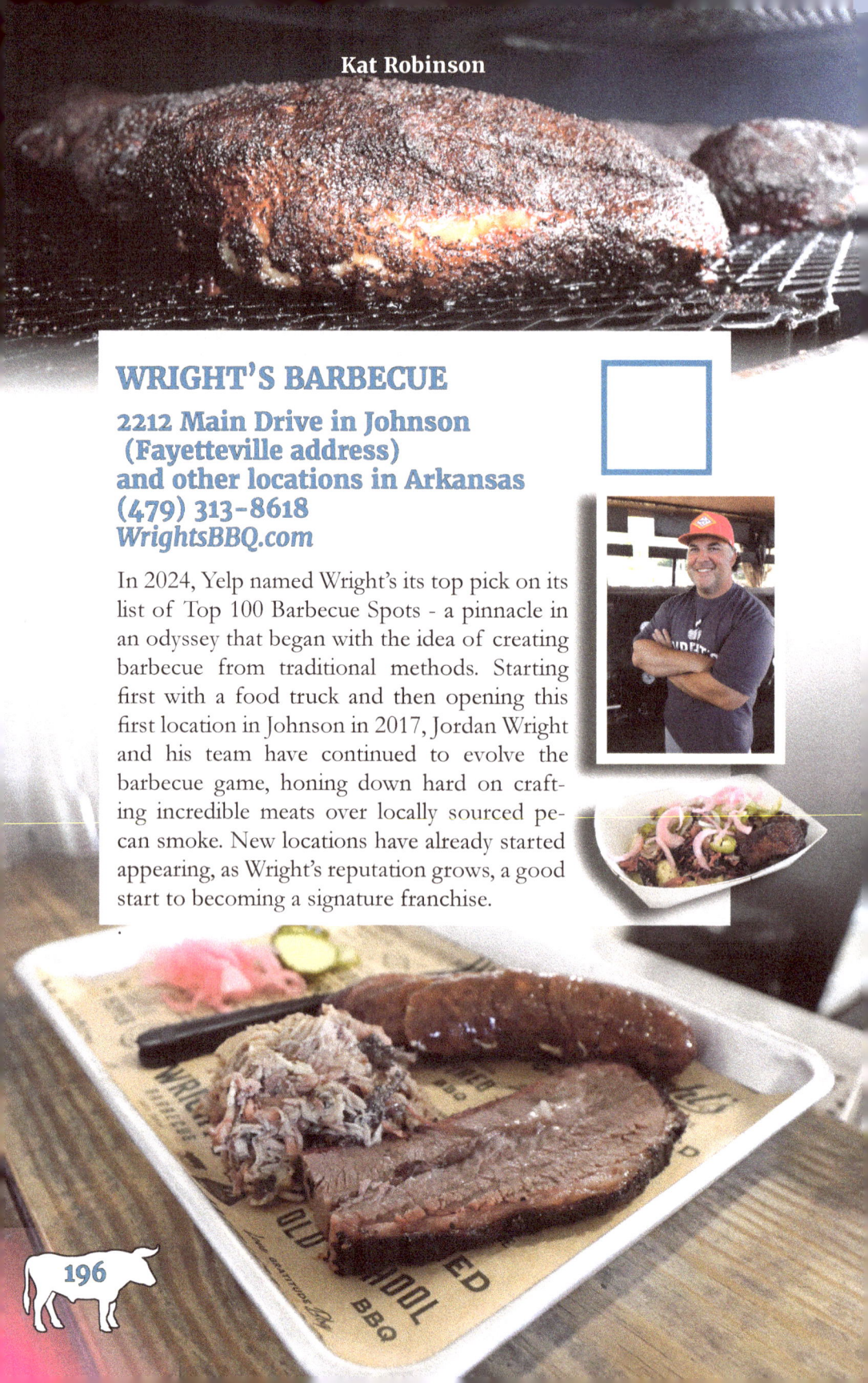

WRIGHT'S BARBECUE

2212 Main Drive in Johnson
 (Fayetteville address)
and other locations in Arkansas
(479) 313-8618
WrightsBBQ.com

In 2024, Yelp named Wright's its top pick on its list of Top 100 Barbecue Spots - a pinnacle in an odyssey that began with the idea of creating barbecue from traditional methods. Starting first with a food truck and then opening this first location in Johnson in 2017, Jordan Wright and his team have continued to evolve the barbecue game, honing down hard on crafting incredible meats over locally sourced pecan smoke. New locations have already started appearing, as Wright's reputation grows, a good start to becoming a signature franchise.

The Arkansas Barbecue Traveler

197

Kat Robinson

YANKABILLY SMOKEHOUSE

327 East Emma in the Mothership Building in Springdale
(833) 468-2867
INeedBBQNow.com

Aaron and Renee Kemper have created the little yellow trailer that could, creating gorgeously smoked meats and an impossibly creamy mac and cheese to cement their position as one of the region's best new barbecue eateries.. Their brisket burger is one of the best burgers I've ever had.

SUNSET GRILL & BBQ

**3418 US Highway 412 in Springdale
(479) 872-9594**

Primarily a diner, it's one of the few places in Arkansas where you can get a barbecue omelet - filled with your choice of pulled pork, chicken or beef with onions, peppers, and Swiss cheese. Sandwiches and dinners available later in the day.

RED DOOR BAR AND GRILL

**188 Pozza Lane in Springdale
(479) 333-2546
Facebook.com/RedDoorBarGrill**

It's hard to miss that big Razorback smoker out front of this bright eatery that offers 12 hour hickory smoked brisket as its headliner. Pulled pork, baby back ribs and smoked sausages also star, along with crispy smoked wings and smokey queso.

MRS. MILDRED'S KITCHEN

**Food truck
1064 East Henri De Tonti Boulevard in Springdale
(479) 334-8677
Instagram.com/Mrs.MildredsKitchen**

Smoked brisket, chicken, and ribs in the Texas style is what this Tontitown area eatery touts - but it's the mac and cheese that gets the biggest raves. Good thing you can get your meat in your mac and cheese. Epic desserts daily, too.

Kat Robinson

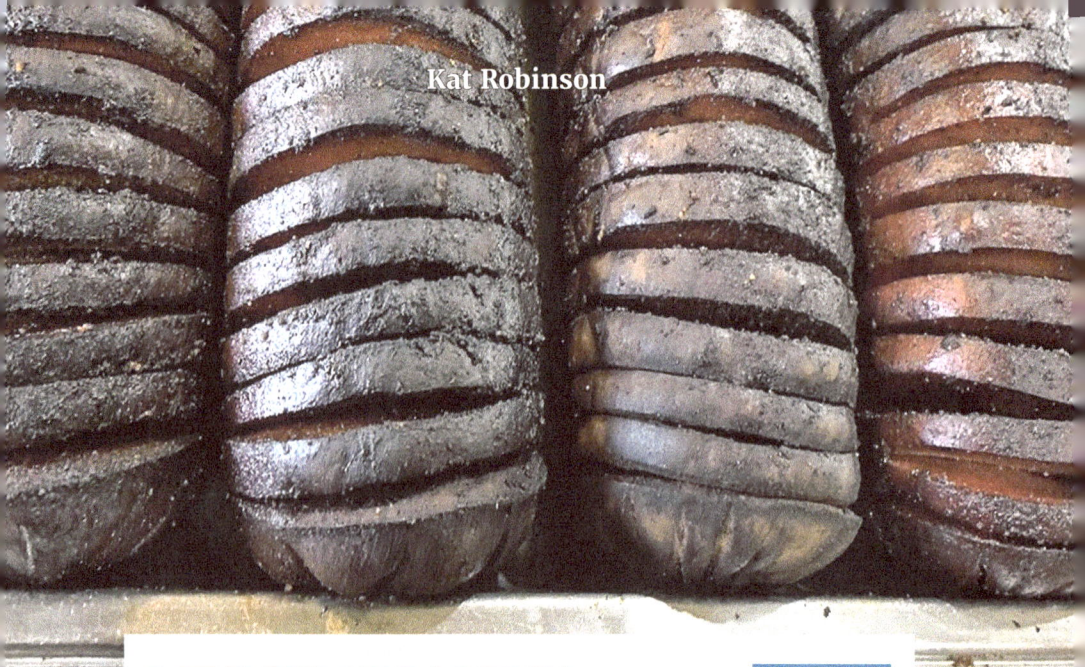

PORK BELLY ROBERTS

600 East Main Street in Siloam Springs
(479) 427-7675

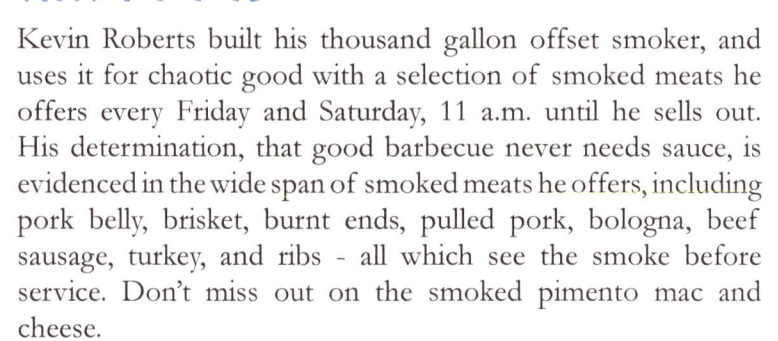

Kevin Roberts built his thousand gallon offset smoker, and uses it for chaotic good with a selection of smoked meats he offers every Friday and Saturday, 11 a.m. until he sells out. His determination, that good barbecue never needs sauce, is evidenced in the wide span of smoked meats he offers, including pork belly, brisket, burnt ends, pulled pork, bologna, beef sausage, turkey, and ribs - all which see the smoke before service. Don't miss out on the smoked pimento mac and cheese.

OZARK MOUNTAIN GRILL
inside Workman's Travel Center

898 West Monroe Avenue in Lowell
(479) 419-9424
WorkmansTravelCenters.com

Ribs, pulled pork and brisket are available as dinners at this oversized restaurant inside a truck stop. Burnt ends and chops and barbecue nachos are also available. 24 hours.

The Arkansas Barbecue Traveler

I'D SMOKE THAT

5079 West Northgate Road in Rogers
(479) 380-4888
Facebook.com/IdSmokeThatFood

Casey Coverdell hit on something spectacular - taking smoked meats and doing exceptional things with them. Coverdell started as the Executive Chef for the Walmart AMP in Rogers. When COVID-19 shut down the world, he turned to this food truck, and success was immediate. The star on his menu is this smoked brisket sandwich with bacon jam, served with the LTOP (lettuce, tomato, onion, pickle) and Cheddar cheese, the top of a lush menu that also includes an incredible smoked chicken caprese that still haunts my dreams. Exceptional.

OZ SMOKEHOUSE

113 West Walnut Street in Rogers
(479) 270-1764
OZSmokehouse.com

Following in his dad's footsteps as a Kansas City barbecue judge and competitor, Jordan Poole brings something marvelous to the table. He learned to smoke meat before he learned how to cook anything else, and it shows with the span of dishes his eatery offers. He may originally hail from Memphis, but his study of Ozark barbecue is evident in a beautiful and barky chopped brisket that's showcased on so many of the items offered here, such as the Brick Street Hero, a brisket and avocado taco with crushed Doritos. Pulled pork and pulled chicken are also stars, as are the lion's mane mushroom bites he has created, lightly dusted in a gluten-free mix, deep fried and served with avocado ranch dressing and Nashville hot sauce, a marvelous vegan item that tastes like, I kid you not, chicken wings.

The Arkansas Barbecue Traveler

Kat Robinson

SMOKIN' JOES RIBHOUSE

200 North 8th Street in Rogers
(479) 621-0181
2504 East Central Avenue in Bentonville
(479) 254-8383
Facebook.com/TheRealSmokinJoes

Longstanding ribhouse that also serves chopped and sliced brisket, pulled and sliced pork, chopped chicken, sliced turkey, hot links and mild links as well as smoked pork tenderloin and half chickens. Smoked prime rib and gumbo also available.

BOAR'S NEST BAR AND GRILL

inside Kingston Centre
4404 West Walnut Street in Rogers
(479) 685-2742

A local bar with entertainment in the form of live bands, karaoke, pool tables, darts and electronic trivia, and a full menu that includes pork belly pops, smoked chicken wings, pork shanks ("pig wings"), plus the traditional smoked brisket, chicken, pulled pork, sausage, and ribs. Almost every dish comes with the option of being topped with a smoked meat.

SAM'S OLDE TYME HAMBURGERS
223 East Locust Street in Rogers
(479) 986-9191
SamsHamburgers.com

Originally opened in 2006 and moved into these current digs in 2009, Sam's has been one of the more popular pull-in spots for folks coming in off Beaver Lake for years. Though the burgers are what get the attention from the outside, within, the smoked ribs have become one of the more popular items. You can have the best of both worlds - Sam's proudly offers single ribs, knowing if you have one, you'll want another.

SMOKEWOOD AMERICAN GRILL
inside XWA

1 Airport Boulevard near Bentonville
(479) 203-9305
FlyXNA.com

Flying in or out of northwest Arkansas? Get your barbecue fix at this concourse eatery, which offers house smoked pulled pork, brisket, and chicken wings on a platter, grab a sandwich, or enjoy brisket in a loaded omelet or breakfast tacos.

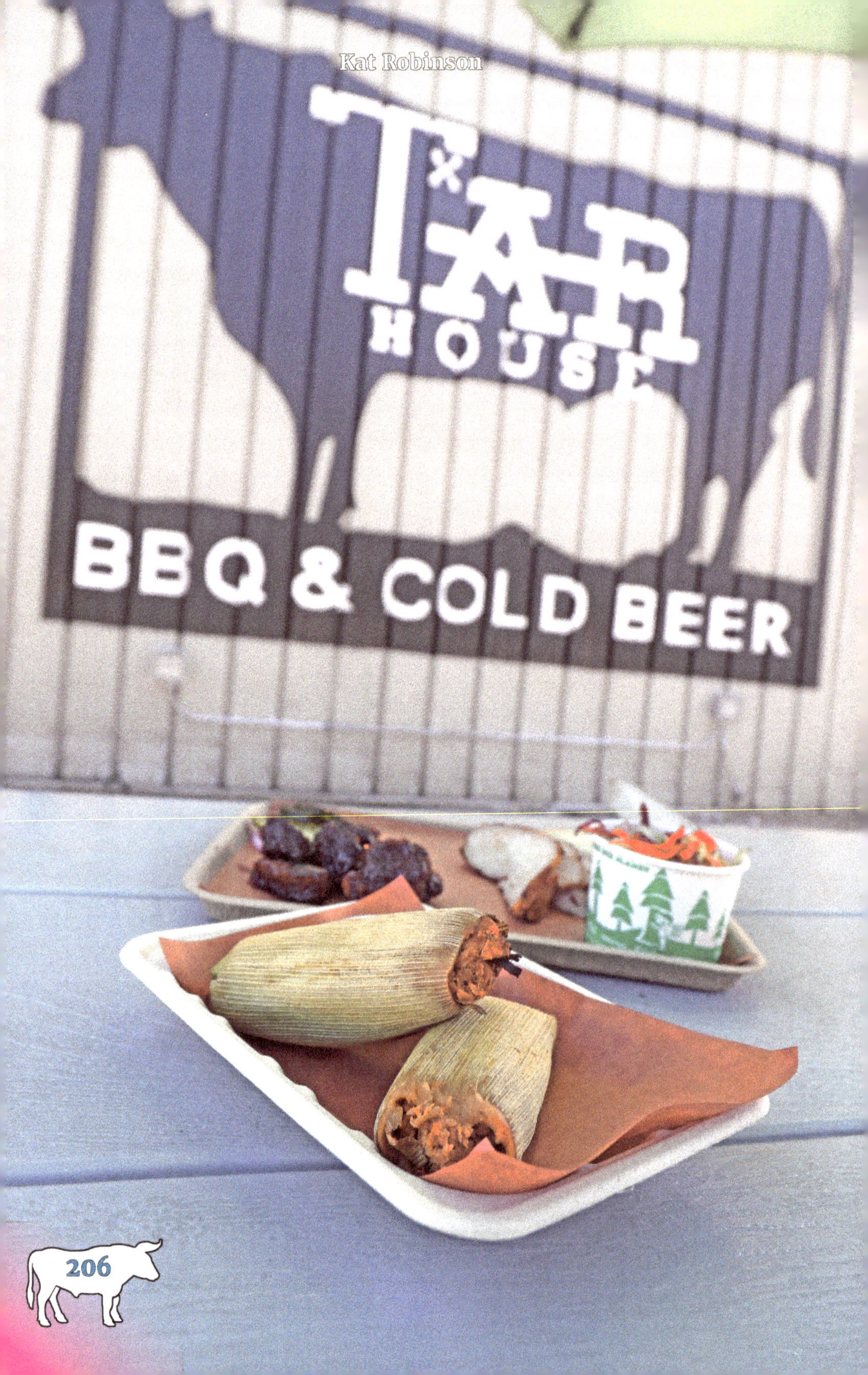
TAR HOUSE
BBQ & COLD BEER

TxAR HOUSE

300 South 1st Street in Rogers
(479) 202-5391
Facebook.com/TxARHouse

These are the best burnt ends I have had in my life. Ever. I don't say that lightly. I've had so many versions of burnt ends over the past year that many just blend in together with each other. But these magnificent, Arkansas Blackapple glazed burnt ends are that perfect balance between sweet caramelized exterior, beautifully smoked interior, excellent beef and expert handling. They're a marvelous creation of Ash, the resident pitmaster, part of a stable of dishes that include beautifully smoked turkey and exceptional, handmade tamales, the flavor of which changes weekly. The business she and Hannah have created here is sewn into the community in which it lives.

BROTHERS MEETHOUSE

405 Southeast 5th Street in Bentonville
(479) 553-7199
BrothersMeethouse.com

Chef Rob Nelson and Pitmaster Alex Glass have created a destination dining experience centered around Arkansas's historic barbecue roots, with a double smoking process in the kitchen that harkens back to pre-refrigeration era barbecue practice in the state. Rob's done as much if not more research on the subject of Arkansas barbecue than I have, with around seven years of vested interest in the creation of the menu. With a team that also includes a world-class mixologist curating a fine selection of house-infused liqueurs, including (I kid you not!) a bacon fat infused vodka, and being one of Arkansas's largest barbecue joints, with seating for 170, Brothers is about to make a name for itself. Some items - like the smoked bread and cornbread pudding, are unique to this place. The brisket is marvelous, the belly bites are already a favorite, but do yourself a favor and try that smoked turkey - it's extraordinary!

The Arkansas Barbecue Traveler

TABLE AT HICKORY INN

1502 North Walton Boulevard in Bentonville
(479) 273-3303
TableAtTheHickoryInn.com

The eatery that Sam Walton cited as his favorite place has a new name and menu. The former Fred's Hickory Inn, opened in 1970, was purchased and revitalized in 2022 by Carl and Lindie Garrett, whi also own Table Mesa Bistro and Tavola Trattoria. The couple kept the restaurant's tradition of producing hickory smoked meats, particularly the famed smoked prime rib, ribs, pulled pork and roasted chicken along with a smoked turkey pot pie, while adding a slate of newer options.

BEACH BBQ

1080 Southast 14th Street in Bentonville
(479) 544-1060
TheBeachBBQ.com

James Beachboard's take on barbecue adds a touch of Mississippi Gulf Coast to the mix. Beachboard's Brississippi is a fine example of this - his 14-16 hour oak smoked brisket chopped fine with added Mississippi pork seasoning makes for an atypical flavor with notes of onion and garlic. With the addition of his fermenty, piquant kimchi slaw and housemade pickles, Beach BBQ's sandwich becomes something that truly stands out.

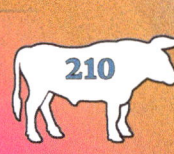

CHOP SHOP BBQ

Mobile food truck and 115 Northwest 2nd Street in Bentonville (479) 685-7211

A friend of Jim and Lisa McDermott asked Jim if he'd take on a food truck at a Father's Day party, and, as Jim tells it, "being about 15 beers in and I'd been cooking all day, I said yes." Though he didn't recall that conversation the next day, he made good on it, and Chop Shop BBQ was born. It was a good call - the long cherry wood smoke he does on his brisket is absolutely gorgeous and shows in the deep pink smoke ring on that brisket. He and Lisa actually run two trucks - a mobile unit and a second location currently behind Bentonville Dive - and they manage to create some spectacular items, like smoked bratwurst, lamb breast, and smoked salmon. The candied jalapenos and pickled onions served alongside are amazing!

Kat Robinson

BEARDED CHOPS MARKET

308 First Avenue Northeast in Gravette
(682) 557-8362
BeardedChopsBBQCo.com

Coby Stauffer only smokes once a week, and contrary to just about every other barbecue purveyor in Arkansas, he serves ONLY on Sundays. The little shop he and Milli have created is an adorable addition to a booming community - a former gax station that's now part gift shop, part sno-cone stand, and part barbecue joint. Her adorable clothing, accessory and knick-knacks fill the shopping space, while in the kitchen Coby is conjuring whatever he's decided to tackle for the day. Some Sundays he'll have hangar steak, others chicken leg quarters, it's whatever he decides. But he just about always has smoked ribs, which are juicy and tender and come tossed in his marvelous glaze. Bearded Chops has recently added take-home prepared meals you can order in advance.

The Arkansas Barbecue Traveler

SMITH AND BETTS BARBECUE

191 First Avenue Southeast in Gravette
(479) 600-9845
SmithBettsBBQ.com

Gravette's Smith and Bett's BBQ is actually two food trucks - one that's stationed at the town's main intersection and the other that's mobile - with a fine selection of meats across the board. Some days there's novel items like smoked meatloaf, there are sometimes steak nights, and there's always brisket, pulled pork, hot links and smoked sausage.

A LITTLE BIT OF TEXAS

Food Truck
(479) 256-9702
Facebook.com/ALittleBitOfTexas

Dean Losh utilizes mesquite in his smoker for a flavor not common to Arkansas. His delectably seasoned chopped beef with thick sauce, onion and pickle makes for a marvelous sandwich. Juicy brisket and ribs are on deck for this winner at the famed Bikes, Blues and BBQ Festival. Losh is also known for taking his barbecue out into the community to feed the homeless.

Kat Robinson

AR TILLERY'S BBQ

700 Blowing Springs Road in Bella Vista
(541) 270-0578
ARTillerysBBQ.com

Rod Tillery moved his family from Oregon during the pandemic, and this year followed a dream and started this mobile barbecue operation. Tillery is using tri-tip instead of brisket and showcases it alongside candied pork belly bites, smoked chicken and the outrageous but craveable Artillery Shells - jalapenos stuffed with smoked beef and cheese, wrapped in bacon, smoked and doused in barbecue sauce. Find the truck out front of Lowe's or in Blowing Spring Park, or see where the trailer will be today on the eatery's website.

MILNER'S BBQ

**1300 North Gaskill Street in Huntsville
(479) 871-0057**

This food truck on the west side of Huntsville doesn't look like much, but the brisket at Milner's BBQ is fall-apart soft with a nice griddle-toasted bun and thick sauce - and they don't scrimp on the meat. Plus, all the sides are homemade, like the cucumber and tomato salad only offered during the summer and the smashed potatoes.

BUBBA'S SOUTHERN PIT BARBECUE

**166 West Van Buren in Eureka Springs
(479) 253-7706
BubbasBBQEureka.com**

Brian and Robin Weinman have taken over the the longstanding local barbecue joint in town, originally began by Bob Wilson in 1978. The restaurant's baby lion back pork ribs are big on the menu, as is sliced or chopped brisket and pork shoulder, hot links, and smoked chicken - the last of which is only available in the evenings. The brisket sandwich in particular, chunky moist chopped brisket, coleslaw on the side, with a default pile of ripply potato chips - is a solid choice from the menu any time Bubba's is open. Try the chili, too.

SADDLE UP

85 South Main Street in Eureka Springs
(479) 239-2124

Opened in 2023, this family restaurant's sole regular barbecue item is pulled pork, though ribs and smoked sausage are often showcased as the daily special.

EUREKA SPRINGS EATS AND TREATS

2051 East Van Buren in Eureka Springs
(479-363-6118
EurekaSpringsEatsAndTreats.com

The menu here is Italian-inspired with pasta, sandwiches and - for some crazy reason, augmented with Memphis-style pulled pork sandwiches where the pork has been dry-rubbed, served with apple butter barbecue sauce on an Italian sweet bun. A pineapple version and one with pulled chicken also available.

ROCKIN' PIG SALOON

2039 East Van Buren in Eureka Springs
(479) 363-6248
RockinPig.com

Local biker-friendly bar that serves dry aged steaks and pizzas along with a selection of smoked brisket and pulled pork dishes like sandwiches and sweet potato fries.

Kat Robinson

SAUCED BARBECUE AND BREWS
139 East Van Buren in Eureka Springs
(479) 239-2044
SaucedBBQEureka.com

Rodney Slane, owner of famed restaurants Grotto Wood-Fired Grill and Wine Cafe and The Filling Station, brought years of experience in upper eschelon Florida restaurants and as a private chef on luxury yachts, to smoke up some high-quality meats. He bought a gigantic smoker at auction, and opened the first iteration of the restaurant in Fayetteville. When COVID-19 came around, Slane relocated his barbecue joint to a shack in the parking lot of Hart's Grocery, where he now showcases a meat-heavy menu. Want brisket? Got that. Pork belly burnt ends? That too. Turkey, sausage, even smoked bologna, all are on this meaty menu.

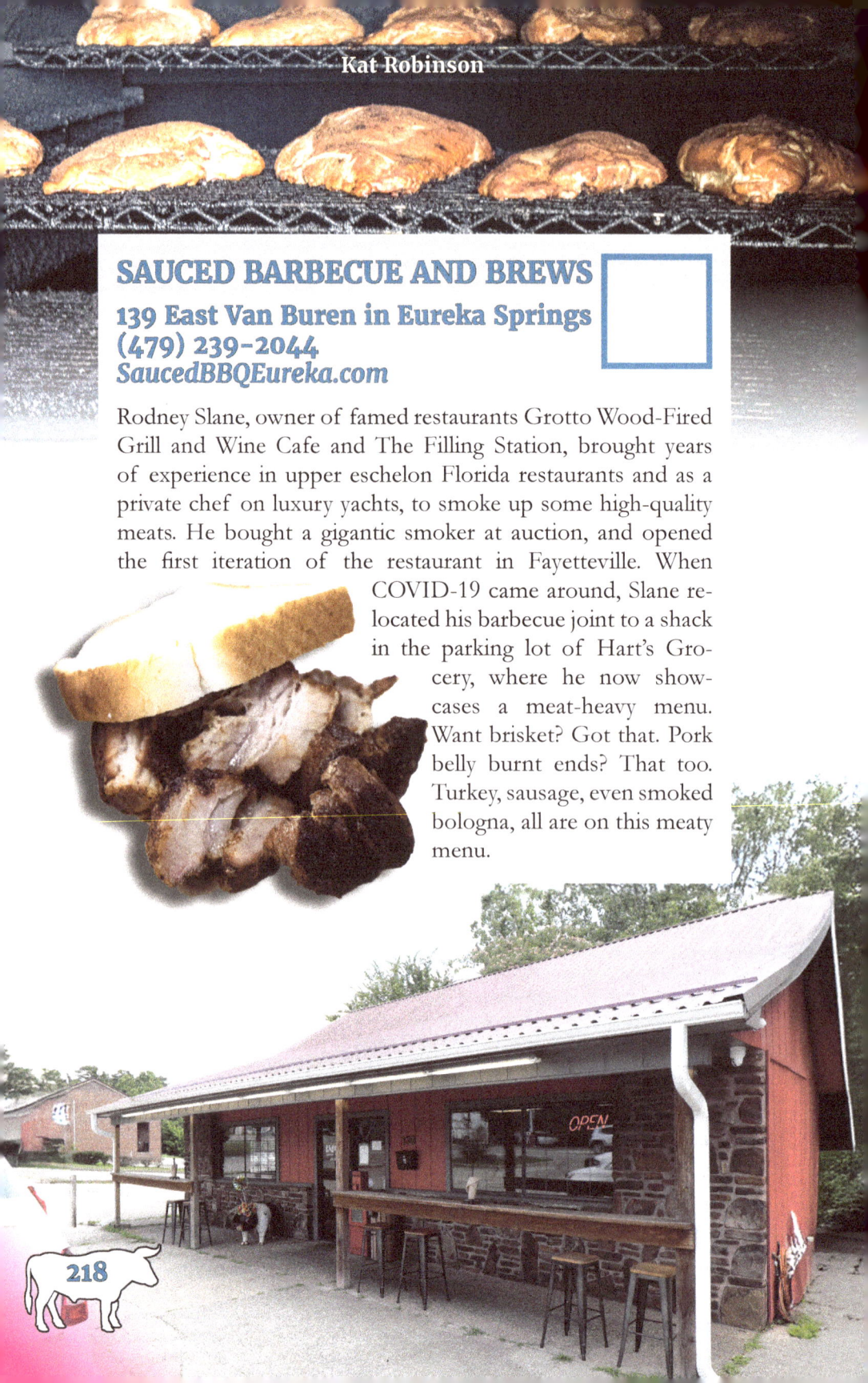

The Arkansas Barbecue Traveler

Hunter, would like for you to have a space to write a few notes, if you wish.

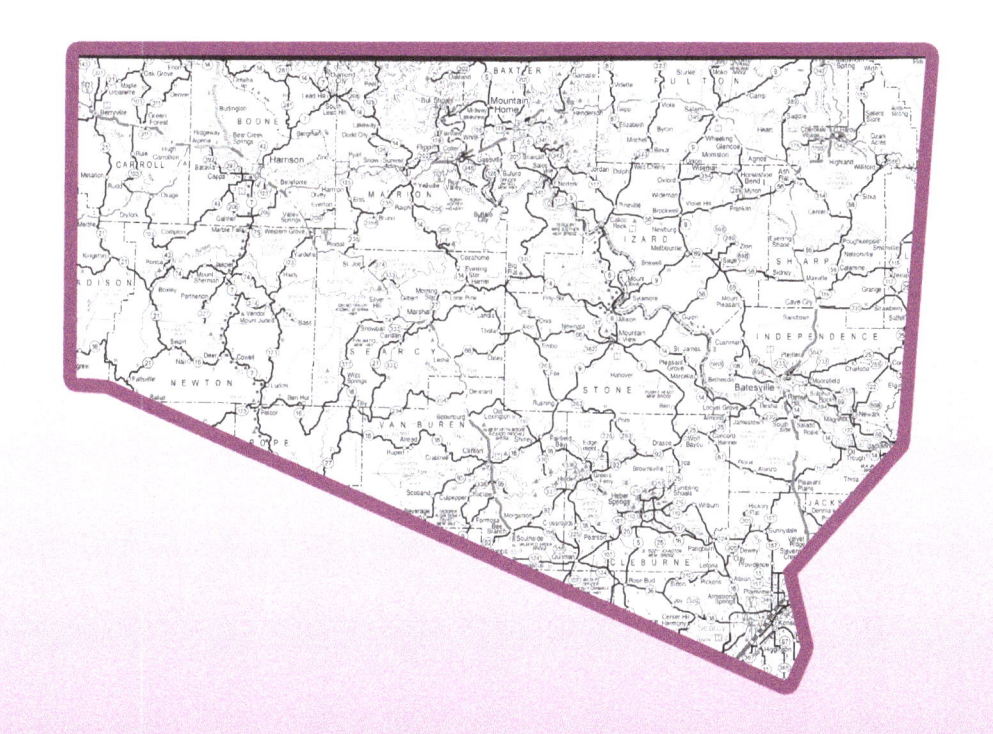

North Central Arkansas

BUB'S COUNTRY STORE

10423 Arkansas 21 in Oak Grove
(501) 732-5196

A classic back country general store serving up smoked ribs, pork chops, chicken and bologna on the regular, with a small array of sides.

JAMIE'S RESTAURANTS

1212 Highways 62/65 North in Harrison
(870) 365-0421

1502 Highway 62 East in Mountain Home
(870) 701-0145

649 Highway 62 in Berryville
(870) 505-2019
JamiesRestaurant.com

BUCKETS SPORTS BAR & GRILL
1406 Highway 62B in Mountain Home
(870) 701-0196

Jamie and Angela Akers started the original Jamie's Restaurant in 2014, after operating the restaurant John Paul in the Hotel Seville. With more than 25 years experience in the business, it was time to put his name on the product. Jamie's main location is now within a massive former Dixie Cafe, offering breakfast, lunch, dinner, desserts and coffee seven days a week. Additional restaurants in Mountain Home and Berryville are already in operation. The barbecue here is slow smoked spare ribs, pulled pork, and pulled chicken, served in dinners and across several menu specialties.

T'S BBQ

108 Lakeshore Drive in Harrison
(870) 741-7675
TsBBQ.net

Handling a large portion of the barbecue needs of an entire town can be a lot - but for T's BBQ in Harrison, it's business as usual. The menu features just about every sort of meat you'd like - pulled pork, sliced brisket, ribs, smoked turkey, jalapeno cheddar sausage, half chickens and ham. The ribs and the catfish are the biggest sellers here, along with Potachos - barbecue meat and cheese loaded tater tots with peppers, sour cream and barbecue sauce - smoked chicken salad, fried pork rinds, and a selection of fried pies that changes daily.

Kat Robinson

HUDSONS SUPERMARKET

**609 North Main Street in Harrison
(870) 741-2171
Facebook.com/
HudsonSuperMarketHarrison**

Barbecue isn't just found in restaurants and at food trucks in Arkansas. In Harrison, you can get your smoked meats about any day of the week by searching out the giant bull. That's where you'll find Hudson's Supermarket, an old-school full-service grocery store with its own smoke shed out by the main drag. Get yourself store smoked brisket, ribs, turkey legs, or even gator sausage, either smoked ahead and chilled for refrigeration or out of the hot case. Plus you can pick up any sides or accoutrements you need - after all, going to Hudson's is a trip to the grocery store.

CRAW BILLY'S SEAFOOD BOIL & BBQ

**12633 North US Highway 65 in St. Joe
(479) 903-2238
Facebook.com/TripleDCabins**

Ken and Sonya Perea boil up hundreds of pounds of crawfish each weekend in the spring and serve a full menu of Cajun and Creole fare - but they also offer Cajun smoked and seasoned baby back ribs.

WHO'DA THOUGHT IT ARKANSAS

**22158 Arkansas Highway 7 in Pelsor
(870) 294-5295**

Out in the middle of nowhere on Arkansas Scenic Highway Seven, you'll find this quaint gas station and lunchroom that's been open since 1950. It's the only place in scantly populated Newton County where you'll find pulled pork on the menu. Assorted sundries and supplies available.

BUFFALO BBQ

Food Truck with indoor dining
1112 North Main in Harrison
(870) 715-5553

This dorable pink barbecue food trailer will catch your eye on Main Street - and then the scent of smoking meats will draw you in. This budding new business started out small but has expanded with the lease of the old Neighborhood Diner, where patrons can now enjoy indoor service. Ribs and brisket were already popular here - now you can also savor harvest skillets with pulled pork, turkey legs, smoked chicken sandwiches and The Cheesy Cajun - mac and cheese with smoked Andouille.

COURSEY'S SMOKED MEATS

152 Courseys Drive in St. Joe
(870) 439-2503

It took until 2020 for Coursey's, the last of our classic restaurants of the time - to join the internet age with a Facebook presence. That being said, the place did just fine from the day Lynn Coursey moved to the Ozarks to retire and opened this shop along what's now US Highway 65 in 1945. Today, the fourth and fifth generation of the family continues to produce double-smoked meats in the old Ozark tradition, with an on-site smokehouse. These days, the hams come smoked the first time from Petit Jean Meats before they're hung here again, but the flavor in that ham, those sausages, the bacon and the turkey remains the same. Check out the original smokehouse building out front, and pick up a snack bag with smoked meat and cheese to go. Jams and jellies also available.

Kat Robinson

The Arkansas Barbecue Traveler

BIG SPRINGS TRADING COMPANY

14237 US Highway 65 in St. Joe
(870) 439-2900
BigSpringsRestaurant.com

Jennifer Jones is continuing traditions that marked barbecue and smoked meats throughout the Ozarks for generations. She's still operating twin smokers (cold smoke and traditional offset hot smoking) at this roadside stop on US Highway 65, and serving up a thick menu built around what goes in and comes out of those smokers. Briskets, sugar-cured hams, bacon, chicken, turkey, pork loin, sausage links, cheeses, a great amount of smoked products are available. Dining in is charming in the beautifully quaint main space and on the porch - or get your sandwiches to-go river packed and ready to travel. Don't forget the smoked cheese.

229

KELLY & NIKKI SMALL'S BBQ
Caterers
(870) 504-0056

Located in Welcome Home, south of Marshall, this partnership's barbecue came on the scene in 2024 with quick notice. Pulled pork is their specialty.

ROCKIN' R BBQ
Food truck in Marshall
(870) 253-9179

Donnie and Jada Ragland's young venture focuses not only on barbecue but on Cajun style seafood as well. Pulled pork and sliced brisket are the main meats in which they work.

WOO PIG MOOIE
4736 US Highway 65 South in Choctaw (Clinton address)
Facebook.com/WPMooie

Jimmy Dooley is taking a tremendous leap of faith. While business was steady at his location in Centerton, he made a choice in the summer of 2024 to do sometehing quite risky - pack everything up and move to a community he has never lived in to start anew. With the burgeoning barbecue scene in northwest Arkansas. Dooley's Centerton restaurant was sometimes overlooked. That autumn, Dooley began the move to tiny Choctaw, south of Clinton, to re-open Woo Pig Sooie in the former digs of Frank's Hickory House Bar-B-Q. Without another brick-and-mortar barbecue restaurant within 30 miles, Dooley hoped his operation would take off. Time will tell. His dedication to learning every day is already showcased in his smoky meats. Van Buren County has welcomed him with open arms.

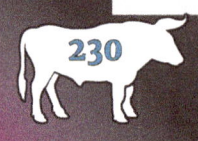

The Arkansas Barbecue Traveler

Kat Robinson

SMOKE HOUSE RESTAURANT

701 West Main Street
 in Heber Springs
(501) 362-7733
Facebook.com/SmokeHouseHeberSprings

A classic long-open diner that's offered pulled pork sandwiches to generations of customers, alongside comfort foods, breakfasts, burgers and pies. Check the wipe boards for daily specials, like the occasional spare rib dinner or smoked meatloaf.

LIL' STACK'S SMOKE SHACK

Beside Clinton RV Park
2521 US Highway 65 South
 in Clinton
(501) 745-2278

A food truck serving brisket, pulled chicken and pulled pork on fries, potatoes, and sandwiches, along with hot links and smoked sausages.

CORDELL BROTHERS BBQ

**301 Southridge Parkway in Heber Springs
(501) 362-5712**

After a career in aviation, Larry Cordell found himself in Heber Springs managing a tool store, then working at the Eden Isle marina. He'd smoke on the weekend, and folks liked what he was doing so much they started pauing him to smoke pork butts, ribs, and shrimp. Word got out, and when the old Brothers BBQ guys looked to get out of the business, they pestered Larry until he agreed to take it on. Since he started running the place in 1989, Cordell's has managed to hang on through a fire that destroyed the original structure, lots of changes in the area, and a couple of generations of locals and vacationers who have discovered his knack for making conversation and good barbecue.

ARROW'S CAFE & BBQ

**9 Pangburn Road in Heber Springs
(501) 206-0444
BBQHeberSprings.com**

South of town, this cafe offers lunch and dinner specials featuring pulled pork and brisket in nachos, quesadillas, baked potatoes, and on sandwich plates. Arrow's Cafe also offers Petit Jean Meats sausages, smoked.

Kat Robinson

SAMMY J'S BBQ

2020 Arkansas Highway 25B in Heber Springs
(731) 394-3130

A cousin to the famed Johns family of Blytheville, Sammy Johns is bringing Arkansas Delta barbecue to Heber Springs. His hickory charcoal smoked pork shoulders are meted out to sandwiches, nachos, and plates and served along with a thin vinegar sauce and coleslaw for that classic flavor. Opened in the summer of 2024, Sammy J's is a standout with a difference in the north central Arkansas town.

The Arkansas Barbecue Traveler

COLDWATER GRILL

**35 Swinging Bridge Drive
in Heber Springs**
(501) 365-3172
CWG501.com

Dry rub baby back ribs, Texas style brisket, beef bologna, turkeys, Boston butts, ham, sausage, burgers, even egg and olive salad and pimento cheese - it all goes on the smoker here! Breakfast includes brisket biscuits and smoked bologna sandwiches, while you can get a hearty bowl of Brunswick stew made with pulled pork and chicken served with cornbread for lunch. Get meat by the pound or pick up a shore lunch for later.

DAVID'S ONE STOP / WILBURN STORE

4549 Wilburn Road in Heber Springs
(501) 270-0222

There's something to be said for gas station barbecue. I had a couple of barbecue purveyors suggest I try out David's One Stop (also known as the Wilburn Store) in the tiny community of Wilburn, between Heber Springs and Searcy. The saucy sandwiches are served on white, seedless buns and are made up by hand in the kitchen in the back when you place your order. The sandwich comes out a little sweet, and the price is cheap.

235

TOMMY'S FAMOUS A PIZZERIA

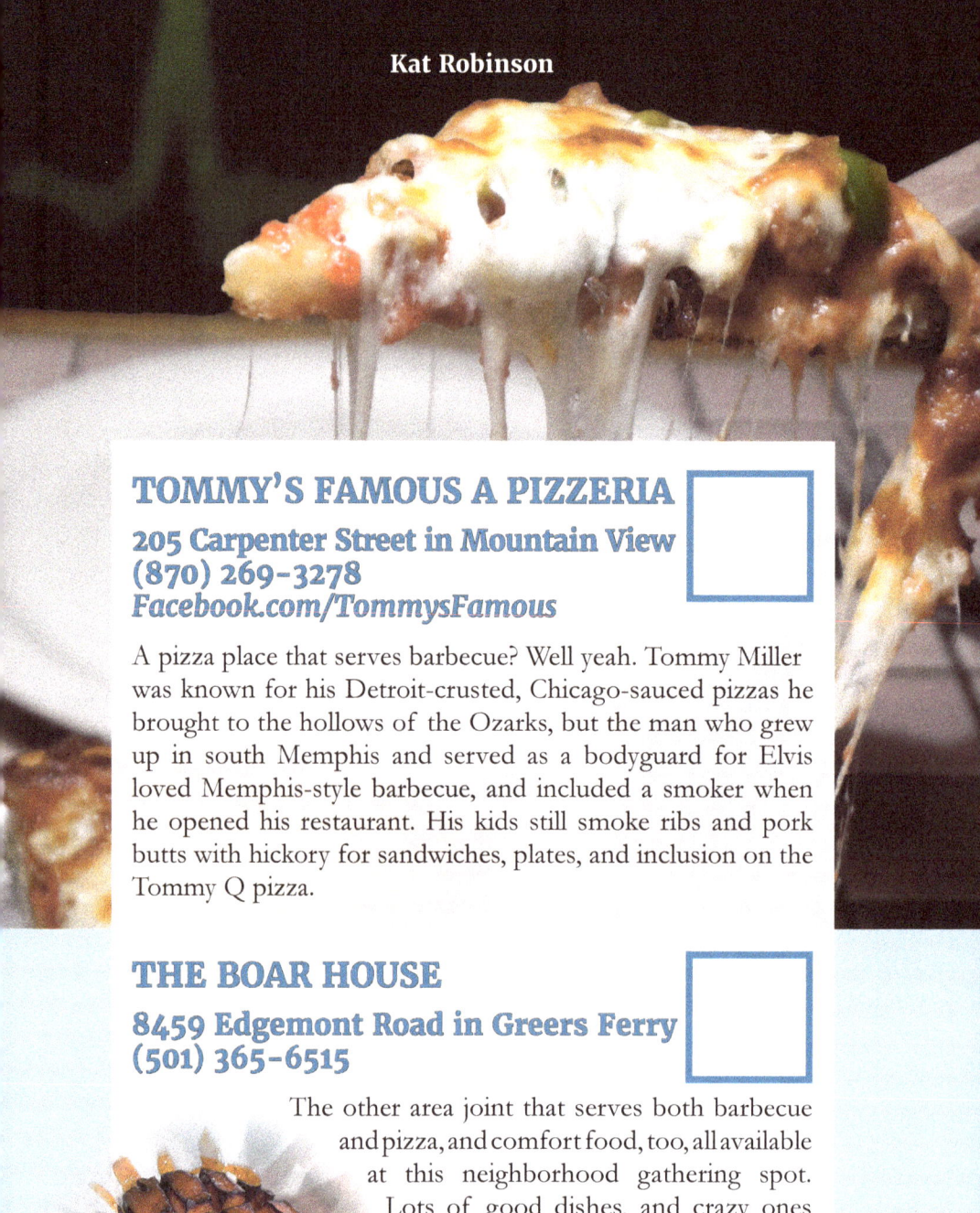

205 Carpenter Street in Mountain View
(870) 269-3278
Facebook.com/TommysFamous

A pizza place that serves barbecue? Well yeah. Tommy Miller was known for his Detroit-crusted, Chicago-sauced pizzas he brought to the hollows of the Ozarks, but the man who grew up in south Memphis and served as a bodyguard for Elvis loved Memphis-style barbecue, and included a smoker when he opened his restaurant. His kids still smoke ribs and pork butts with hickory for sandwiches, plates, and inclusion on the Tommy Q pizza.

THE BOAR HOUSE

8459 Edgemont Road in Greers Ferry
(501) 365-6515

The other area joint that serves both barbecue and pizza, and comfort food, too, all available at this neighborhood gathering spot. Lots of good dishes, and crazy ones too, like the Bloomin' Bologna - a scored slab of bacon smoked and sauced for serving. Pulled pork, brisket, smoked chicken are all on the menu here - even a pizza with barbecue sauce under the cheese!

The Arkansas Barbecue Traveler

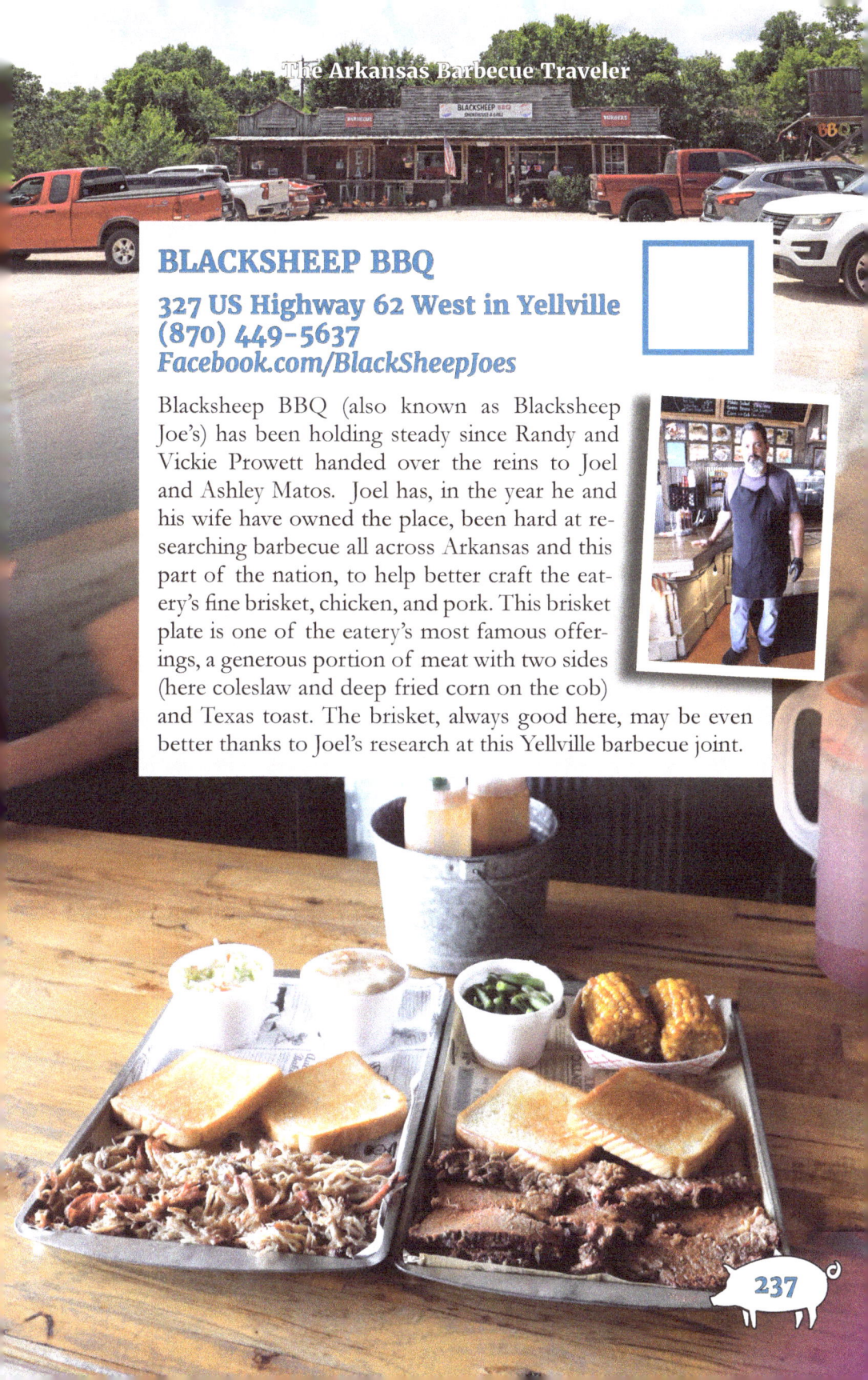

BLACKSHEEP BBQ

327 US Highway 62 West in Yellville
(870) 449-5637
Facebook.com/BlackSheepJoes

Blacksheep BBQ (also known as Blacksheep Joe's) has been holding steady since Randy and Vickie Prowett handed over the reins to Joel and Ashley Matos. Joel has, in the year he and his wife have owned the place, been hard at researching barbecue all across Arkansas and this part of the nation, to help better craft the eatery's fine brisket, chicken, and pork. This brisket plate is one of the eatery's most famous offerings, a generous portion of meat with two sides (here coleslaw and deep fried corn on the cob) and Texas toast. The brisket, always good here, may be even better thanks to Joel's research at this Yellville barbecue joint.

237

CAROLYN'S RAZORBACK RIBS

369 US Highway 62 in Yellville
(870) 449-7427

This is the Cave Man Dinner, a mass of meat served with sauce at Carolyn's Razorback Ribs in Yellville - four of those famed ribs, a pile of smoked sliced chicken, a pile of chopped brisket, and sauce if you need it. The half size of this is the Community Plate, and it's still substantial. A number of other presentations, from nachos to grilled cheese, also available.

ANCHOR POINTE RESORT & RESTAURANT

204 Wagon Wheel Lane in Peel
(870) 436-5401
AnchorPointeResort.com

Brisket and pulled pork are served on sandwiches and in dishes at this restaurant along Bull Shoals Lake, a short couple of steps from the Peel Ferry. Rib sandwiches and plates also on the eveening menu.

KT'S SMOKEHOUSE

406 East Main Street in Gassville
(870) 435-5080

Moulton "Mo Mo" Storey and his wife Katie moved to north Arkansas in 2001 to open KT's. Though he passed in 2016, Katie Cunningham Storey keeps this business alive and thriving. This place isn't just an eat-in restaurant. Cases along the wall hold frozen whole smoked chickens, sausage, gumbo, smoked boudin, pork butts, and breakfast sausage while the refrigerator next to it has bowls of barbeue sauce, fresh farm eggs, pickled eggs, and housemade dressings, all ready to take home. Sit down, though, and enjoy a rack of St. Louis style pork ribs, sliced smoke ham, smoked chicken sandwich or a slice of peanut butter pie. Go early, though - meats tend to run out by the end of the day.

Kat Robinson

HOLY SMOKES BBQ
400 Arkansas Highway 201 in Mountain Home
(870) 425-8080

Matt Wood's operation smokes meat in all sorts of ways. I have long lauded the award-winning peanut butter pie from this Mountain Home establishment, but the quality and span of smoked meats at this Twin Lakes region joint cannot go unnoticed. Turkey, chicken, brisket, pastrami, ribs, pork butt, smoked prime rib - there's always something on the smoker and it's all done well. Nachos, sandwiches, sides, all on point. Even if you never make it into the restaurant, chances are you'll encounter this exceptional barbecue at events throughout the region, since Holy Smokes is big on bringing out its mobile trailer and working catering jobs, too.

The Arkansas Barbecue Traveler

HEART OF THE OZARKS BBQ AND SWEETS

71 Hillbilly Land in Mountain Home
(870) 736-6555

This mobile eats and sweets trailer brings smoked chili, bacon wrapped smoked meatloaf, and crazy items like the Spicy Hawaiian Clucking Oinker to the party. An extraordinary selection of sweets, from cobblers and brownies to "Banana Pudding on Crack" are always on the menu.

BOB'S BBQ AND BILLIARDS

210 Bomber Boulevard in Mountain Home
(870) 232-0363
Facebook.com/PoolForFun

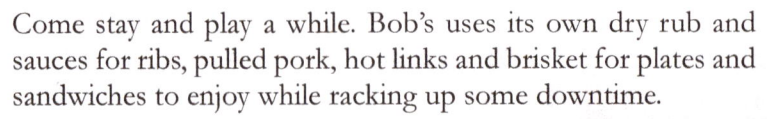

Come stay and play a while. Bob's uses its own dry rub and sauces for ribs, pulled pork, hot links and brisket for plates and sandwiches to enjoy while racking up some downtime.

WOODS RIVER BEND RESTAURANT

80 Main Street in Mammoth Spring
(870) 625-9357
Facebook.com/WoodsRiverBendRestaurant

Enjoy a morning or afternoon overlooking the start of the Spring River while dining on ribs or pulled pork sliders. If you ask nice and you're in that time between breakfast and lunch, you can get your ribs with eggs and biscuits.

SMOKIN' RICK'S BBQ

206 East Main in Hardy
(870) 751-0970
Facebook.com/SmokinRicksBBQ

While you're waiting for your pulled pork dinner or sandwich, hang out in one of Spring River Country's best arcades. The meat here is pork or chicken, or you can get a rack of ribs.

JOHNSON'S COUNTRY COOKIN

745 East Main Street in Melbourne
(870) 368-5454

This oversized family restaurant serving one of the Ozark's most secluded metropolises offers brisket, ribs, and chicken on the regular, with a pulled pork sandwich and a special on ribs on Friday and Saturday nights.

Kat Robinson

ROAD HAWGZ BBQ

127 US Highway 62 in Ash Flat
(870) 243-4258
Facebook.com/RoadHawgzBBQ

Pulled pork, brisket and chicken leg quaraters are common on this menu, which also features pork burritos filled with meat, beans, slaw and nacho cheese sauce. A simple menu for a spot that's the perfect crossroads stop, within eyesight of where US Highways 62, 167 and 412 all meet.

BOB AND SANDY'S BEACH CLUB BBQ

5 JoJo Street in Hardy
(870) 856-2593
Facebook.com/BobandSandysBBQ

The oversized hilltop dining room plays host to all sorts of meetings and family gatherings - and for good reason. For more than 40 years, Bob and Sandy Gilliland's shop has stood as a comfortable hub for Spring River Country happenings. Beef, pork, and chicken are smoked and served alongside classic sides. Grab your own drink and condiments while you wait, then catch a seat at a window for a gorgeous view of the river below.

The Arkansas Barbecue Traveler

BAILEY'S FAMILY RESTAURANT

**208 North Main Street in Cave City
(870) 916-2195
Facebook.com/BaileysCountryCookin**

Pulled pork sandwiches are on the menu - not just traditional sized sandwiches but a massive beast called the Pigzilla - two pounds of pulled pork on an oversized housemade bun. Ribs and brisket also circulate through the daily specials routine.

GYPSY WILLOW SCRATCH KITCHEN AND OYSTER BAR

**417A US Highway 167 in Cave City
(870) 384-2261**

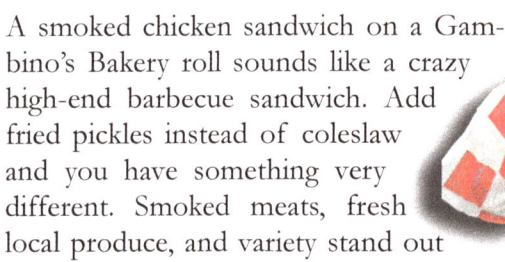

A smoked chicken sandwich on a Gambino's Bakery roll sounds like a crazy high-end barbecue sandwich. Add fried pickles instead of coleslaw and you have something very different. Smoked meats, fresh local produce, and variety stand out at this marvelous stand where the menu evolves almost daily.

ROCKIN' HOG SMOKEHOUSE

2121 Batesville Boulevard in Southside
(870) 251-2229
Facebook.com/RockinHogSouthside

Since 2001, this local hangout has offered brisket, chicken, ribs, sausage, and pulled pork on a single Pit Master Sampler and separately in a number of dishes. Its biggest seller is actually pie - for the many varieties offered here. The Smokin' Hog burger, a beef patty topped with brisket and bacon, is also tops.

BIGGER BURGER BETTER BBQ

2170 North Central Avenue in Batesville
(870) 307-9227

There's a lot to love at Bigger Burger Better BBQ in Batesville, from great burgers to excellent appetizers like the smoked meat stuffed jalapeno poppers. But folks swear by the pulled pork sandwich, where the pork is extra juicy and the bun soaks up that sweet mix of sauce, coleslaw and drippings to form an excellent and rib-sticking sandwich.

Kat Robinson

FOX CREEK BBQ

129 Lawrence Street in Batesville
(870) 698-0034
FoxCreekBBQ.com

Patrick Collins was a deputy with the Independence County Sheriff's Office for 30 years. He and his wife Melinda purchased Fox Creek in 2017 - she passed in 2020, but he still keeps going, not only using his Kansas City competition circuit experience to serve up excellent smoked brisket, pork, chicken, sausage, bologna, wings, and ribs, but to run Fox Creek as a hub of community life for downtown Batesville. It's not just the good food he serves in the old historic train depot; it's also the commitment to helping others out through good works. Patrick is so much part of this community, his alter ego - Santa - shows up from time to time to lead parades and bring toys to kids and folks stuck in the hospital during the holidays.

The Arkansas Barbecue Traveler

Kat Robinson

COWBOYS BAR-B-QUE

4101 Harrison Street in Batesville
(870) 698-8500
Facebook.com/CowboysBarbque

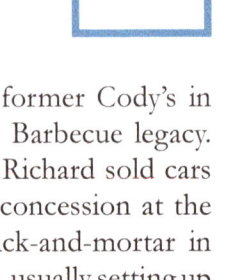

Pam and Richard Gramling took over the former Cody's in 2001, renamed it, and started the Cowboys Barbecue legacy. Pam used to work in medical coding, while Richard sold cars for a living. He spent six years operating a concession at the Arkansas State Fair while Pam ran the brick-and-mortar in Batesville. Today they still run that food trailer, usually setting up in Southside nearby. They have the original restaurant for dine-in and drive-thru, too, selling pork, sausage, brisket, chicken, Polish and ribs. Customers go for sandwiches and loaded baked potatoes and for the restaurant's famed peanut butter pie.

MOORE'S DAIRY CREME

511 West Sixth Street in Newark
(870) 799-3980
Facebook.com/MooresDairyCreme

Most folks know this place as the local dairy bar that's stood for more than 70 years. But Moore's has become locally known for good barbecue, too. Originally started in 1954 on one side of the home owned by C.L. and Joanne Moore, it was moved to its current location later. Their son Charles and his wife Mary took over in 1977, running it until 2017, handing it down to their daughter and son-in-law, Melissa and Jesse Parker. This local haunt still has arcade games and a pool table, the ice cream is rich thanks to a high butterfat mix, and pulled pork is smoked daily for sandwiches, nachos and the Stuffed Pig, a pile of curly fries topped with grilled onions, pulled pork, cheese and barbecue sauce.

EDDIE'S BBQ SHACK

Regional food truck
(870) 308-5120
Facebook.com/EddiesBBQShack

This local truck travels as far as DeWitt and Batesville, home-basing in Searcy much of the year. Specializing in smoked chicken for sandwiches and nachos, ribs, and often hot wings.

Kat Robinson

KNIGHTFIRE BBQ

**1403 East Race Avenue in Searcy
(501) 322-9971
EatKnightFire.com**

Matthew Knight's journey to a brick-and-mortar barbecue establishment started on the farm. Rice, beans, corn, wheat - Knight spent years growing crops and working fields. He spent time working with utility companies. He got married, moved to the area, got divorced. All the while, he smoked meats - and folks kept asking him to cook, so he did. Knight ended up starting his own food truck in 2018, which became so quickly popular he ended up opening his first brick-and-mortar in 2022. At the time of this writing, he is relocating to a larger place where customers will be able to dine in and enjoy a cold one with their meal.. They're in for a treat - with soft and flavorful briskets, packed sausages, smoky ribs, a cheese and sausage box, and an always-changing seasonal menu incorporating unusual presentations for those meats - like a PB&J (here, pork, brisket and jalapeno) and loaded sweet potatoes with green onions and rub.

The Arkansas Barbecue Traveler

GLENN'S SMOKEHOUSE

**1016 South Main Street in Searcy
(501) 279-1211
3177 Arkansas Highway 16 in Pangburn
(501) 827-9671
GlennsSmokehouseSearcy.com**

Charles and Gena Glenn started up their operation in Searcy in 2014, and keep expanding on it to bring classic barbecue to this section of the state. In addition to the original location on South Main and a mobile food truck (often set in Branford, as you saw in the Upper Delta section of this book), the Glenns have recently opened a new, larger place on Arkansas Highway 16 out towards Pangburn. The best way to enjoy the pulled pork, brisket, chicken, or sausage here is in a Pig Pie (with Fritoes) or a Pig Sundae (atop coleslaw and baked beans).

THIS GUY'S SMOKE N GRILL

**2030 South Benton in Searcy
(501) 305-4227
Facebook.com/
ThisGuysSmokeNGrill**

Thurman McCloskey spent ten years cooking for the Whistle Stop Cafe in Searcy. When owners Mark and Lorri Petty decided to close, they sold him the space and turned it into This Guy's in 2019. Managing to hang on through the pandemic, Thurman's killing it with ribs and chicken.

SMOKIN' T'S SOUTHERN KITCHEN
Food truck in White & Woodruff Counties
(501) 827-7711

A barbecue meets cajun food trailer first opened in 2020, this large black truck with a smoker offers barbecue loaded dishes like fries and nachos with pulled pork, brisket, and smoked bologna. Also known for its smashburgers.

BARB'S BAR-B-Q
905 Pleasure Avenue in Searcy
(501) 268-3418

Texas native Barbara Hill bought the former Pasley's Bar-B-Q in 1984 and turned it into her own with their help. They stayed on and worked side by side with her. She still goes and sources her own hickory for her pit, where she smokes a couple dozen pork butts each day for six to seven hours. The difference in her barbecue comes down to a combination - pork plus sauce plus slaw. It's a messy, colorful concoction, a pork sandwich topped with both the bright tomato red sauce and a strong mustard coleslaw that's pungeantly yellow and that only she knows.

A place for notes.

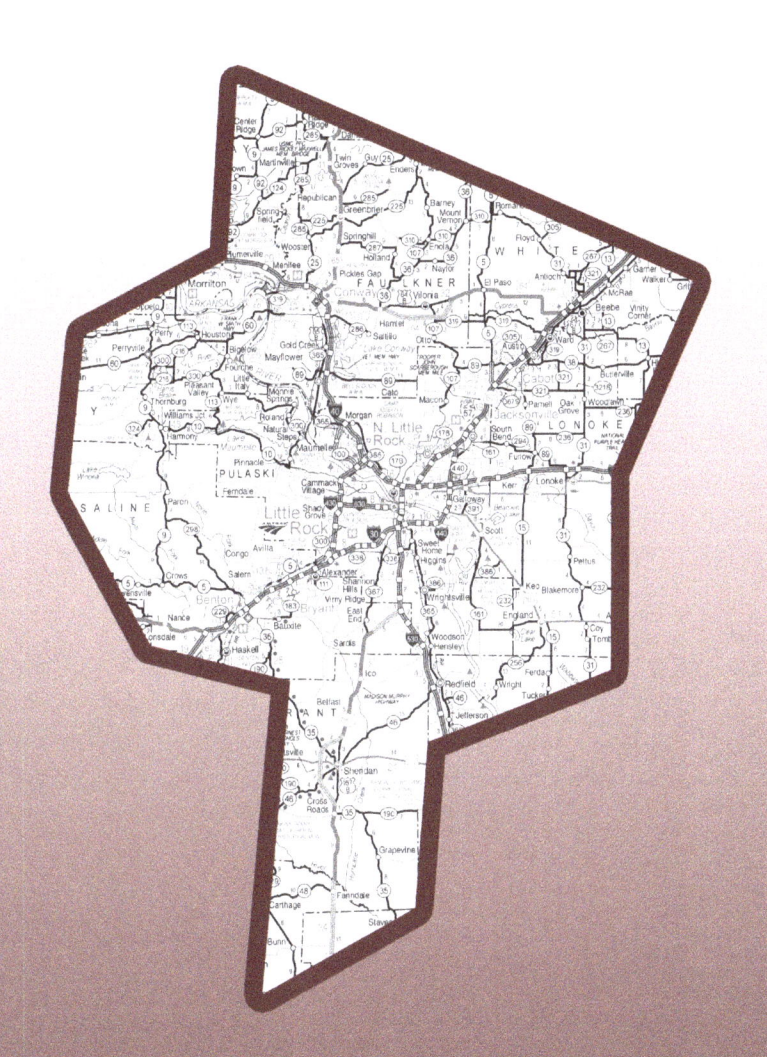

Central Arkansas

SUTTLE'S ROAD HOG BBQ

2008 West DeWitt Henry Drive in Beebe
(501) 882-1034
Facebook.com/SuttleRoadHogBBQ

Originally a food trailer beginning in 2004, the Suttles family has steadfastly continued to up their game. When you visit the restaurant these days, you can see the original trailer Bill and Glenda Suttles used, right next to the cavernous edifice they opened in 2015. Bill, who's retired from the railroad, figured out barbecue when he and his wife were band boosters - they'd sell barbecue to raise money for band trips. He perfected his skills by reading and consulting with other barbecue smokers. Today, his daughter Sara runs the house, while Bill is content to talk your ear off as you enjoy the ribs, pulled pork, brisket, smoked chicken and Polish with a slice of one of the dozens of pies in the case up front.

CAMPGROUND GRILL

3202 Campground Road in Austin
(501) 941-0103
Facebook.com/CampgroundGrill

Opened in 1980 by "Uncle" Phil White, this local secret is at the heart of, yes, an actual campground in the Austin community near Cabot. Camground Grill has long been known for its fried chicken - and it still offers the delicacy. But along the way, the folks there added apple and chocolate fried pies, catfish and hush puppies, and pulled pork barbecue. Pork butts here are smoked with applewood. Try the Burgerque sandwich - which is pulled pork packed into onion rings stacked on a burger patty between buns.

MEAN PIG BBQ

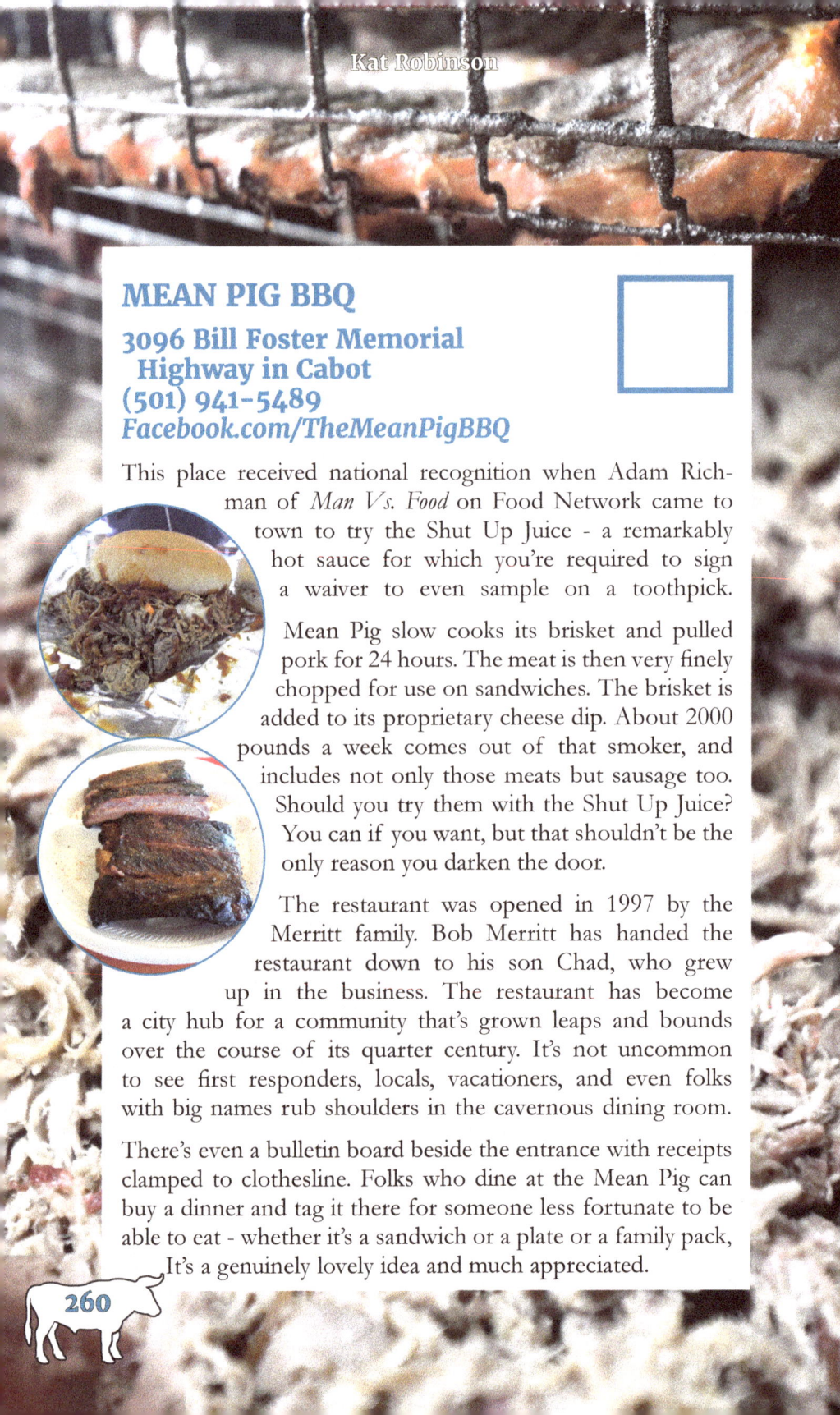

3096 Bill Foster Memorial Highway in Cabot
(501) 941-5489
Facebook.com/TheMeanPigBBQ

This place received national recognition when Adam Richman of *Man Vs. Food* on Food Network came to town to try the Shut Up Juice - a remarkably hot sauce for which you're required to sign a waiver to even sample on a toothpick.

Mean Pig slow cooks its brisket and pulled pork for 24 hours. The meat is then very finely chopped for use on sandwiches. The brisket is added to its proprietary cheese dip. About 2000 pounds a week comes out of that smoker, and includes not only those meats but sausage too. Should you try them with the Shut Up Juice? You can if you want, but that shouldn't be the only reason you darken the door.

The restaurant was opened in 1997 by the Merritt family. Bob Merritt has handed the restaurant down to his son Chad, who grew up in the business. The restaurant has become a city hub for a community that's grown leaps and bounds over the course of its quarter century. It's not uncommon to see first responders, locals, vacationers, and even folks with big names rub shoulders in the cavernous dining room.

There's even a bulletin board beside the entrance with receipts clamped to clothesline. Folks who dine at the Mean Pig can buy a dinner and tag it there for someone less fortunate to be able to eat - whether it's a sandwich or a plate or a family pack, It's a genuinely lovely idea and much appreciated.

VP'S BBQ & SOULFOOD CATERING SERVICES

3225 Carmichael Road in Cabot
(501) 500-4147
Facebook.com/VPSBBQ

Dwayne Borden's food hustle is all about a remarkably moist brisket, pork burnt ends, smoked chicken, and whatever genius meat he comes up with each day. Borden's family has Arkansas roots, but this generation comes out of St. Louis, with that amazing influence on its ribs. Not just a barbecue truck, VP's offers greens, yams, mac and cheese, fried cabbage, barbecue beef baked beans and other Southern comfort foods. Check out their Facebook page to find out where they're serving each day.

SMOKIN' BUNS BBQ & CATFISH

25401 Arkansas Highway 107 in Jacksonville
(501) 988-2867
SmokinBuns.net

Originally built by Cory Nicholson in 2008 over the course of two months, the Jenkins family purchased the place in January 2023 and moved right in, making this place very much their own. The biggest seller isn't barbecue but catfish, strangely enough. That being said, the place has a reputation for excellent ribs and Piggy Pies - Fritos covered in pulled pork, smoked beans and coleslaw. Those beans are smoked right along with the meats in the rotisserie, where the drippings from all the meats fall right into the pot.

FARM 2 TABLE PROJECT

**Food trailer and at
25 Prickly Pear Loop in Holland
(501) 796-1083
FreshEatN.com**

Patrick and Sheila Colb and their team have created this organization to bring nutrient dense meals to families in need. It started as a project called Chicken For The Homeless back in 2019. When the first families received assistance, more came forward, so the program expanded - but rules that went into place during the pandemic shut it down. In 2024, the program was restructured and reborne as the Feed The Need Program, and anyone can come take part and not be turned away. To fund the project, the Colbs are smoking meats that are sold through Farm 2 Table Project and a food truck, bringing pork belly, ribs, brisket, and other tasty smoked items out for good eats, and a good cause.

KITCHENS BBQ & MORE

294 South Broadview Street in Greenbrier
(501) 581-2315

Just opened in summer 2024, this family operation has jumped right in to providing barbecue in a community that was in need of a smokehouse. With a full slate that ranges from pork belly burnt ends and smoked chucken to deviled eggs and homemade desserts, the eatery is getting a reputation for being a great spot to dine in or carry home your dinner.

JOE T'S SAVORY MEATS

169 Clinton Road in Conway
(501) 428-2235

Joseph Taylor's new operation opens on Saturdays in Collier's Used Car lot in the Saltillo community. While Joseph has been smoking bologna and pulled pork a good while, he just recently jumped into the food scene with this operation. Homemade sauces and rubs, pulled beef and chuck roasts and the aforementioned bologna and pork are all features here.

VINCENT'S BBQ

**2850 Prince Street in Conway
(501) 329-1280**
EatVincentsBBQ.com

Vince and Jennasyn Scherrey's operation began in a food truck, then moved brick-and-mortar, first in Morrilton and then Conway. Chef Vince utilizes a hickory pit to prepare brisket, ribs, pulled pork and smoked bologna for the dishes offered here. When I asked for the best dish in the house, I was surprised to be presented with this well-composed, smoked then fried bologna sandwich made with locally produced Petit Jean bologna.

WADE'S BBQ

**310 Salem Road in Conway
(501) 428-7987**
Facebook.com/WadesBBQ

Glen D. Winston has spent a lifetime cooking for others, or as he says, "giving the gift of food." He's been part of a food ministry team that travels to Kenya often, since 2004. When he returned from a trip there in 2019, he says God told him it was time to start his own business. He named it after his father, who passed when he was 13. He hand-built his own trailer and studied barbecue in several states before coming back here to begin on his own. With plans to eventually go brick-and-mortar not just in Conway but across the MidSouth, he's a man with a plan. His brisket and ribs are marvelous, and his wife Eva's pecan and sweet potato pies are bliss.

The Arkansas Barbecue Traveler

SHORTY'S BAR-B-QUE

1101 Harkrider Street in Conway
(501) 329-9213
Facebook.com/ShortysinConway

Outside of the prices, not much has changed at Shorty's BBQ since it originally opened in the 1970s. The classic barbecue shop started by Shorty Wilson continues today under the consistent efforts of Wayne and Keith Leach. Here the barbecue sandwiches are as they were back all those decades ago, where the meat falls apart pot roast style in sauce, where beef and pork sandwiches are the same price, and where you can get your sandwich or plate accompanied by a good old-fashioned ice cream shake. Cash only.

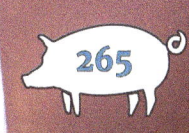

HOG PEN BBQ

1265 Sutton Street in Conway
(501) 329-9213
Facebook.com/HogPenBarBQ

Dennis and Mavis Forte started up this landmark shop in 1999, and the couple has stuck with the recipes that have put it on the map. The dry rubbed ribs, the homemade coleslaw and baked beans, homemade sausage and fresh desserts every day have been a winning combination for them. The spice blend used on Hog Pen's fish is light and sublime. And the Twice Cooked Chicken - which is smoked and then flash fried - is craveably delicious. The downside is the dining area - there are just a few tables - but most folks take orders to go. Just be aware - while the sign is on the road, the entrance is on the back side of the building. You'll be glad you found it.

The Arkansas Barbecue Traveler

267

Kat Robinson

OL BART'S SOUTHERN EATS

1220 Old Morrilton Highway in Conway
(501) 613-7142
OlBartSouthernEats.com

Bart Likes is using post oak to create a tender brisket that's got a glorious smoky tone to it, soft but not too buttery, flavorful but not so loud as to interrupt the flavors elsewhere on the plate. This location of Ol' Bart's (there's a second in North Little Rock) showcases his smoking skills through the power of tacos (it's a thing!) and a selection of traditional smoked meats.

UNCLE TIM'S FOOD TRUCK

218 Highway 286 East in Conway
(501) 932-1171
Facebook.com/UncleTimsFoodTruck

Timothy Ester's operation brings soul food barbecue to the table - in this case, on the veranda he's set up with his food truck and kitchen on a fenced lot. Catfish and fried buffalo ribs star here, as do the St. Louis style pork ribs that come from the smoker. Barbecue links, pulled pork and country fried wings are all popular.

STOKED BBQ FOOD TRUCK

Regional food truck
(501) 472-1943

This family-run operation serves up pulled pork, chicken, smoked sausage and pulled beef sandwiches and quesadillas along with Trash Can Nachos. Soft serve ice cream is also available - though the Swine Sundae does not (fortunately) include it, rather being a cup of barbecue with coleslaw, beans and sauce. Usually found in Mayflower or Quitman.

TIN MAN BBQ

Food truck in Conway
(501) 690-7975

Joe Vandiver spent years as a sheet metal worker before opening this silver food trailer that offers, as he says "barbecue with heart." Pork and brisket are smoked with hickory, while Joe uses oak and pecan when he offers chicken leg quarters. He tends to set up anywhere from Conway and Mayflower to Maumelle and North Little Rock.

VOLSTEAD PROPER

2205 Dave Ward Drive in Conway
(501) 358-6501
Facebook.com/VolsteadProperSmoked

Chef Steve Binotti, who has risen through the ranks from One Eleven at the Capital to Petit and Keet and Cypress Social, now heads the kitchen at this comfort casual concept based on smoked meats, with pulled pork, ribs, brisket, chicken and salmon presented alongside ham hock collards, cheesy corn grits, and brisket chili. The smoked wings are not to be missed.

Kat Robinson

ALMOST FAMOUS BBQ

258 Highway 64 East in Conway
(501) 450-3036
AlmostFamousConway.com

Al Meyer opened this joint on what used to be a rural stretch of US Highway 64 between Conway and Vilonia back in 1999. He's seen a lot of progress since then, but continues to operate this Cajun-influenced barbecue joint as a respite for folks who want some down time and down home good eats. Meyer had intended for this to be a meat market and sandwich shop, but there was a need he was able to meet. While he's worked in restaurants for more than 40 years, it was traveling and competing with a team at Memphis in May some 30-odd years ago that got him hooked on smoking meats. He already enjoyed making red beans and rice, gumbo, and crawfish, so it was just a natural progression. Today you can get Al's ribs, brisket, and sausage any day - and during the spring, pick up a mess of crawfish, too - as long as it's not his miracle blue crawfish he personally plucked out of a live order, who's been living a quiet retirement in an aquarium by the front door.

SMOKESTACK BBQ

818 Arkansas Highway 365 in Mayflower
Online ordering only at Smokestack1994.com

The original Smokestack BBQ was opened in 1994 by Kent Stubbs. In 1997, Stubbs decided to go to catering only. He retired and sold the business to his nephew, Gary Logan Jr., in 2020. Today, Logan - who is a full time elementary school principal - only works in smoked meats, open just a few times each year. A quarter of all proceeds from sales of turkeys and hams at Thanksgiving goes to feed the homeless. Prepay only.

H&H BBQ FOOD TRUCK

Arkansas Highway 10 in Perryville
(501) 499-3602

This simple red food trailer offers pulled pork, chicken, brisket, and ribs in dinners or sandwiches with baked beans, potato salad and coleslaw. H&H proclaims "it's all good from the hoods," mostly operating from a lot across the street from Harp's Grocery.

FAT BLAINE'S BBQ

**20309 Highway 113 in Roland
(501) 330-1906
Facebook.com/PresumptuousPigBBQ**

Blaine Burgess, who spent years working the competitions as Presumptuous Pig, now has a residency at Wye Mountain Farm, where he serves up smoked meats each Saturday. Smoked items vary, but usually include smoked turkey, pork butts, brisket and burnt ends. Try the chili!

BROTHERS IN CHRIST BBQ

**Roland area caterers
(501) 352-0197
Facebook.com/BrothersinChristBBQ**

A group of men smoking meat to help fund small churches in the Roland area - serving up brisket, ribs, pulled pork and catfish for these upstarts.

JORDAN'S BBQ & CATFISH

**110 North Reynolds Road in Bryant
(501) 847-6167
JordansBBQ.com**

Gary and Paula Jordan began this landmark restaurant in Bryant in 1985, watching over the years as the community around them blossomed into a full-scale city. Though Gary passed in 2023, Paula continues along with daughter Heather, son-in-law Josh Stivers, and a crew that's like family, smoking beef, pork, ham, turkey, sausages and St. Louis style ribs. Catfish is really good here. Don't miss the smoked sausage foot long with peppers and onions.

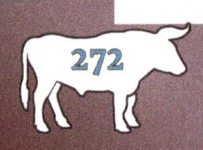

The Arkansas Barbecue Traveler

FIRE DANCER BBQ

3403 Meeting Street Suite 500 in Bryant
(501) 352-0806
Facebook.com/FireDancerBBQ

A competition barbecue team, occasional food truck AND a shop to pick up rubs, sauces, pickles and such. These guys understand good barbecue and always place well. Teammate Emily Bench won top place at the 2024 World Food Competition with her desserts, too - a good reason to follow this team!

BREITWEISER'S DELI

1113 West South Street in Benton
(501) 776-0391
Breitweisers.com

Hubbard Breitweiser and his son Carl began this local sandwich shop back in 1976. They sold it to the Gay family a while back, and today Tracy Gay continues its operation, not only handling the well-reputed meat market but smoking briskets, ribs, tenderloins, pork butts, boneless chickens, and hams, for cold sandwiches and plate lunches and for folks to take home for dinner. Take home a bottle of the proprietary barbecue sauce while you're at it.

SIMKINS MUDDY SOUF BBQ
Food truck
(469) 601-4331

Moses and Angela Simkins are all over the place with their mobile food truck as of late. Anywhere in a couple county radius of Pulaski County seems fair game. The couple bring chicken, brisket, and pork to events and food truck lots,. Moses cooks everything on the smoker, including wings, baked beans with brisket, sweet corn, and fried cabbage. This operation was originally a side hustle in 2022 but the popularity has grown, with nachos being the biggest seller.

PJ'S PIT AND GRILL
Pre-order pick-up operation
(501) 278-7609

A by-appointment pickup barbecue service where you message your order during the week and pick up on Sundays. It's how Jason Kindrix is building his pitmaster's dream of owning a barbecue business. Brisket, ribs and pulled pork are available each week, with Creole smoked turkeys offered seasonally. Flavors like whiskey apple smoked pulled pork and Italian herb smoked chicken occasionaly getable.

KREAM KASTLE DRIVE IN
15922 US Highway 70
southwest of Benton
(501) 209-2450

Ray and Heather Queen, who purchased the famed Salem Dairy Bar just a few years ago, brought back this longstanding dairy bar along the highway to Hot Springs to instant success. The eatery's been packed since opening day, with a new leader on the menu board - ribs, which the Queens smoke over hickory. Pulled pork is also popular on sandwiches, salads, and nachos.

The Arkansas Barbecue Traveler

275

Kat Robinson

BLUE PIG CRAFT BBQ
1933B Shoemaker Road in Sheridan
(870) 942-2880

Sheridan's newest barbecue property, started up by Kristina and Jeremy Funderburg...was originally a joke. Back in 2016, the couple was trying to source enough food for a get-together and tried their hand at smoking. It was so good, they went looking for a food truck the next week. The name comes from Jeremy, who's a retired police officer. The couple smoke up a soft brisket, fall-apart pork, chicken and ribs and lots of different configurations - quesadillas, sandwiches, baked potatoes and nachos. Try the lemon whip.

WRIGHT'S RANCH HOUSE
109 North Rock Street in Sheridan
(870) 917-2121

This larger version of the original from White Hall has become a family destination with an eclectic menu that includes things like fried bologna sticks and cornbread salad. The brisket sandwich with slaw is about as traditional as you can get. A house sampler encompasses all the smoked meats - beef, pork, smoked sausage, and loin back ribs.

UNCLE HENRY'S BBQ
202 South Rock Street in Sheridan
(870) 942-3937

Henry and Janice Ford began this place as a produce market back in 1983 to keep their family - with their seven children - going. Over time, those meats Henry smoked out back started getting notice, and he began offering them for lunch and for pick-up. Today, walking into Uncle Henry's is like walking back into a 1980s era cowboy country store, complete with saddles and cattle skulls. All those hickory smoked meats - pork, ham, chicken, hot links, brisket, bologna, and ribs - are available by the sandwich, plate or pound. Those sandwiches are huge, two-handed affairs. Cowboy beans are a hit here, and you can choose between mustard potato salad or a sour cream version. Check the case for pie.

Kat Robinson

FAT BOYS KILLER BAR-B-Q

**14611 Arch Street
south of Little Rock (Landmark)
(501)-888-4998**
FatBoysKillerBBQ.com

Have you had your pork pulled lately? The suggestive tagline for this joint Mike and Teresa Brewer opened nearly two decades ago, works for this small, memorabilia packed shop out near Landmark, heading out Arch Street from Little Rock. They offer all the hits - ribs, pork, chicken, beef and sausage - with lots of options for sides, like okra, onion rings, and Maxine and Cheese (an inside joke, I'm told). The Spudtastic is a huge baked potato packed with baked beans, barbecue meat, sauce, cheese, coleslaw and onion. Dessert is going to be a fried pie with or without ice cream.

BIG BABY'S BBQ

**Food truck
(501) 515-0344**
Facebook.com/BigBabysBBQandMore

Greg Owens has a great set-up and he likes taking it on the road. His Triple B has become a sensation, with folks sighting the black and yellow trailer as far off as Scott, Warren, England and Pine Bluff. His chopped chicken and pork offered on fries, nachos, or a sandwich is just marvelous, a uniform size and cut that leads to a great mouthfeel. Catch Triple B for catfish and ribs, too.

SMOKE N JOE BOX

4823 Rixie Road in Sherwood
(501) 256-6229
Facebook.com/SmokeNJoeBox

Looking for smoked ox tails, turkey legs, chicken wings, brisket, and award-winning ribs in central Arkansas? Smoke N' Joe Box has you covered. Kevin Cotton's lounge may not be large, but it's packed with Razorback red and team memorabilia, and you can pick up some remarkable eats. Check Facebook daily.

SCOTT STATION

15235 US Highway 165 in Scott
(501) 961-1100
Marlsgate.com/Resturant
(spelling correct for link)

Beau and Martha Ellen Talbot purchased the charming shop in 2022, and named it after the old train station that once stood nearby. They use wood from felled pecan trees in the area for the smoke, and offer ribs, pulled pork and chopped beef barbecue with or without a pungent yellow mustard slaw and vinegary sauce. Get the old Fischer's Restaurant style onion rings if you can, and don't miss out on a slice of peanut butter pie.

BOSS HOG BBQ

Food truck in Jacksonville
(501) 554-0824

It's just an old truck-towed tin sided food trailer in the parking lot of the Family Dollar Tree - but it serves up extraordinary cherry wood smoked brisket, pork, and chicken, chopped fine and sauced for sandwiches. Barbecue spaghetti, pork jerky, smoked rice pudding and smoked peach cobbler are standouts on the limited menu.

BARBECUE SHACK

1000 South Arkansas Highway 161 in Jacksonville
(501) 982-1009

The longstanding spot with its smoking cannon has served more than a quarter century of barbecue lovers. In 2023, Adam and Brittany Trevino purchased the business from Gary Green and refreshed the menu, refocusing on beef, particularly Texas style salt-and-pepper brisket and changing over from hickory to post oak in the smoker. Still a great place for a filling lunch - just look at the size of this brisket loaded baked potato!

SAUCY PIG

119 Country Club Boulevard in Sherwood
(501) 580-7246

This brisket comes from one of the coolest smokers I've seen in practice - where the hickory and pecan is fed in through the top and stocks the smoker for 14 hours! It's on the back end of Saucy Pig, a food truck run by Ben and Sarah Hurst and family. Ben was in the car wash and oil change business for 15 years, but had always wanted to smoke meat for a living. He competed in barbecue competitions for a long time, and he would barbecue at the car wash, running fundraisers for the Arkansas Food Bank and other non-profits. One night, he sat down and worked out things with Sarah, his sister Kelly and her husband Steve, and came up with Saucy Pig. They have a good thing going - that brisket is fall-apart soft! Pulled chicken and pork, homemade sides and excellent cheese dip are all on the radar here.

FEASTROS FIRE AND GRILL
4218 East Kiehl in Sherwood
(501) 864-7860

Originally opened as a food truck in 1998 with time at Prothro Junction, this place has spent time both as a barbecue cart and a southern food buffet over the course of time - but now does menu service. Mark Spaight's menu includes ribs, beef, pork and rib tips alongside plenty of other meals.

NORTH OF THE ROCK BAR-B-Q
Food truck in Sherwood
(501) 920-8069

Moist and delectable burnt ends. Deep fried corn on the cob. Smoked cream cheese. This food truck always has something tasty to offer. Find it in front of Whit Davis Home and Hardware or some place close along Kiehl Avenue. Facebook updates with daily location.

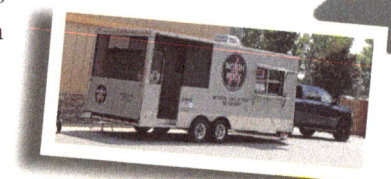

The Arkansas Barbecue Traveler

PIG-N-CHIK

7824 Highway 107 in Sherwood
(501) 834-5456
PigNChikBBQ.com

Pig-N-Chik has evolved over the years - back in the 1990s it spent time as a food trailer before moving into its spacious, wood paneled JFK storefront. Kerry Gore took over in 1997 and maintains the place today. Turkey, chicken, beef, and pulled pork are all hickory smoked, and portions are generoun. There's also a dish of smoked catfish that's worthy of your attention.

PANTHER MOUNTAIN BBQ

14406 Smalling Rd & MacArthur Drive in North Little Rock
(501) 681-6706

Tony Lord's upstart operation specializes in award-winning pulled pork, pulled chicken, smoked mac and cheese and nachos. Tony was on the barbecue circuit for years before starting up his food truck - winning 40 trophies over that time. He also does catering and can come up with some pretty incredible ideas - like smoking an inside out breakfast burrito filled with cream cheese.

SWEET POPPA'S CAFE

5231 East Broadway in North Little Rock
(501) 615-8810
SweetPoppasCafe.com

Open in the location of the White Pig Inn, which had been the oldest barbecue operation in Central Arkansas, Sweet Poppa's is the place to go in the area for a barbecue breakfast, with pulled pork and brisket burritos a staple. At lunch, it's choppped beef, chopped pork, or rib sandwiches. There are also ribs and rib tips, chicken wings, and whole smoked chickens.

GRAND KIBB'S BBQ

**6230 Baucum Pike
in North Little Rock
(501) 955-1110
Facebook.com/KibbsBarBQue**

For those of us who have fallen in love with Kibb's BBQ, we're so lucky. Grand Kibb's BBQ is an offshoot of the Stuttgart and Pine Bluff restaurants, located out past Rose City towards far eastern North Little Rock. Gwen will set you up well - ribs and rib tips in your sauce of choice, chopped beef sandwiches, chopped pork sandwiches, or a cheeseburger. The simple menu in the old Dub's Hamburger Heaven dairy bar is all you really need. Those sandwiches with that coleslaw and sauce (I choose medium, the hot's a little too spicy for me) are remarkably satisfying.

Kat Robinson

BJ's MARKET CAFE

704 Market Plaza in North Little Rock
(501) 945-8884
BJsMarketCafe.com

The market part of BJ's opened up in 1975. In 2006, the restaurant was added, and the crowds came. Today, second generation operator Jeanna Whitley and her daughter Dede Chapman manage this classic eatery, overseeing the baking of pies, making of casseroles, and maintaining of standards across its country menu. Wednesdays are smoked chicken days, while Thursdays are rib days. The eatery's offerings go quick and are apt to run out.

CHICK N' BUTTS

Regional food truck
(501) 258-1397
Facebook.com/ChickNButtsBBQToGo

They could be at North Little Rock's The Filling Station, they could be at the White County Fairgrounds, they could be right close to you right now. This food truck gets around, utilizing rubs from Fire Dancer BBQ and Oklahoma Joe smokers. Chris and Phil Disterdick started the operation in 2012 as a barbecue competition team. In 2022, Chris and his wife Kim started up the food truck, Chick 'N Butts BBQ To Go, offering smoked pulled chicken and pulled pork sandwiches, Piggy Parfaits, loaded spuds and what they call Meat Crack - sausage, boudin and cream cheese.

OL' BART SOUTHERN EATS AT DIAMOND BEAR BREWERY

600 North Broadway Street in North Little Rock
(501) 406-7819
OlBartSouthernEats.com

At the time of this writing, this location of Bart Like's barbecue chateau lies within a space created around the production of Diamond Bear Beer, the first major local brewery in Arkansas. While the future of the brewery is in question, with the building being up for sale, Ol' Bart Southern Eats plans to stay, offering smoked wings, brisket, bologna, chicken, sausage, and pulled pork from its menu alongside brews from several Arkansas breweries and distilleries.

HOGG'S MEAT MARKET

3901 JFK Boulevard in North Little Rock
(501) 758-7700
HoggsMeatMarket.com

When the longtime local meat market moved from its old home on Camp Robinson, it expanded into a full scale restaurant, too, offering a variety of items prepared from its own products. Hogg's is now smoking turkey and pork butts for lunch and dinner service; and as always has fresh meat, housemade sausages and its own proprietary dry rub for sale so you can smoke your own meats at home.

HAYGOOD BBQ

Food truck in Central Arkansas
(501) 944-9822
HaygoodBBQ.com

Primarily a central Arkansas operation, you'll find Haygood's at so many local festivals. Whether it's Hillcrest Harvestfest, Pops on the River, Juneteenth or your local corner, this bright red truck brings pulled pork, brisket, ribs, and smoked turkey legs (sometimes stuffed) to the celebration.

SO GOOD SOUL FOOD CAFE

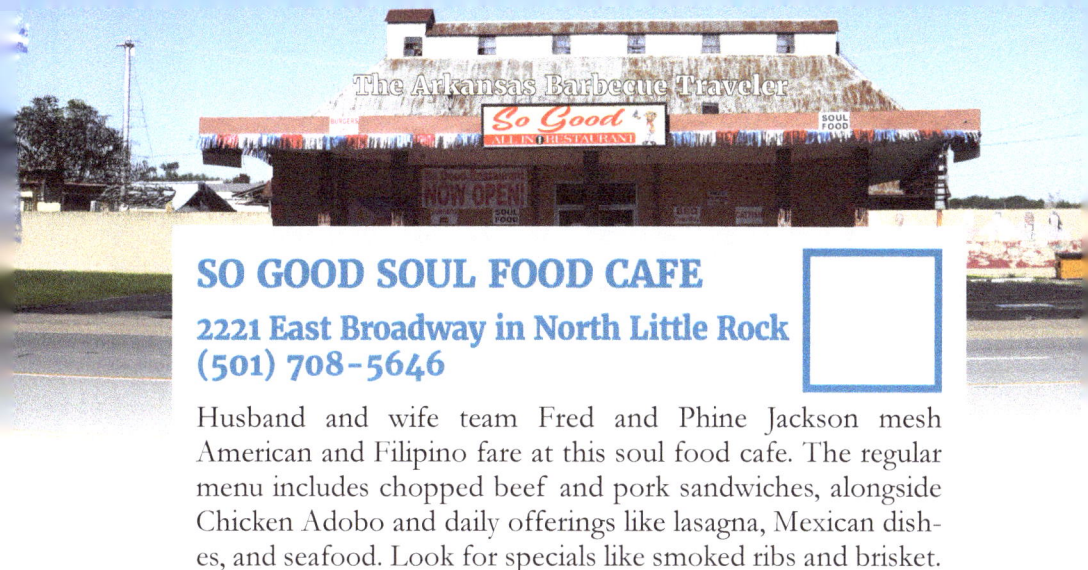

2221 East Broadway in North Little Rock
(501) 708-5646

Husband and wife team Fred and Phine Jackson mesh American and Filipino fare at this soul food cafe. The regular menu includes chopped beef and pork sandwiches, alongside Chicken Adobo and daily offerings like lasagna, Mexican dishes, and seafood. Look for specials like smoked ribs and brisket.

MICK'S BAR-B-Q

3609 MacArthur Drive in North Little Rock
(501) 791-2773

Originally opened in 1991. Mick's is known most for its hickory smoked ribs, pork butts and briskets. The two-window walk-up and drive thru offers a three bone rib sandwich, hot links and smoked chicken too, along with deviled eggs, jerk chicken, hand patted burgers and fried pies. The ribs are St. Louis style, everything's available for catering, and sometimes there are smoked turkey legs, too!

Kat Robinson

SMOKE SHACK BAR-B-Q

20608 Highway 365 North in Maumelle (501) 803-4935
Facebook.com/SmokeShackBarBQ

I could write a whole book about Joe Finch. Joe had 11 restaurants around Arkansas. He ended up with recipes from The Shack, which had stood in downtown Little Rock in a couple different places beginning in 1934 and ending in 1988. He used those recipes at a couple of his eateries. The Smoke Shack is the last of these. Finch sold the Maumelle operation to former KFC franchisee Doug Thompson in 2002. Doug didn't change a thing. The restaurant, tagged on to the end of Razorback Pizza, shares a back room with that eatery. The smoking operation carries on 24 hours a day, pulled pork alternating with brisket, ribs, and turkey. Smoke Shack is the sole place where I've observed sauce offered hot, temperature-wise, ladled from a pot in the main dining room. It's thick, not too sweet, and unlike any other. Instead of coleslaw, get yours with finely shredded cabbage.

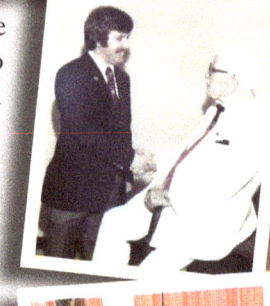

290

The Arkansas Barbecue Traveler

COUNT PORKULA

10840 Maumelle Boulevard in North Little Rock
(501) 246-5669
CountPorkula.com

The whole shebang started with a rusted out smoker and a dream to make Little Rock's best barbecue, back in 2008. Today, that dream is realized in this location on what is referred to as the "Boulevard of Barbecue Dreams," where massive slices of brisket, heaping piles of pulled beef or chopped beef on buns, pulled chicken nachos and so much more are brought to table in this massive dining room. Kelly Lovell and Walt Todd's top meat is brisket, not the pork I would have expected from the name, and it's prepared and served nude on its own merits, with a cumin-brown sugar sauce if you really want it. Ribs, if you go that way, are baby backs; sandwiches come default with slaw, and the signature dill pickle pasta salad is a bright and surprising counterpoint.

LINDSEY'S HOSPITALITY HOUSE

**207 Curtis Sykes Drive
 in North Little Rock
(501) 374-5707
LindseysBBQNMore.com**

The original Lindsey's Bar-B-Q dates back to 1956, when Bishop D.L. Lindsey Sr. decided he wanted to offer a lunchroom that served barbecue and home cooking. The menu grew, the hours spread, and in 1989, the operation moved a block over. The new space offered room for gatherings and meetings, thus the name expanded well to what the Lindsey family offered with every dish - hospitality.

Today, Lindseys son Donnie and Donnie's wife, Eleanor, run this classic restaurant, with its thick menu of comfort foods, smoked meats, pies and specials. Beef and pork sandwiches automatically come with coleslaw. Hot link sandwiches come with slaw and baked beans on there, too. Ribs, fried chicken, smoked chicken, and a slew of sides from beans and coleslaw to greens, yams, potato salad, onion rings, black-eyed peas, steamed cabbage and fried okra all grace the menu. They also have one of my favorite sweet potato pies in the world, along with coconut and pecan and a handful of fried pies. When I go, though, I go for that smoked chicken, so moist and flavorful all the way through, a true Arkansas delicacy.

The Arkansas Barbecue Traveler

293

AUTISTIC TOUCHED BBQ

Catering and pick-up
(501) 266-0242
Facebook.com/AutisticTouchedBBQ

A catering operation by a couple raising three autistic sons, offering barbecue along with tacos and fajitas, baked potato bars, breakfasts, brunches, and dinners. Smoked chicken, mac bowls topped with pulled pork, smoked sausages, brisket and burnt ends are all options.

TRACY B'S FOOD TRUCK

801 South Chester in Little Rock
(231) 944-5102

In the course of a year, Tracy Blankenship has developed a devoted following based on a magnificent cheese sauce - which goes well with the smoked pork she uses in her marvelous mac and cheese. She also offers a selection of pork sliders for a quick bite.

HUSKY LEW'S BBQ

400 East Third Street in Little Rock
(501) 626-1129
HuskyLewsBBQ.com

Just opened in spring 2024, Lewis Dillahunty has pushed hard to bring Arkansas barbecue to the River Market district with research, energy, and a passion for smoking. His saucy ribs, with a nod to Memphis, are already massively popular, as is his Goldslaw (mustard coleslaw). Brisket and pulled chicken also popular here.

PIMPIN' PIG BBQ

Regional food truck
(501) 519-6868

This brand new food truck is out and about across central and northern Arkansas, serving barbecue parfaits, pulled pork sandwiches, Piggy Pies, smoked bologna sandwiches and such.

BLACK ANGUS CAFE

**5100 West Markham in Little Rock
(501) 228-7800
BlackAngusCafe.com**

Originally opened in 1960 by Oliver Harper, this eatery's become famous for its chargrilled burgers and steaks. Over the years it moved from its original Fair Park and Markham location, to University Avenue, to Rodney Parham out in West Little Rock and now back to its original Fair Park plot, along the way maintaining a high quality of chargrilled eats and sides. On Thursdays, barbecue is the special, pulled pork and smoked chicken and barbecue ribs. You can get a smoked ham sandwich or pulled pork sandwich from Karla Creasy and her crew any day they're open.

PHONZIE'S 1 STOP HOG SHOP

**Food truck in Little Rock
(501) 594-0066
Facebook.com/Phonzies1Stop**

Phonzie and Laticia are doing their best to serve the community. They travel all over the state to different festivals, plating up extraordinary ribs and barbecue nachos - and they're helping others, too - promoting other food trucks and businesses and spreading the word on ways to help.

PULL UP AT BIG DAVE'S

**Caterer in Little Rock
6214 East Roosevelt Road
 in Little Rock
(501) 414-6476
Facebook.com/PullUpAtBigDaves**

Big D spare ribs are at the heart of the menu here, with both dry rub and sauce for an extra round of flavor and a little extra mess. It's all right - it's tasty. Nachos come with your choice of chopped chicken, chopped beef, or pulled pork. Catering pans to feed 12-16 people or more should be ordered 48 hours in advance.

Kat Robinson

296

The Arkansas Barbecue Traveler

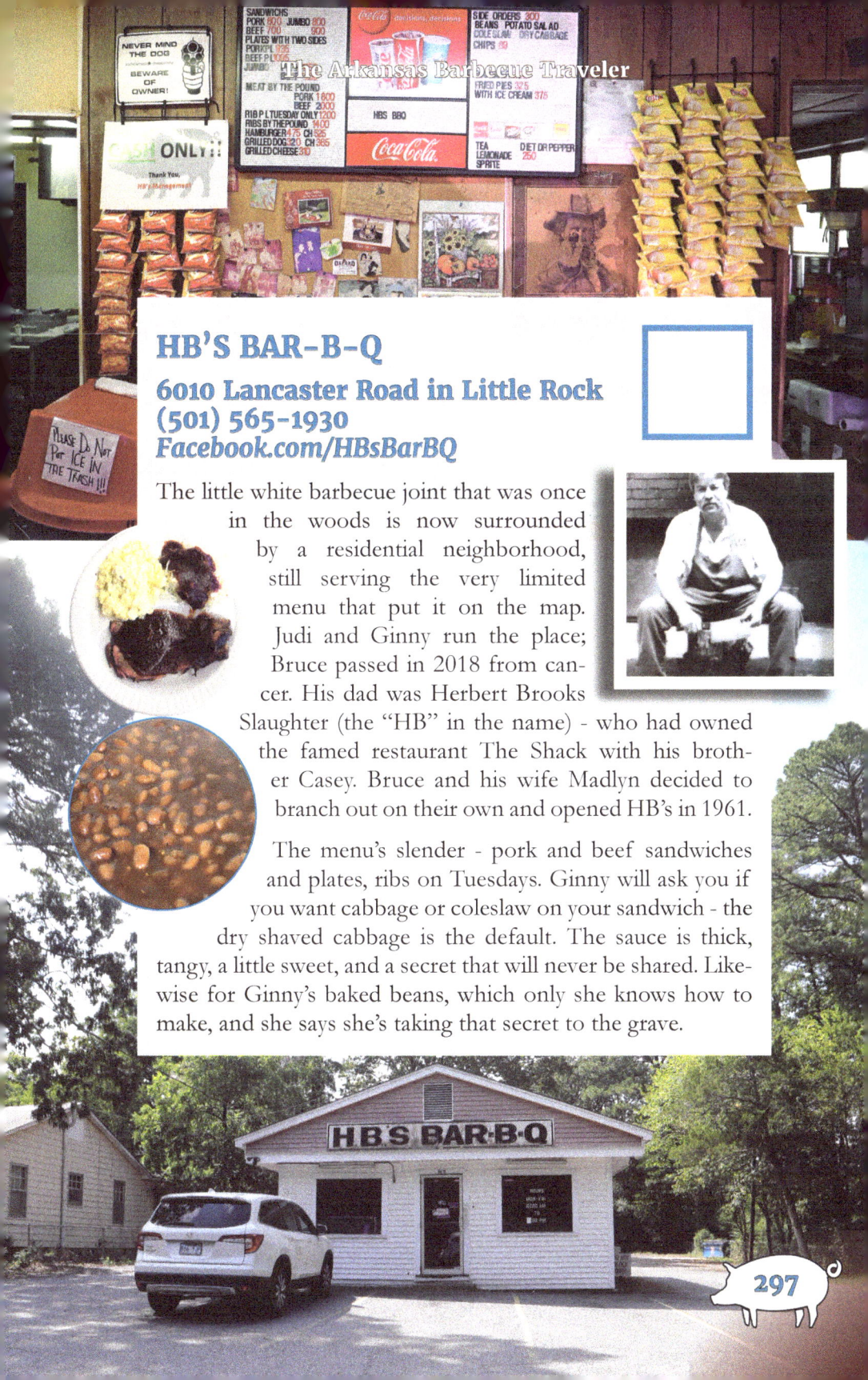

HB'S BAR-B-Q

6010 Lancaster Road in Little Rock
(501) 565-1930
Facebook.com/HBsBarBQ

The little white barbecue joint that was once in the woods is now surrounded by a residential neighborhood, still serving the very limited menu that put it on the map. Judi and Ginny run the place; Bruce passed in 2018 from cancer. His dad was Herbert Brooks Slaughter (the "HB" in the name) - who had owned the famed restaurant The Shack with his brother Casey. Bruce and his wife Madlyn decided to branch out on their own and opened HB's in 1961.

The menu's slender - pork and beef sandwiches and plates, ribs on Tuesdays. Ginny will ask you if you want cabbage or coleslaw on your sandwich - the dry shaved cabbage is the default. The sauce is thick, tangy, a little sweet, and a secret that will never be shared. Likewise for Ginny's baked beans, which only she knows how to make, and she says she's taking that secret to the grave.

SMACKEY'S

Caterer and Event Planner
(501) 240-5219
SmackeysBBQ.com

Chef Chad Mackey takes barbecue to elegant levels with his catering service. After five years at Arkansas Heart Hospital. Mackey moved into the AR Kitchen Complex space in Little Rock and began his work, smoking his award-winning brisket and other meats for catering jobs. Though he makes a great number of dishes and offers several different menus to his clients, that brisket stands out as one of his greatest hits. Mackey also offers meal planning options aimed at good health.

POKEY D'S

Caterer
(501) 310-2930
PokeyDs.com

Sliced beef brisket, smoked pork tenderloin, smoked chicken, ribs and rib tips, even pulled pork and chicken are all on the menu with this catering service ran by Sheila and Steve Leeks. Though they focus on weddings and special events, Pokey D's can also offer various box lunches and grazing boards for advance order.

BITE YO FINGER BBQ

Caterer in Little Rock
(501) 765-4738

Larry and Nick Harris offer food so good, you have to bite your finger to keep from hollering praise - or perhaps the flavor's so good, you bite your finger trying to get it into your mouth. Either way, it's excellent. Smoked chicken, ribs, mac and cheese and greens are all popular here. Set up and ready to handle big catering jobs as well as appearances around town.

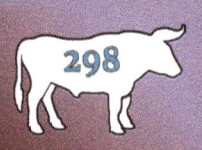

BURGE'S IN THE HEIGHTS

5620 R Street in Little Rock
(501) 666-1660
SmokedTurkeys.com

The Little Rock location for the Arkansas classic Burge's in Lewisville opened in 1977. While the two restaurants share the smoked turkey and ham that put both on the map,, the menu itself is a bit different here. Being a lunchroom instead of a dairy bar means no walk-up window. Instead, customers queue up to place their order and then sit and wait for it to be brought to table. Turkey crack - I mean, turkey salad - is one of the more popular dishes, being made with the excellent smoked turkey Burge's produces. Getting that smoked turkey salad can be done with several options, including the Leftover Plate - which includes sliced tomatoes, a peach half with cottage cheese, and crackers. Turkey, ham, chopped beef, sliced pork (one of the few places in Arkansas that offers its pork sliced) and smoked hot links are all available for plate lunches. The turkey is so well known and beloved that, during the holidays, Burge's runs two lines - one for dine-in customers, the other for people picking up their birds for Thanksgiving and Christmas. They always run out before the end of the season.

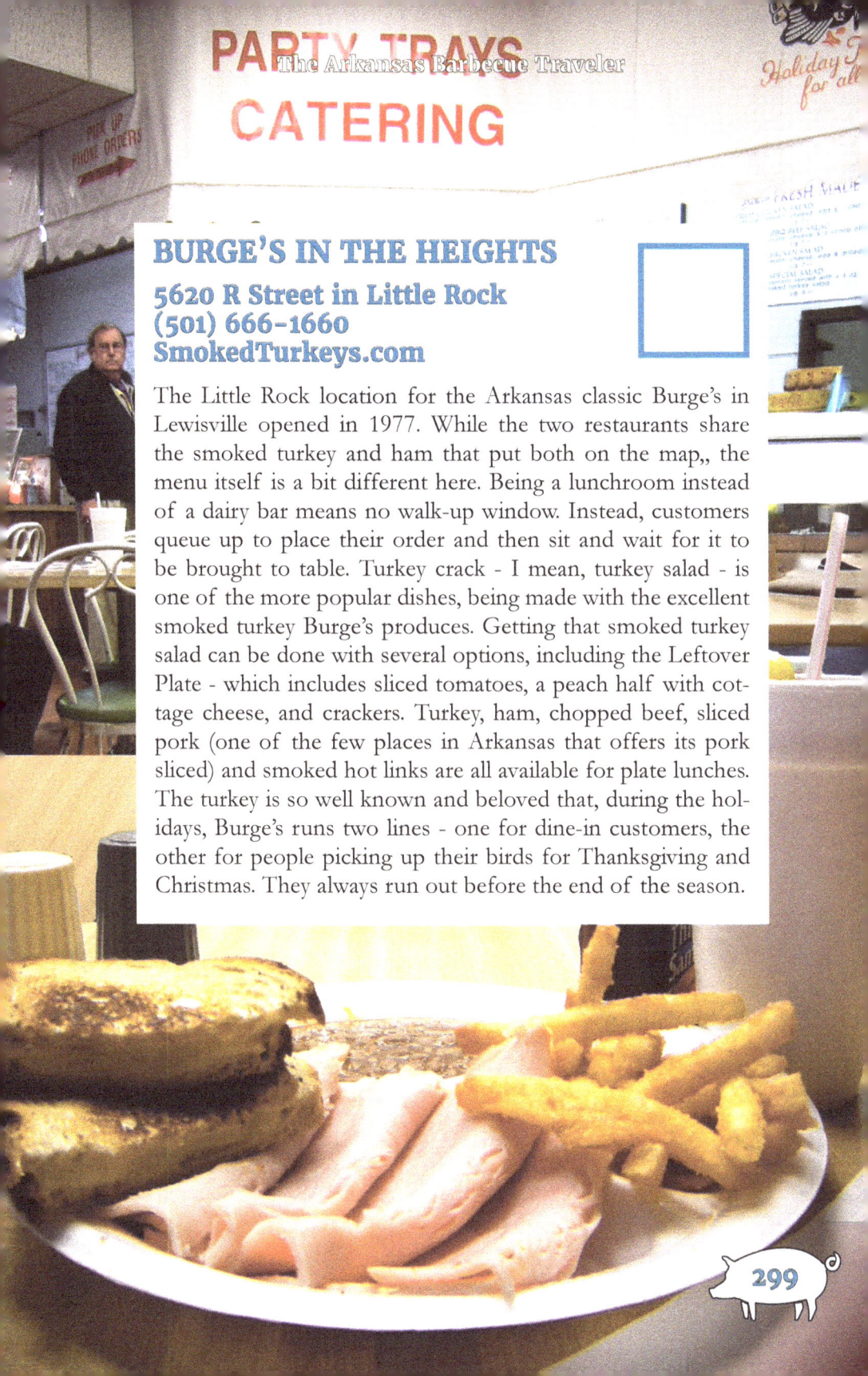

PLATNUM BBQ

400 President Clinton Avenue in Little Rock's River Market Pavilion
(501) 457-3128
Facebook.com/PlatnumBBQ

Angia and Kevin Cox opened this place in 2017 on the east end of the River Market Market Hall. Angia went to culinary school and was a caterer. She decided to take on this restaurant when she saw the space open while on a date night with her husband, Kevin. The space works both as a lunchroom and a homebase for her catering. Pulled pork, brisket, sausage, chicken and ribs are all offered in plates and sandwiches, alongside lunch specials each day.

SMOKIN' HOUZE BBQ

Food truck at 11200 West Markham in Little Rock
(501) 251-8146

Pulled pork and ribs are always available at this trailer open usually just in the evenings. Smoked turkey legs and stuffed turkey legs also offered.

KOOL'S BBQ and CATERING

Food truck at 6817 Colonel Glenn in Little Rock
(501) 912-4111

Rufus Duff sells ribs, turkey legs, lamb chops, pork chops, soul food - he has it going on with catfish and sides, too. Kool's travels as far as Conway but can usually be found in Little Rock. Look for "The Big B," a plate with a Kandyland Burger, five honey gold wings, chicken turkey cheese and Ro*Tel casserole, fries with Kandyland sauce and a large rib - an excellent way to experience a little bit of everything.

CAPITOL SMOKEHOUSE

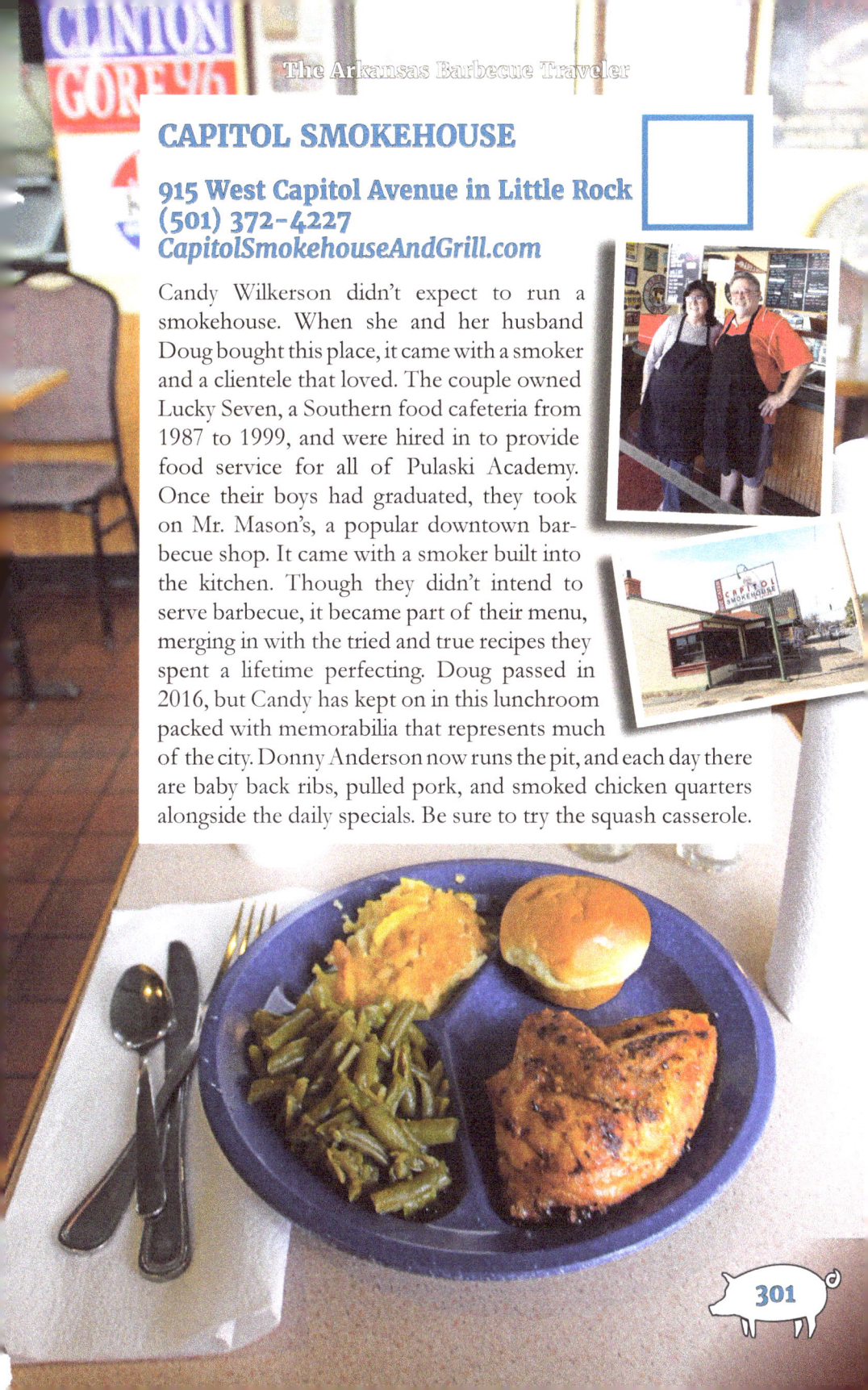

915 West Capitol Avenue in Little Rock
(501) 372-4227
CapitolSmokehouseAndGrill.com

Candy Wilkerson didn't expect to run a smokehouse. When she and her husband Doug bought this place, it came with a smoker and a clientele that loved. The couple owned Lucky Seven, a Southern food cafeteria from 1987 to 1999, and were hired in to provide food service for all of Pulaski Academy. Once their boys had graduated, they took on Mr. Mason's, a popular downtown barbecue shop. It came with a smoker built into the kitchen. Though they didn't intend to serve barbecue, it became part of their menu, merging in with the tried and true recipes they spent a lifetime perfecting. Doug passed in 2016, but Candy has kept on in this lunchroom packed with memorabilia that represents much of the city. Donny Anderson now runs the pit, and each day there are baby back ribs, pulled pork, and smoked chicken quarters alongside the daily specials. Be sure to try the squash casserole.

DOWN HOME BLUES BBQ

Food truck
11200 West Markham in Little Rock
(501) 309-5500

If you see smoke on West Markham, chances are Ronnie Duff has turkey legs and pork butts on the back of the truck. Those turkey legs are something else - cooked low and slow overnight, falling off the bone tender. You can get them on their own or stuffed with dressing or Alfredo or whatever's the special. Brisket, pulled pork - the Duff family's work here is excellent and much appreciated.

MARIE'S BBQ

2803 Broadway in Little Rock
(501) 590-2912
Facebook.com/MarieBBQ

Currently anchored at the former David Family Kitchen location on south Broadway, this barbecue and burger truck specializes in pulled pork, brisket, and ribs along with soul food classics like butter roll, peach cobbler and strawberry banana pudding. The burgers are massive.

SIM'S BAR-B-Q

**2415 Broadway in Little Rock
(501) 372-6868
1307 John Barrow Road in Little Rock
(224-2057)
7601 Geyer Springs Road in Little Rock
(501) 562-8844
*SimsBBQAR.com***

A classic since 1937, Sim's Barbecue in Little Rock serves its ribs, pulled pork, brisket, chicken portions and such with its signature thin, sweet sauce. Ribs come with white bread for gripping bones and sopping sauce. And if you take home a pound of barbecue, it comes with a half a loaf of bread. You'll need every slice.

TERRI-LYNN'S BBQ & DELI

10102 North Rodney Parham Road in Little Rock
(501) 227-6371
Facebook.com/TerriLynns501

Originally opened in 1959 by Harry and Mary Gilberson and named for their daughter Terri-Lynn, this local deli is one of those local joints that's never advertised, that's serving a neighborhood customer base, and which is always packed at lunchtime. New owner Tim Jackson plans to change very little about the place - other than a paint job and a little touch here and there. It's hardly noticed - the long smoked beef and pork are still as good, the corned beef and pastrami made inhouse haven't changed a bit, the same folks are still coming through the door. This is where you get your old school coleslaw on the sandwich barbecue with tamales on the side. Get a slice of pecan or chocolate pie when you go.

The Arkansas Barbecue Traveler

THREE SAMS BARBECUE JOINT

10508 Mann Road in Mabelvale
(501) 407-0345
Facebook.com/ThreeSamsBBQ

Sammy and Annette Jones opened this place in the early 00s - naming it for their trio, Big Sam, son Little Sam, and Gigi, Annette's nickname. They built a classic barbecue joint into the small town on the outskirts of Little Rock, and became well known for good service, excellent smoked meats, and a marvelously light peanut butter pie. They may not be behind the counter any more, but that same family atmosphere has not changed. Andrew Mueller bought the place in 2022 and works the smoker - Martine Dionne is who you'll see up front, greeting customers and infusing the place with attention and charm. This local treasure has suffered fires and been hit by a car but keeps on keeping on. Get the onion rings.

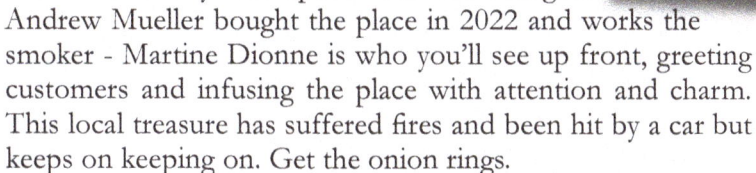

BAD DOG BBQ LLC

Competition cooking & catering
(870) 500-0514

Kyle Sadler's operation isn't available often at this point in time - he's on the road throughout the year representing well in competitions. But from time to time, he opens up orders for smoked chicken, pork butt, bologna, brisket, and ribs with vastly wonderful returns. Look up Bad Dog BBQ on Facebook (black and purple logo) or call above for inquiries.

BACK HOME BBQ

West Markham and South State Streets in Little Rock
Opening in 2025

Adam Murray's new concept close to City Hall and not far from the beloved Doe's Eat Place will serve Texas-style barbecue with brisket, pulled pork, spare ribs, chicken, turkey, and house-made sausages, weighed by the pound. Murray already owns three Home Plate BBQ restaurants in China - his associuation with partner Chase Rittelmeyer influenced his decision to plant this new operation here. The pit will be run by Curtis Guerrero, formerly of Pinkerton's Barbecue in Houston.

BLUE EMBER SMOKEHOUSE

Locations across Arkansas
BlueEmbreSmokehouse.com

A new upstart franchise with its first location in Fort Smith, offering house smoked meats on platters, sandwiches, salads and potatoes. There are four at the time of this writing - Fort Smith, Jonesboro, Texarkana (Texas side) and Little Rock - offering up brisket, pulled pork, chicken, turkey, ribs, pork burnt ends and two different types of sausage. It's all ordered by weight, with your sides ordered separate. Greenwood restarateur Mark Dean and business partner Earl Richardson, who are franchisees for Colton's Steak House, are hoping to continue expansion of this concept across the region.

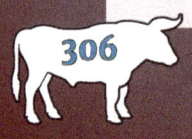

WHOLE HOG CAFE
Arkansas barbecue franchise
WholeHogCafe.com

With more than a dozen locations across four states, this is what many people think about when they hear "Arkansas barbecue." It started with three guys - Mike "Sarge" Davis, Ron Blasingame, and Steve Lucchi - who entered the 2000 Memphis-in-May World Championship Barbecue Cooking Contest. They took their meat smoking hobby there and came home with a second place trophy for "The Southern Gentlemen's Society." A couple of years and a couple of competitions later, they came out on top as World Champions, winning first place in the whole hog category.

This lead to the guys opening a little barbecue trailer - and that lead to the first restaurant. And the second. And so on. Today, with locations both in and out of Arkansas, Whole Hog Cafe has become one of our state's big names in barbecue. Pork ribs and butt, ribs, brisket, turkey, chicken, and sausages are all on point here. With six sauces, there's something to please everyone.

All barbecue related companies listed in this book

270 Diner	130	Big T's General Store	130
3 Heethens BBQ	94	Bigfoot's Backwoods	
3 J's Wings and More	144	BBQ Food Truck	130
313 Blues Cafe	67	Bigg Butts BBQ	37
A Little Bit of Texas	213	Bigger Burger Better BBQ	247
A Poor Man's Heaven	109	BigMac's Barbeeque	121
A&S City Cafe		Biscuit Row BBQ	73
(AKA Atkin's City Cafe)	59	Bite Yo Finger BBQ	298
Al's Real Pit Bar-B-Q	168	BJ's Market Cafe	286
Allen's Barbecue Company	124	Black Angus Cafe	295
Almost Famous BBQ	270	Blacksheep BBQ	237
Anchor Pointe Resort		Blue Ember Smokehouse	306
& Restaurant	238	Blue Pig Craft BBQ	276
Angry Possum	14	Boar's Head Cafe	175
AR Tillery's BBQ	214	Boar's Nest Bar & Grill	204
Arrow's Cafe & BBQ	233	Bob & Sandy's Beach	
Art's BBQ & Burgers	163	Club BBQ	244
Autistic Touched BBQ	294	Bob's BBQ and Billiards	242
Back Home BBQ	306	Bonds Grocery &	
Back Street BBQ and More	158	Highwater Landing	67
Bad Dog BBQ LLC	306	Boss Hog BBQ	280
Bailey's Family Restaurant	246	Bowles Bar-B-Que	48
Bar-B-Q Barn	22	Breitweiser's Deli	273
Barb's Bar-B-Q	255	Briggs BBQ, Cooking	
Barbecue Shack	280	& Catering	85
Barbecue Shack East	23	Brothers in Christ BBQ	272
Beach BBQ	210	Brothers Meethouse	208
Bearded Chops Market	212	Brown's Delta Bar-B-Q	17
Bearded Guy BBQ & Eats	129	Brown's Southern	
Beau's Bayou Smokehouse	181	Smoke BBQ	103
Bendi's Diner	77	Bruce Terri Drive In	
Benny Bob's BBQ	44	and Catering	162
Betty B's Smokehouse		Bub's Country Store	222
BBQ	56	Bubba Brews on Lake	
Big Baby's BBQ	278	Hamilton	138
Big Bear BBQ	105	Bubba Flay	82
Big Boys BBQ	87	Bubba's Southern Pit	
Big D's Station and		Barbecue	216
Hey Hawgz BBQ	128	Bubbie's	93
Big Daddy D's BBQ &		Buckets Sports Bar & Grill	222
D's Sweet Treats		Buffalo BBQ	226
Enterprises	166	Bulldog Drive In	100
Big Fork Mall	130	Bulldog Restaurant	12
Big Gilley's Smokehouse		BullsDenGrill	85
and Diner	115	Burge's Hickory Smoked	
Big Gun's Pit BBQ	61	Turkeys and Hams	111
Big Jake's BBQ	114	Burge's in the Heights	299
Big O Ribs	49	Burger Shack	71
Big Poppa's BBQ	177	Burl's Country	
Big Springs Trading		Smokehouse	131
Company	229	Burt's BBQ	54

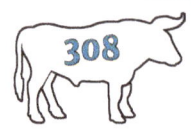

Butcher Boys Meat Market and Deli	170
C&C Meat Packing Company	110
Campground Grill	259
Candley's Cookin' #1&#2	103
Candy Apple's BBQ	28
Capitol Smokehouse	301
Carolyn's Razorback Ribs	238
Central BBQ	182
Charbroiler Restaurant	158
Chat & Scat	176
Chick N' Butts	286
Chop Shop BBQ	211
Church Street Grocery	149
City Park	195
Clampit's Country Kitchen	132
Cleveland Corner Store	149
Coldwater Grill	235
Cordell Brothers BBQ	233
Count Porkula	291
Country Express of Mena	128
Coursey's Smoked Meats	227
Cowboys Bar-B-Que	250
Craig Bros Bar-B-Q Cafe	79
Craig's Bar-B-Que	145
Craw Billy's Seafood Boil & BBQ	225
Crayton's BBQ	106
Crazy Horse BBQ	59
Cunningham's Barbecue	150
Cypress Corner Bar-B-Q	70
Dads' BBQ	34
David's One Stop/ Wilburn Store	235
Dee's BBQ at Southland Road Store & Diner	71
Delta Q + Deli	55
Demo's Smoke House BBQ	28
Dermott BBQ	89
Dixie Pig	40
Down Home Blues BBQ	302
Downtown Bar & Grill	72
Drip Drop BBQ Shop	139
Eddie's BBQ Shack	251
Endlsey's Burger Shack	95
Eureka Springs Eats and Treats	217
Farm 2 Table Project	262
Fat Blaine's BBQ	272
Fat Boys Fine Foods	126
Fat Boys Killer Bar-B-Q	278
Fat Daddy's	35
Fat Daddy's Bar-B-Que	154
Feastro's Fire and Grill	282
Fire & Lightning Catering/ Tyler's Craft BBQ	183
Fire Dancer BBQ	273
Flavorsmith's Craft BBQ	191
Fox Creek BBQ	248
G's Meaty Buns	194
GC's BBQ Catering	148
G&G Deli	119
Geronee's BBQ Express	58
Girls Gone BBQ	188
Gladish's BBQ	24
Glenn's Smokehouse	254
Glenn's Smokehouse Food Truck	13
Glenwood Fish Nest	127
Glory Grill	60
Grand Kibb's BBQ	285
Greene's Beans Buns & BBQ	17
Grumpy's Burger Barn	177
Gypsy Willow Scratch Kitchen and Oyster Bar	246
H&H BBQ Food Truck	271
H2Que BBQ	29
Harold's Bar-B-Que	18
Hart's Backroad Grub	108
Harvey's Que	72
Haygood BBQ	288
HB's Bar-B-Q	296
Heart of the Ozarks BBQ & Sweets	242
Herman's Ribhouse	192
Hickory Hut	100
Hillbilly Junction	18
Hog Pen Barbecue	47
Hog Pen BBQ	266
Hog Wild Bar-B-Q	37
Hogg's Meat Market	288
Holy Smokes BBQ	240
Holy Smokes BBQ Food Truck	34
Home Plate Cafe	132
Hometown Grill	63
Hoot's BBQ	88
Howell's BBQ	102
Hudson's Supermarket	225
Husky Lew's BBQ	294
Hwy 270 Grill	145
I'd Smoke That	201
Ironhorse BBQ & Steakhouse	23
J&N Bar-B-Que	26

J&S Grocery, Grill and Bait Shop	66
Jackson's Holy Smokes BBQ	95
Jamie's Restaurants	222
JC's Bar-B-Q Place	171
Jefferson's Mobile Grilling	138
Jerry Neels Bar-B-Q, Catfish & Catering	165
JJ's BBQ	104
Joe T's Savory Meats	263
Jones Bar-B-Q Diner	69
Jordan's BBQ & Catfish	272
Juicy Pig BBQ	109
Kelley's Kickin' Chicken	63
Kelly & Nikki Small's BBQ	230
KI BBQ and Fish	87
Kibb's Bar-B-Q #1 of Pine Bluff	83
Kibb's Bar-B-Q #1 of Stuttgart	77
Kibb's Bar-B-Q #2 of Pine Bluff	83
Kibb's Bar-B-Q #2 of Stuttgart	78
Kings Backyard BBQ	39
Kitchens BBQ & More	263
KnightFire BBQ	252
Kool's BBQ and Catering	300
Kream Kastle Drive In on US 70	274
Kream Kastle of Blytheville	43
Kristy's Cook Shack	118
KT's Smokehouse	239
L&Y Carwash and Barbecue	91
Legends BBQ Smokehouse	27
Legends Restaurant at Saracen Casino	84
Lil D's BBQ	82
Lil' Stack's Smoke Shack	232
Lindsey's Hospitality House	292
Links at Chaffee Crossing	161
Lion's Den Drive In	76
Little Piggy BBQ	49
Lorado Smokehouse and Grill	30
Lucky Luke's BBQ	187
Mad 2 Me BBQ Shack	105
Mama K's	145
Marie's BBQ	302
McClard's Bar-B-Q	135
McDonald's Grocery & Deli	106
Mean Pig BBQ	260
Mick's Bar-B-Q	289
Mike's Paradise Grill & BBQ	55
Milner's BBQ	215
Momma Louise's BBQ, Burgers and More	58
Mona Jo's Kitchen & Grill	96
Moore's Dairy Creme	251
Mortuary BBQ and Grill	100
Mr. J's BBQ	114
Mr. Whisker's	144
Mrs. Mildred's Kitchen	199
Naaman's World Championship BBQ	113
Naughty BBQ	155
Neumeier's Rib Room	167
Nick's Bar-B-Q and Catfish	52
Nooner's Diner	148
Norman's 44 Restaurant	123
North of the Rock Bar-B-Q	282
Oinky's BBQ	21
Ol Bart Southern Eats of Conway	268
Ol' Bart Southern Eats at Diamond Bear Brewery	287
Old Hickory Sauce Company	101
Ole Hickory Bar-B-Q	15
Ole Sawmill Cafe	57
Ouachita Bar and Grill	133
Ouachita Valley Meats	126
Outlaw BBQ	118
OZ Smokehouse	202
Ozark Mountain Grill at Lowell	200
Ozark Mountain Grill at the I-40 Travel Center	175
Panther Mountain BBQ	284
Papa Mike's BBQ	116
Pauley's Pit Stop	106
Penguin Ed's BBQ	184
Penguin Ed's Historic B&B BBQ	184
Phonzie's 1 Stop Hog Shop	295
Pig Barn BBQ	164
Pig-N-Chik	283
Pig-N-Pepper	165
Pimpin' Pig BBQ	294
PJ's Pit & Grill	274

Platnum BBQ	300	Sim's Bar-B-Q	303
Pokey D's	298	Simkins Muddy Souf BBQ	274
Pop's Place	85	Simply Smoked	160
Poplar Grove Bar-B-Q	75	Smackey's	298
Pork Belly Roberts	200	Smith and Betts Barbecue	213
Pork N Stuff	38	Smitty Smoke BBQ,	
Prime Country Meat Market	117	Ribs & Catfish	74
		Smok'd TX BBQ	195
Pull Up at Big Dave's	295	Smok'n Mule BBQ	195
Que49 Smokehouse	33	Smoke House Restaurant	232
Ragin' Cajun Louisiana Kitchen	116	Smoke N Joe Box	279
		Smoke N' Willie	182
Ramsey's B.B.Q.	50	Smoke Shack Bar-B-Q	290
Ray's of Monticello	92	Smokeez BBQ	176
Ray's Rump Shack	36	Smokehouse BBQ Newport	14
Ray's World Famous Bar-B-Que	65		
		Smokehouse Deli	154
Red Door Bar & Grill	199	Smokestack BBQ	34
Red Oak Filling Station	141	Smokestack BBQ 1994	271
Red's Restaurant	97	Smokewood American Grill (inside XNA)	205
Reid's Hometown BBQ	156		
Rib Cage BBQ	140	Smokin' Buns BBQ & Catfish	261
Ribs and More	57		
Ridgewood Brothers BBQ	152	Smokin' Houze BBQ	300
Rineyville Smokers LLC	16	Smokin' in Style	136
River Bend BBQ, Seafood and Steaks	89	Smokin' Joe's BBQ	13
		Smokin' Joe's Pit Stop BBQ	101
Road Hawgz BBQ	244		
Roadside Bar-B-Que	66	Smokin' Joe's Ribhouse	204
Robertson's Smokehouse	98	Smokin' Raven	20
Rockin' Hog Smokehouse	247	Smokin' Rick's BBQ	243
Rockin' Pig Saloon	217	Smokin' Rick's Hickory House	120
Rockin' R BBQ	230		
Rollin' Smoke BBQ	159	Smokin' T's Southern Kitchen	255
Rolling Pit BBQ	141		
Ronda's Roundhouse	183	Smoky Bs BBQ & Wing Kraze	172
Rub 'Em Tender BBQ	173		
Saddle Up	217	Sno White Dairy Bar	53
Salty Dalty's BBQ	147	So Good Soul Food Cafe	289
Sam's Olde Tyme Hamburgers	205	South Side Smoke Shack	185
		Southern BBQ Hilltop	31
Sammy J's BBQ	234	Southern Unorthodox	45
Sargent's Sunoco Gas & BBQ	174	Stoked BBQ Food Truck	269
		Stu's Clean Cookin'	172
Sassy's BBQ and Grille	190	Stubby's Hik'ry Pit Bar-B-Q	142
Sassy's Red House	190		
Sauced Barbecue and Brews	218	Stumpy's Backyard BBQ	62
		Sunset Grill & BBQ	199
Saucy Pig	281	Survivor-Que	174
Savory Avery	125	Suttle's Road Hog BBQ	258
Scott Station	279	Sweet Poppa's Cafe	284
SCR BBQ	53	Sweetpea's Smokehouse	127
Shorty's Bar-B-Que	265	T's BBQ	223
Silver's NC BBQ	166	T's Place	83

Table at Hickory Inn	210	Uncle Henry's BBQ	277
Terri-Lynn's BBQ & Deli	304	Uncle Tim's Food Truck	268
The Backyard Barbecue Company	107	Vaughn's Pit Stop BBQ	25
		Vincent's BBQ	264
The Blitzed Pig	138	Volstead Proper	269
The Boar House	236	Von's Tasty Wings & Soul Food	48
The Buck Stop Meat Store	93		
The Flaming Pig BBQ & Mobile Catering	99	VP's BBQ & Soulfood Catering Services	261
The Ranch House at James Ranch	20	Wade's BBQ	264
		Walk Baby Love BBQ	123
The Swamp	80	Wes's BBQ Burger Plus	186
The Vault 1905 Sports Grill	170	Who'da Thought It Arkansas	225
The Wood Shed BBQ & Catering	86	Whole Hog Cafe	307
		Williams Bar-B-Q	64
This Guy's Smoke N' Grill	254	Willie's Place	99
Three Sams Barbecue Joint	305	Woo Pig Mooie	230
Tin Man BBQ	269	Woods River Bend Restaurant	243
Titletown Feed House	160		
TJ's Place	101	Woody's Bar-B-Q Sauce Company	50
Tommy's Famous A Pizzeria	236	Wright's Barbecue	196
Top's Bar-B-Q	61	Wright's Ranch House of Sheridan	276
Track's BBQ	99		
Tracy B's Food Truck	294	Wright's Ranch House of White Hall	86
Trey's Deli & Grill	53		
Trina's Diner: A Touch of Soul	123	Yank's Famous Barbeque	44
		Yankabilly Smokehouse	198
Triple Cross BBQ	96	Yessuh BBQ & More Catering	31
Trish's Smokin' Bar-B-Q	119		
TxAR House	207		

Special thanks for assistance with this book:

Arkansas Department of Parks, Heritage and Tourism
Arkansas Department of Transportation
Arkansa State Archives
Arkansas State Parks
Central Arkansas Library System
Experience Fayetteville
Fort Smith Convention & Visitors Bureau
Fort Smith Museum of History
Historic Arkansas Museum
Southern Tenant Farmers Museum
The Writers Colony at Dairy Hollow
Crescent Dragonwagon
Leif Hassell
Hunter Robinson
Kitty Waldon
Grav Weldon
Blake Woodson

Kat Robinson is an Arkansas author and food historian specializing in covering restaurants, food and culinary traditions in The Natural State. With more than a dozen titles to her name, Robinson has established herself as the state's expert. The author of *Arkansas Food: The A to Z of Eating in The Natural State* and *101 Things to Eat in Arkansas Before You Die* has dedicated her time and efforts to researching and cataloguing everything from historic eateries to home cooking methods. Her books span both a burgeoning restaurant scene and a repertory of recipes that showcase the foods and cuisine from decades of home cooks, church groups, rural communities and metropolitan clubs.

Robinson's documentaries, *Arkansas Dairy Bars: Neat Eats and Cool Treats* and *Make Room for Pie,* are both available to watch through *PBS.org.* She is the co-chair of the Arkansas Pie Festival and a founding selection committee member for the Arkansas Food Hall of Fame. She has written for *Food Network* and *Forbes Travel Guide* and has been cited as an expert in Arkansas cuisine by *Saveur, Gastro Obscura, Eater, USA Today,* and *The Wall Street Journal.* She lives in Little Rock, Arkansas.

Books by Kat Robinson

**Arkansas Pie:
A Delicious Slice of the Natural State**
History Press, 2012

Classic Eateries of the Ozarks and Arkansas River Valley
History Press, 2013

Classic Eateries of the Arkansas Delta
History Press, 2014

Another Slice of Arkansas Pie: A Guide to the Best Restaurants, Bakeries, Truck Stops and Food Trucks for Delectable Bites in The Natural State
Tonti Press, 2018

**Arkansas Food:
The A to Z of Eating in The Natural State**
Tonti Press, 2018

101 Things to Eat in Arkansas Before You Die
Tonti Press, 2019

102 More Things to Eat in Arkansas Before You Die
Tonti Press, 2019

43 Tables: An Internet Community Cooks During Quarantine
Tonti Press, 2020

**A Bite of Arkansas:
A Cookbook of Natural State Delights**
Tonti Press, 2020

Arkansas Dairy Bars: Neat Eats and Cool Treats
Tonti Press, 2021

**Arkansas Cookery:
Retro Recipes from The Natural State**
Tonti Press, 2021

**The Great Arkansas Pie Book:
Recipes for The Natural State's Famous Dish From Our Favorite Restaurants, Bakeries, and Home Cooks**
Tonti Press, 2023

This book:
**The Arkansas Barbecue Traveler:
A Roadside Companion for Hungry Wanderers**
Tonti Press, 2024

And coming Spring 2024:
The Arkansas Barbecue Classics
Tonti Press, 2025